New Testament: Christian Scriptures

*Catholic High School
Teacher's Edition*

**by
Marie Thérèse Buggé, O.S.U.**

General Editors
John S. Nelson, Ph.D.
Catherine Zates Nelson

Special Consultants
Peter F. Ellis
Judith Monahan Ellis
Rev. James T. Mahoney, Ph.D.
Rev. Peter Mann
Sr. Ruth McDonell, I.H.M.
Sr. Rosemary Muckerman,
June O'Connor; Ph.D.

Contributors
Elinor R. Ford, Ed.D.
Eileen E. Anderson
Eleanor Ann Brownell
Joyce A. Crider
Mary Ellen McCarthy
William M. McDonald
Joan McGinnis-Knorr
William J. Reedy
Joseph F. Sweeney

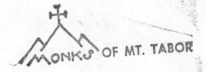

The content of this program reflects the goals of *Sharing the Light of Faith* (NCD).

A Division of
William H. Sadlier, Inc.
New York
Chicago
Los Angeles

Nihil Obstat
Rev. Donald J. Tracey
Censor Librorum

Imprimatur
✠ Raymond J. Gallagher, D.D.
Bishop of Lafayette-in-Indiana

March 4, 1981

Acknowledgments
"I Will Try." Copyright © 1976, Damean
Music and Franciscan Communications,
1229 S. Santee St., Los Angeles, CA
90015. Reprinted with permission.

Assistant Project Director:
    Sr. Ruth McDonell, I.H.M.
Project Editor: Gerard F. Baumbach
Managing Editor: Gerald A. Johannsen
Design Director: Willi Kunz
Designer: Grace Kao

Home Office:
11 Park Place
New York, NY 10007

ISBN: 0-8215-2927-7
123456789/987654321

Contents

3

Additional Chapter Features:

- **Student Involvement:** recurring opportunities for sharing concerns, raising questions, internalizing experiences.
- **Challenges:** questions and activities which reinforce and extend the learning experiences of the chapter.
- **Prayer Reflection:** opportunities for personal prayer and communal sharing based on the theme of the chapter.

Authors

John S. Nelson, Ph.D.
Moral Growth
Lifestyles
General Editor:
Journey in Faith Series

Director, Division of
Adolescent Religious Development
Fordham University

Catherine Zates Nelson
General Editor:
Journey in Faith Series

Co-Author of Sadlier
Lord of Life Series
Grades 7 & 8

Paul E. Bumbar
Faith

Supervisor of Child Care
St. Agatha's Home of the
New York Foundling Hospital
Nanuet, N.Y.

Anthony J. Cernera
Social Issues

Assistant Director, Bread for
the World Educational Fund

Sr. Regina Coll, C.S.J.
Death and Dying

Campus Minister
Queen's College, N.Y.

Judith Craemer
Old Testament:
Hebrew Scriptures

Teacher, Los Angeles Unified
School District
Los Angeles, CA

Patricia Curley
Social Issues

Chairperson, Religion Department
St. Helena's Commercial High
School, Bronx, N.Y.
Chairperson Bread for the World
Bronx Chapter

Sr. Mary Dennison, r.c.
Church

Assistant Director of the
Graduate School of Religious
Education
St. Thomas University
Houston, TX

Gloria Durka, Ph.D.
Faith

Associate Professor of Religious
Education and Theology, Graduate
School of Religion and Religious
Education, Fordham University.
Director of Division of Family
Ministry

Peter F. Ellis, S.S.L.
New Testament:
Christian Scriptures

Professor of Biblical Theology
Graduate School of Religion
and Religious Education
Fordham University

Judith Monahan Ellis
New Testament:
Christian Scriptures

Religious Education Coordinator
St. Denis – St. Columba Parish
Hopewell Junction, N.Y.

Thomas V. Forget
Social Issues

Chairperson, Manhattan
Chapter, Bread for the World

Rev. Robert J. Hater, Ph.D.
Ministry in Catholic
High Schools

Theologian for Studies in Spirituality
and An Active Spirituality for a
Global Community Program
Cincinnati, Ohio

Brennan R. Hill, Ph.D.
Jesus

Director of Parish Programs
Office of Religious Education
Diocese of Albany, N.Y.

Gloria Hutchinson
Prayer and Worship

Free lance writer
Former high school teacher
and religious education
coordinator
Brunswick, ME

Rev. James T. Mahoney, Ph.D.
Church

Assistant Superintendent of
Schools for Religious Education
Diocese of Paterson, N.J.

George McCauley, S.J., D. és Sc. Rel.
Prayer and Worship

Associate Professor of
Theology, Graduate School
of Religion and Religious
Education, Fordham University

Nadine McGuinness, C.S.J.
Old Testament:
Hebrew Scriptures

Director of Master's Program
in Religious Studies
Loyola-Marymount University
Los Angeles, CA

Rev. Frank J. McNulty, S.T.D.
Lifestyles

Professor of Moral Theology
Immaculate Conception Seminary
Darlington, N.J.
Vicar for Priests
Archdiocese of Newark
Mahwah, N.J.

Joanmarie Smith, C.S.J., Ph.D.
Death and Dying

Associate Professor of
Philosophy, St. Joseph's
College, Brooklyn, N.Y.

Joanne Roach Stickles
Lifestyles

Religious Education Coordinator
Most Holy Name Parish
Garfield, N.J.

Consultants

Dr. Elinor R. Ford
Vice President and Publisher
William H. Sadlier, Inc.

Joyce A. Crider
Assistant Editor in Chief
William H. Sadlier, Inc.

William M. McDonald
Project Director
Journey in Faith Series
William H. Sadlier, Inc.

Eleanor Ann Brownell
National Consultant
William H. Sadlier, Inc.

Sr. M. Jeannine Curley, R.S.M.
Secondary Religion Chairman
Religion Department Chairman
Immaculate Conception
Diocese of Memphis, TN

Rev. Peter Mann
Theologian and Producer
Diocesan Television Center
Uniondale, NY

June O'Connor, Ph.D.
Assistant Professor of Religious
Studies
University of California
Riverside, CA

Sr. Dominga M. Zapata, S.H.
Consultant: Spanish Division
Archdiocesan Center of CCD
Chicago, IL

Eileen E. Anderson
Vice President and
Assistant Publisher
William H. Sadlier, Inc.

William J. Reedy
Vice President and
Director of Catechetics
William H. Sadlier, Inc.

Ruth McDonell, I.H.M.
Assistant Project Director
Journey in Faith Series
William H. Sadlier, Inc.

Mary Ellen McCarthy
Regional Sales Manager
William H. Sadlier, Inc.

Rev. John E. Forliti, D.Min.
Director of Religious Education
Archdiocese of St. Paul and
Minnesota, MN

**Sr. Rosemary Muckerman,
S.S.N.D.**
Supervisor, Secondary Schools
Archdiocese of Los Angeles, CA

Sr. Marie Paul, O.P.
Associate Director of Youth
Ministry/Catechesis
Archdiocese of Newark, NJ

Joseph F. Sweeney
Vice President and
Editor in Chief
William H. Sadlier, Inc.

Gerard F. Baumbach
Assistant Director of
Catechetics
William H. Sadlier, Inc.

Joan McGinnis-Knorr
Director of Market Research
Manager of Consultant Services
William H. Sadlier, Inc.

Rev. Michael J. Carroll
Assistant Superintendent of
Schools
Archdiocese of Philadelphia, PA

Rev. James F. Hawker
Director of Religious Education
— Schools
Archdiocese of Boston, MA

Dr. Samuel M. Natale, S.J.
Associate Professor
Psychology and Management
Col. of Business Admin.
St. John's University, NY

Lawrence J. Payne
Director, Office of Black
Ministries
Diocese of Galveston-Houston,
TX

Introduction

The *Journey in Faith Series* is offered to contemporary Catholic youth and to those who minister with them to assist in the study of the Catholic Faith. It provides the catechetical component of youth ministry in Catholic high schools and parish schools of religion. The series addresses the needs of youth at a critical stage of their faith development. Each of the texts provides opportunities for the sharing of faith experience and the building of Christian community.

The *Journey in Faith Series* is designed to meet wider youth ministry goals such as:

● That both young people and adults realize that they are a ministering community, that is, people who help each other in their journey of faith.

● That each one become more knowledgeable about the community's doctrines, heritage, rites, symbols, values, and great persons. As a community we share rich traditions.

● That in this shared journey each one find his or her own way of praying, serving, and becoming his or her own best self. We are a community who cherishes the uniqueness of each of its members.

The *Journey in Faith Series* was prepared by a catechetical team whose members have journeyed in faith with young people in schools and parishes.

Many of the team members are biblical scholars, theologians, psychologists, and educators. They offer from their disciplines the best of today's thinking for responding to faith questions and for sharing faith experiences.

The Series directly reflects the goals of *Sharing the Light of Faith: National Catechetical Directory for Catholics of the United States*. The Series applies in a practical way the wisdom of *Sharing the Light of Faith*. From this document, may we cite one passage in particular to express what is central to *Journey in Faith*:

"The source of catechesis, which is also its content, is one: God's word, fully revealed in Jesus Christ and at work in the lives of people exercising their faith under the guidance of the magisterium, which alone teaches authentically. God's word deposited in scripture and tradition is manifested and celebrated in many ways: in the liturgy and 'in the life of the Church, especially in the just and in the saints'; moreover, 'in some way it is known too from those genuine moral values which, by divine providence, are found in human society.' Indeed, potentially at least, every instance of God's presence in the world is a source of catechesis." (#41)

The *Journey in Faith Series* is true to *Sharing the Light of Faith* in another way. In matters of doctrinal substance, it is clearly and explicitly Catholic. It makes use of a wide variety of learning processes.

The Series recognizes and respects the enormous range of backgrounds and experiences of those who may be using these books. It does not shy away from its task of evangelizing and catechizing explicitly the Good News that is Jesus Christ.

The Series strikes a balance between *input* from the catechist or youth minister and *discovery* by the young person through individual and group activity.

Again, to cite *Sharing the Light of Faith*:

"It is significant that many adolescents apparently stop thinking about religion long before they consciously reject it. Various reasons are suggested. . . . To the extent that these explanations are valid, the answer seems to lie in adapting catechesis to the mental age of young people, and allowing them to question, discuss, and explore religious beliefs. . . . If such steps as these are taken; if young people are provided with models of faith which they perceive as credible and relevant; if they are challenged to confront the fullness of religious truth — then there is reason to hope that, as they grow older, adolescents will progress in faith and religious practice and suffer no delay in the process of religious maturation." (#200)

To assist catechists, this series includes a handbook which relates the *Journey in Faith Series* to the catechetical component of youth ministry programs in schools and parishes.

Student Materials

The texts pictured in the top row were designed primarily for ninth and tenth grades; those below for grades eleven and twelve. However, they are not limited to these levels and could be used in the curriculum wherever appropriate.

Moral Growth: A Christian Perspective, John S. Nelson, Ph.D.
This text focuses on the dynamic relationship between personal and moral growth. The processes of decision-making and the stages of personal development are examined as ways by which this growth takes place.

Old Testament: Hebrew Scriptures, Nadine McGuinness, C.S.J., Judith Craemer
This text presents important themes of the Hebrew Scriptures which speak to some life questions of Christians today: human relationships and law, personal and social morality, the dignity of persons, the recurring Passover experience in our lives.

Prayer and Worship: Praise the Lord with Gladness, George McCauley, S.J., D. és Sc. Rel., Gloria Hutchinson
This text encourages students to examine concepts and practices of prayer — both individual prayer and the liturgical prayer of the Church. The emphasis is on the sacraments and prayer which express the relationship of a life lived in God's presence.

Death and Dying: A Night Between Two Days, Joanmarie Smith, C.S.J., Ph.D., Regina Coll, C.S.J.
This text explores death as experienced by all humans, as reacted to in various religious traditions, and as understood in the light of Christian faith. In Catholic Christian tradition this text explains that the resurrection of Jesus is the promise of new life.

Lifestyles: Shaping One's Future, Rev. Frank J. McNulty, S.T.D., John S. Nelson, Ph.D., Joanne Roach Stickles
This text is designed to assist students in coming to a deeper appreciation of their sexual and vocational identity. The student is challenged to consider the various vocations which reflect a mature Christian lifestyle.

Social Issues: A Just World, Anthony J. Cernera, Thomas V. Forget, Patricia Curley
Examining the Scriptures as the foundation for our involvement in and concern for the value of human life, this text helps the student to examine ways to solve some of the complex social issues of our time.

Support Materials

New Testament: Christian Scriptures, Peter F. Ellis, S.S.L., Judith Monahan Ellis
This text helps the student to understand the value of the Christian Scriptures as a source of knowledge to establish a relationship with Jesus. The New Testament writings exemplify what it means to be a member of the Christian community.

Church: Our Faith Story, Sr. Mary E. Dennison, r.c., Rev. James T. Mahoney, Ph.D.
Through a study of Christian Scriptures and Church life, this text develops the "story" of the Church as the community of Christ. The students are encouraged to see how their own personal stories form part of the Christian community's story.

Spirit Masters
The *Journey in Faith Spirit Master Paks* are available through William H. Sadlier, Inc. These worksheets are designed to encourage dialogue about the themes of the chapter. The teacher will find them a resource for facilitating the student's journey of faith. The Pak also includes an attitudinal and informational survey to be used by the students at the beginning of the course.

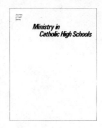

Jesus: God's Son with Us, Brennan R. Hill, Ph.D.
This text helps the students to answer the two questions put by Jesus to his first disciples: "Who do people say that I am?" "Who do you say that I am?" In so doing, they are helped in developing their own faith in who Jesus is and what meaning he has in their lives.

Faith: Becoming True and Free, Gloria Durka, Ph.D., Paul E. Bumbar
This text presents faith as an ongoing, developing process. Students are helped to see the gift of faith as the dynamic force which shapes our personalities and relationships.

Ministry in Catholic High Schools, Rev. Robert J. Hater, Ph.D.
This book helps teachers reflect on their role as ministers in the Catholic High School. Models for ministry are offered and analyzed. Concrete suggestions are presented to improve and expand that ministry.

About This Guide...

Each chapter of this Guide builds upon the following components:

Objectives: what we intend the students to know, to feel, to do as a result of this learning experience. We recognize that, in sharing faith and moral values, individual freedom plays an important role. Hence some of our objectives may be beyond empirical measurement or verification.

Orientation: a sense of the chapter — its relationship to what precedes and what follows, its internal flow, logic, and structure. The orientation's purpose is to maintain a good progression from chapter to chapter and within the chapter itself.

Life Experience Focus: a statement of how the content and process of the chapter arises from or is related to the wider life of the adolescents. According to its subject matter, a chapter may stay totally within the life experience of the students or it may begin with their life experience, move on to items from the Christian community's tradition, then return in reflection and application to their everyday lives.

Background on Content: a statement for the teacher, in more technical terms, of the theology, biblical scholarship, or human sciences which underlie the substance of the chapter. The authors of this series have tried to present the best of recent scholarship in nontechnical language for the students.

Teaching Notes: practical indications on how to present the chapter section by section. For ease in reference, Teaching Notes for each chapter are divided into three parts and they follow the section headings found in the student text. One feature of the Teaching Notes is the reference to the *Journey in Faith Spirit Master Pak* which contains 24 worksheets for use throughout the course. They are reproduced in miniature at the back of this Guide, and they may be obtained from William H. Sadlier, Inc.

Prayer and Worship Experiences: possibilities for personal prayer or communal celebration at different moments of the learning experience. This section may refer not only to the "Prayer Reflection" at the close of each chapter in the student text, but also to other items in the chapter where prayer is appropriate.

Service Projects: ways in which students can live out the knowledge and attitudes which have become more their own through the learning experience. There are difficulties of programming service activities for adolescents; such a dimension, however, is very important to their growth in faith, and carrying their faith into civic and secular life.

Independent Study Projects: items which lend themselves to library research, further reading, oral or written presentations. The student texts are designed more for group learning than for individualized instruction, yet they are open to personalized assignments.

Resources: selected audiovisual and print material for use by the teacher and, at times, by the students. These materials represent some of the sources researched by the authors of both the student's text and the teacher's guide.

Outline of the Text

The focus on this text is to acquaint the student with some of the earliest Christian writings — the letters of St. Paul, the four gospels, and the Acts of the Apostles.

The text takes five approaches to St. Paul's writings: Paul as a traveling apostle in the Acts of the Apostles, the letter writer in the letters to Philemon and the Thessalonians, the trouble shooter in the two letters to the Church at Corinth, the theologian in his writings to the Galatians and the Romans, and finally as the prisoner in the letter to the Philippians.

The study of the four gospels explains how each evangelist presents differently the good news experienced in the teaching and the person of Jesus Christ.

The entire focus of the course comes together in the last chapter with a powerful round-table discussion which illustrates the differences of approach between the gospel writers and St. Paul.

The following overview is given to provide the teacher with the scope of the entire text:

Chapter One — **Christianity's Most Important Book** acquaints the students with the focus and content of the New Testament and its importance on human history.

Chapter Two — **Paul, the Traveling Apostle** explores the Christian communities which Paul visited, their problems, and their cultures.

Chapter Three — **Paul, the Letter Writer** compares the letter writing style of Paul to the style of today and examines the styling components of Paul's letters.

Chapter Four — **Paul, the Trouble Shooter** presents Paul as solving practical and pastoral problems in the early Christian communities.

Chapter Five — **Paul, the Theologian** deals with the theology of Paul as expressed in the Letters to the Galatians and the Romans.

Chapter Six — **Paul, the Prisoner** details the sufferings and trials of Paul as expressed in the letters which he wrote from prison.

Chapter Seven — **Introduction to the Gospels** presents similarities and differences in the Synoptic Gospels.

Chapter Eight — **Mark: Realist's Gospel** challenges the reader to face the realities of hardship and suffering.

Chapter Nine — **Matthew: Idealist's Gospel** presents the vision of Christian living as found in Jesus' words and actions.

Chapter Ten — **Luke: Joyful Gospel** highlights the enthusiasm experienced by Jesus' followers and the first Christian communities.

Chapter Eleven — **John: New Life Gospel** explains how those who believe in Jesus are called to share in divine life itself.

Chapter Twelve — **Conclusions: A Discussion** describes an imaginary discussion between Paul and the gospel writers about how each understands the person of Jesus.

1

Christianity's Most Important Book

Objectives

Knowledge: To develop a sense of the value of the Christian Scriptures in searching for the truth about life; to help students to understand the importance of history and the importance of those men and women who make history.

Attitude: To encourage students to develop an appreciation for the importance and impact of Jesus on the history of the world; to appreciate the Christian Scriptures as their main source for discovering the truth about their own lives.

Practice: To assist students to determine which people have influenced and contributed to their own history and to decide what place Jesus has in that influence; to search out situations in their own lives in which knowing the truth was critical for making the right decision.

Orientation

The many ideas in this chapter set the stage for a serious study of the Christian Scriptures. The content is not difficult for students to grasp; at the same time it is important that the teacher delineate the main concepts both while reading through the first chapter and while summing up before proceeding to Chapter 2.

The influence of the person Jesus on history will have greater or lesser impact on the students to the degree that they realize how their own lives are very much influenced by people and events in their own history. "The Historical Me" (text page 5) is designed to allow students the opportunity to realize the influence of people and past events on their own personal lives.

The exercise at the end of this section (text page 5) lends itself to a lively group discussion. It would be well for the teacher to utilize this opportunity to involve the students thus stimulating their interest, participation, and sharing at the very beginning of this course.

"Calendars" (text pages 6–7) introduces the fact that several calendars have existed throughout history. Each calendar dated from an important event in the history of a particular people.

Why most of the world abandoned these calendars and adapted to our present uniform calendar is explained in the section "Dionysius Exiguus" (text page 7). The birth of Jesus was the most important event in the history of the world; therefore, Jesus becomes the center of history.

The heart of this first chapter can be found in the remainder of the chapter beginning with the section "In Search of Truth" (text pages 9–10). In this core material sacred Scripture is presented as the treasury of truth wherein questions asked from the beginning of time can be answered. Sacred Scripture answers questions about life:

- with regard to *ourselves,* it reveals our value as persons in the sight of God (John 3:16);
- with regard to *our world,* it unfolds the beauty of God's gift to us and calls us to use our world responsibly, to treasure this gift by building up one another in love, thereby building up our world (Romans 8:19);
- with regard to *God,* it reveals a Father whose love is faithful and forgiving (Luke 12:22–34).

The Christian Scriptures are important because they reveal the God of the Israelites in a special and unique way through Jesus his son. It is this Jesus who reveals to all the truth of the reliability of God's love for us.

Life Experience Focus

When we look at the subject not only of this chapter but of the whole book and try to align it with the life experience of the early adolescent (ages 13–15), we find both lines of convergence and lines of divergence.

May we recognize first of all the divergence. Early adolescence is an inward-looking, self-centered stage. This is perfectly normal and, if not overdone, healthy. It is difficult to interest young people this age even in present-day events, not to speak of things that occurred in the past. On the other hand, adolescents have increased powers of reasoning and reflection to see how events which apparently have little to do with them do in fact figure importantly in their own personal stories.

The thrust of this chapter is to indicate how the Christian Scriptures can profoundly influence the shape our lives are taking today. Here and elsewhere the teacher's approach is to interweave two sets of stories: that of the adolescent in his or her group and that of the faith community as recorded in the Christian Scriptures.

Background on Content

Anyone who takes Christianity seriously must also give serious attention to the Christian Scriptures. It is by reading, studying, and praying the Christian Scriptures that one's mind becomes one with the message of Christ, one's heart becomes one with the heart of Christ and one's life in our world. Crucial to a study of the Christian Scriptures is the faith response of the reader. That faith response is open to all regardless of intellectual ability or status on the social ladder. God's gift is for all; the response is the individual's. The simplest to the most profound of men and women have come to the deepest of insights about the Christian Scriptures and make these insights operative in their personal lives. Something other than intellect is the key here.

Having said the above is not to disregard the importance of scholarship. The study of the New Testament is a tremendous tool for opening one's mind to the treasures contained in the writings of the Christian Scriptures, leading one to a close relationship with God. The Christian Scriptures contain the key to our questions about life, about relationships with ourselves, with the world, and with God. Therefore any study of the Scriptures should clarify these questions and at the same time elicit from us a deeper faith commitment to the God of the Scriptures.

With this in mind it is important for any teacher of Christian Scriptures to be knowledgeable of recent biblical scholarship and to have some general idea of the literary forms used by the Christian Scripture writers against the cultural background of their times. The synoptic gospels are so named because they very much tell the same story in the same way. The reader is invited, as it were, to stand in the crowd and somehow participate in the lives of people encountered, the events that occurred, and the sayings of the main characters. These narratives, now referred to as the Gospels of "Matthew," "Mark," and "Luke" relate a great deal about the authors, their audiences, and their concerns. There is an interrelatedness among the three evangelists. Biblical scholars point to Matthew and Luke's dependence on Mark as a primary source, but they also indicated another source "Q," a common source not Markan, consisting mainly of sayings and used for a teaching purpose. In addition to Mark and Source "Q," Matthew and Luke each had their own special material.

The fourth evangelist, "John", wrote a drama, in which the reader is an observer to the unfolding of sacred events. Both John and Paul wrote *letters* addressed to a specific audience but meaningful for all audiences. The Letter to the Hebrews stands alone in the literature of the Christian Scriptures; its author unknown, the "letter" bears little resemblance to a letter other than the greeting found at its conclusion (13:22–25). A *theological* sermon, Hebrews was written for an audience of Jewish believers for the main purpose of exhorting them in their Christian faith.

Although the authors of the Christian Scriptures write at different times for different audiences, using different literary forms, all are united in their efforts to deal with problems of faith. By reflecting on their faith experiences of Jesus and on that of the Christian community, each writer tries to help believers cope with life's situations by believing in the power of the Risen Christ in their lives. It is precisely this aspect of all scriptural literature which makes it so relevant and meaningful for all people of all ages.

For further information on the content of this chapter an excellent guide would be the "Study Helps" printed in the Sadlier publication of the *Good News Bible* (see *Resources* in this Guide chapter). These study guide essays, written by prominent biblical scholars, include important background crucial to understanding the Bible.

Teaching Notes 1

Future and Past

1. Introduce the chapter by discussing "Future and Past" (text page 4) with the students. Ask the students to identify some characteristics that they feel will be considered quite common by the turn of the century. Then ask them to identify some things that people living around the year 1900 may have expected to happen in the future decades of this century. By looking at both the past and the future, the students can begin to identify for themselves the influence that history and expectations of humankind have had on the lives of people through the ages, including people today.

2. Continue the group's discussion by asking the students these questions:
● How do you think the past helps to explain what is happening in the present?
● What books, movies, or sayings that you may have read, seen, or heard long ago left an impression on you that cannot be ignored or forgotten?

The Historical Me

"The Historical Me" (text page 5) enables the students to reflect upon the people who have contributed to making them who and what they are. By looking at several of these people—by discovering them

through a brief "self-search"—the students can begin to realize that they are their own history.

a. Allow the students time to reflect on the many influences that have shaped them as persons. The following questions can be helpful for reflection:
● What is the ethnic and cultural background of my family? How have I allowed these influences to become part of the person I am?
● In what way have my friends (from neighborhood, school, etc.) helped to make me the person I am?
● How has my family contributed to the person I am and am becoming?
● How do the area where I live and the salary my family lives on contribute to the kind of person I am?
● What other influences are special to me?

b. In small groups, encourage the students to share their reflections on the influences that have shaped them as persons. Emphasize as needed the concept that each of us is a history; in this sense, we look to ourselves to determine who we are, where we have come from, and where we are headed. While the groups are together, discuss the exercise on text page 5. Use this as a focal point to summarize all that the students have done in dealing with their own self-histories.

Calendars

Discuss with the students the fact that different people have used different methods to determine how far they have come from their past, or from what they considered to be their origins. Use the material in the text under "Calendars" (text page 6) to show this. Realize, however, that the fact that there have been calendars other than our own may not be a new idea for some students. Ask these students to contribute whatever information they have about calendar-dating within various cultures.

Dionysius Exiguus

1. The section entitled "Dionysius Exiguus" (text page 7) points out to the students why the Roman calendar is no longer followed. Discuss with the students some reasons why a decision to change from one calendar to another would have monumental implications. What kind of event would precipiate such a change? Surely it would not be a minor historical happening that would result in a change in a most basic way of identifying past history. The impact of Jesus, then, can be measured (at least in part) by this major adjustment in the calendar.

2. Ask the students to brainstorm some reasons Dionysius might have had for doing what he did. Encourage them to consider the kind of faith this person must have had to center all of history around the person of Jesus.

3. To personalize this material, ask the students the following questions:
● Do you know people today whose lives center on Jesus?
● Do you see anything distinctive about their lifestyles? About their relationships with others?
● How would you describe the "meaning" Jesus has for their lives?

The World Says Yes!

1. "The World says Yes" (text page 8) can be used to alert the students to the extent of change brought about by the new calendar. The example of the difficulty involved in trying to adopt the metric system is a good one. Perhaps the students could identify other examples that show what can happen when a major shift occurs.

2. Have the students do the exercise at the end of this section. Then ask:
● How is the Dionysian calendar different from the Roman calendar?
● What might have been some of the problems encountered when the people first tried to adjust to the Dionysian calendar?
● What kinds of "adjustments" can we make today to keep our lives focused on Jesus?

3. Summarize with the students the chief points discussed so far from each of the sections listed above. Guide the discussion to a concluding focus on the person of Jesus—the central character of world history.

Teaching Notes 2

Text Pages
8–14

The Greatest Influence

1. Jesus' impact on all human history is clearly understood after reading "One Solitary Life" (text pages 8–9). Jesus has had such universal appeal these 2000 years because he touches people at the core of their being and reveals to them the truth about their existence and purpose in life.

2. *Worksheet #1* may assist the students in reflecting on their personal journey in life.

In Search of Truth

1. Before beginning the next section, "In Search of Truth" (text page 9), discuss with the students their understanding and experiences of truth:
- What is meant by truth?
- What values does today's world place on truth?
- We like people we deal with to be truthful—why?

2. Truth or honesty is an essential element to good and deep human relationships. But more important than these everyday relationships are the larger questions asked by persons from the beginning of time, questions about life, its purpose, their destiny and their relationship with God. *Worksheet #1* may help the group to surface some of their basic questions as they begin this study

of the Scriptures.

3. Jesus speaks about life through the words of the evangelists in the Christian Scriptures. To give the students an example of how truth is revealed through Jesus, take Luke's parable of the Good Samaritan (Luke 10:25–37). Students most likely are familiar with the sequence of events.
- Have the students give a general outline of the events of this parable, as they remember it (use the blackboard for the outline).
- Have one student read the account from Luke and ask one or two students to add any details omitted from the original outline.
- What truth(s) do you think Jesus is trying to teach by telling this story?

Some possible responses are:
- The outcast of society (the Samaritan) does the more favorable thing in God's eyes: God's love is operative through all who are open to him.
- All persons are neighbors; race, creed, color should be no barrier to living Christ's life of love (this is especially true when we happen to be the person "mugged"; in that position we gladly accept help from anyone).

4. A careful study of the Christian Scriptures will reveal the truth about the most serious questions people ask about hemselves, their world, and their God. This course should open up to the students the immense treasures in a book with which they are vaguely familiar.

Encounters of a Third Kind
The Human Person

1. After reading the section "The Human Person" (text page 12) have half the students do the exercise that deals with the qualities of a "perfect" person; the other half of the group should list the qualities of perfection that are God's.

17

2. God's love and acceptance of us speaks of our tremendous value in his eyes. Jesus calls us to be perfect as God is perfect (Matthew 5:48). Using the two lists—the "perfect" person and the perfection of God:

● Have the students express their feelings as to the feasibility of really trying to be perfect as God is perfect.

● What do they think Jesus had in mind when he made that challenge (Matthew 5:48)?

This Spaceship Earth
Relationship Among Persons

1. With reference to "This Spaceship Earth" (text page 14), help the students to delineate ways in which people have fulfilled God's will—or not—by discussing:

● how we rule the earth in our little corner of the world;

● how we beautify it (or how we deface it);

● how we treasure the gifts of the earth (or how we abuse these gifts and take them for granted).

2. Place the word "earth" on the board. Have the students reflect on the ways in which Jesus used the earth in the gospels; some responses might be:

● as examples to teach an important lesson (Parable of the Sower, Mark 4:1–9; Parable of the Weeds, Matthew 13:24–30, etc.);

● as a means to heal others (John 9:1–15);

● to reveal himself as the Son of God (John 6:6–12).

Teaching Notes 3

Text Pages 15–19

Gods and God

1. Before beginning the section "Gods and God" (text page 15), have the students brainstorm about God:

● What is the first word that comes to mind when I say "God"?

● What feelings are aroused when I say "God"?

2. Jesus presented his friends with a whole new understanding of God. He calls God his Father, *Abba,* and he teaches us to approach God as our Father.

● What images of God are presented in the story of the Lost Son? (Luke 15:11–32)

● What message is there in this story about God's relationship with each of his sons and daughters, with me in particular?

A Perspective on Life

1. It is especially difficult during the course of one's lifetime to see individual events in their true perspective; this is even more true of the young adolescent who is also very idealistic. With regard to "A Perspective on Life," (text page 16) the following exercise might prove beneficial before reading the student text:

● List in the order of priority (#1=highest priority) the persons who are most important in your life.

● Allow the students to share their lists in small groups and their reasons for placing people where they did.

2. After reading the section "A Perspective on Life" have the students place Jesus somewhere on their list. It would be important that they realize they need not put him on top, but that they *honestly* place him here they feel he actually is on their priority list. Allow them time to reflect on *why* they put him *where* they did and then share these reflections in their small groups.

3. The last section of this chapter lists the sacred writings in the Christian Scriptures. At this point it would be beneficial to have the students view the filmstrip "How the Bible Was Put Together" (see *Resources* for this Guide chapter) both as a review of the Hebrew Scriptures and as an introduction to the Christian Scriptures.

4. Students might find helpful the following summary of important points of this chapter:

a. *Each person is uniquely a product of his or her own personal history:* no one lives in total isolation. It is important to recognize the richness of each individual's background, that richness developing from proper utilization of both the good and the bad to form the fabric of one's life before God.

b. *Jesus has made a dynamic impact on the history of humankind:* not only is the world's calendar centered upon Jesus, but people from all over the world have lived and died for him during the past 2000 years.

c. *Jesus leaves us in the Christian Scriptures the answers to the questions deepest in our hearts:* basically, we seek happiness and peace in our relationship with ourselves, our world, and God. The Christian Scriptures show us how to achieve this inner peace and happiness.

Prayer Reflection

1. In preparation for the "Prayer Reflection" (text page 19), surface the students' understanding of Hebrews 4:12 by discussing:
● To what extent is God's word accurately imaged as a double-edged sword?
● How do you personally react to this image?
● Is there another image which you prefer? If so, please explain.

2. The "Prayer Reflection" says in part that "the study of the Christian Scriptures which I am about to undertake is no ordinary study." Invite the students to think about ways in which this statement may be true for them. This exercise can be done privately.

3. The beginning sentence of the "Prayer Reflection" can serve as a brief prayer in itself often during this course of study. Encourage the students to pray it privately whenever they begin to read and/or study the Scriptures.

Prayer and Worship Experiences

1. The Scriptures are the word of God to us. Using the song "Is There Any Word from the Lord?" (see *Resources* for this Guide chapter), have the students reflect on the words of the song as it is being played. Two students can alternately read John 1:1–5. 10–12, 14, 16 and then allow a few moments of silence; any who wish can then share their reflections on the scriptural passages with the rest of the group. End with the "Prayer Reflection" (text page 19).

2. Using Psalm 33, coordinate slides (see *Resources* for this Guide chapter) of people and nature with the verses. This beautiful psalm of praise and trust can be used effectively to begin a study of the Christian Scriptures. "The words of the Lord are true . . . " (vs. 4), especially his Word, Jesus, who reveals the truth of God's love for each of us. End with the "Prayer Reflection" (text page 19).

3. *A Prayer Journal:* You may wish each tudent to have a personal Prayer Journal in which to write down prayerful reflections at the end of each chapter.

Service Projects

1. The Scriptures are often precious to people who for some reason can no longer read them themselves or perhaps have never been able to do so: the elderly, those with sight impairment, the educationally disadvantaged. There are recordings of the Scriptures for such people; however, many of them would prefer the kind of live reading which your students can provide. Invite some students to form a group which under direction will provide a live reading of the Scriptures to such persons as those who are mentioned above.

2. To help your group in its study of the Christian Scriptures, ask some of its members to volunteer to research maps and visuals which pertain to St. Paul and to the four evangelists. As the group begins each new topic, these materials could be displayed as an aid to everyone's learning.

Independent Study Projects

1. The fact that people look upon certain writings as sacred is wider than the Judaeo-Christian tradition. Assist some students in researching books considered as sacred in other religions. Invite them to report their findings to the group.

2. Part of our Christian belief is that the Scriptures are "the Word of God." This raises such questions as: How did God's inspiration affect the writers of the Scriptures? Direct some students to research information on this topic from such sources as the opening essay in the *Good News Bible* (Catholic Study Edition) and *The Jerome Biblical Commentary* (see *Resources* for this Guide chapter).

Resources

Audiovisual

"How the Bible Was Put Together." sound filmstrip. Episode 8 of *Understanding Scripture.* R0A, 1696 No. Astor St., Milwaukee, WI 53202.

Joy in Creation. Slides. Winston Press, Minneapolis, MN.

Print

Good News Bible, (Catholic Study Edition). New York: W.H. Sadlier, 1979.

F. Gast, O.C.D. "Synoptic Problem" #40 in *The Jerome Biblical Commentary.* Englewood Cliffs: Prentice-Hall, 1968.

J. Kselman, S.S. *"Modern New Testament Criticism"* #41 in *The Jerome Biblical Commentary.*

X. Leon-Dufour, S.J. *The Gospels and the Jesus of History.* New York: Doubleday and Company, 1970.

_____. *Dictionary of Biblical Theology.* New York: Seabury Press, 1973.

P. Perkins. *Reading the New Testament, An Introduction.* NJ: Paulist Press, 1977.

N. Perrin. *The New Testament, An Introduction.* New York: Harcourt Brace Jovanovich, 1974.

2 Paul, the Traveling Apostle

**Text Pages
20–35**

Objectives

Knowledge: To help the students to understand that Paul's conversion encounter with the risen Jesus on the road to Damascus was a reversal of his whole life; that it was the origin of his passionate and lifelong drive to convert the whole world.
Attitude: To enable the students to appreciate Paul's fascination with Jesus by reflecting on the radical changes that took place in his life in order to devote himself to the work of making Jesus known to others.
Practice: To assist the students in finding ways in their everyday lives to express their own commitment to Jesus.

Orientation

The main objective of this chapter is to introduce the students to the person of Paul and, in a sense, to get inside his person, allowing Paul's mind and heart to be understood and experienced in their own minds and hearts. Paul should become so real to them that his message will ring true in their own lives.

Paul's encounter with the risen Jesus on the road to Damascus explains the radical change in his thinking and living. It is from this encounter that Paul's message gets its thrust and meaning. It will be important to convey the importance of this event to the students not only to help them understand the reversal in Paul the Jewish Pharisee, but also to help them appreciate the strength of his convictions as conveyed in his letters. This experience influenced Paul's theology, a fact to be remembered in Chapters 2, 3, 4, 5.

In "Paul the Persecutor" (text page 20) the emphasis is on the total dedication with which Paul gave himself to a cause. Paul persecuted the Jews who seemingly denied the oneness of Yahweh by acknowledging Jesus as God's Son. Here it would be well to emphasize the Jewishness of Paul and his commitment to the Jewish Law (*The Jerome Biblical Commentary* #79:10 and 13).

The section entitled "Experiences Which Transform" (text pages 23–24) concentrates on Paul's conversion experience, the decisive factor dominating the rest of his life. Students should be made aware, not only of the drama of this incident, but especially of the impact this turning point had on Paul's life and his message to the Gentiles. The story of Helen Keller (text pages 23–24) is an example of a contemporary woman who encountered a similar turning point when she met Anne Sullivan. The students should come away with the realization that conversion experiences are possible when one is open to the Lord's action in and through people around them, and that once conversion takes place, one's life is turned inside out (*JBC* #46:16−17−18; #79:12−13−14). Jesus became everything for Paul. He was so caught up in the person of Jesus that there was no facet of his life which was not impregnated with the mind of Christ.

For Paul "Life is Christ!" (text page 25). It is important that the students recognize in this section the passsionate energy that possessed Paul because he had become fascinated with Jesus.

Because he was caught up with Jesus, with his message and way of life, Paul had to spread this fascination to others. In "Paul the Community Builder" (text pages 26−29), students should see the intimate connection between a deep conviction and/or experience and the burning zeal that constrains one to share this with others. Paul's experience of Jesus made him an apostle, building communities of believers.

Fascination with Jesus often gets one into trouble with a world whose values differ greatly from those of Jesus. "The Troublemaker" (text pages 30−31) is a section which reveals precisely this fact in Paul's life following his conversion. Important to the students' understanding is the realization that standing for Christ is costly. Because Paul was caught up in Jesus he risked all in the way of human values in order to share the "riches of Christ" with others. Spreading the good news got Paul into trouble. Living the gospel message then or today meets with opposition because it makes others feel uncomfortable. To be Christ in our world often makes one seem a troublemaker.

Life Experience Focus

A recent ecumenical study done by the Boys Town Center for the Study of Youth Development at Catholic University tried to answer two questions about adolescents in 10th grade: 0f those who are worshiping regularly, what are the key influences? Of those who are active in the life of the parish or congregation, what explains this involvement?

With regard to regular worship, the study showed that no factor equals in importance the attitude and example of the adolescent's parents. With regard to active involvement, three factors have special weight: parental attitude and example, involvement by the friends of the adolescent, and the positive qualities of the parish's or congregation's youth minister. One element is constant: the influence of some significant other, the help of some facilitating person. Early adolescents *identify,* that is, they try on for size the lifestyle of someone(s) whom they admire and they grow into what they imitate.

This chapter builds upon the process of identification in two ways:
- It presents Jesus as the significant other in the life of Paul—the one who made all the difference to him.
- It presents Paul as a person himself who embodies an ideology worth making one's own, as a significant other whose lifestyle to some extent can be tried on and imitated by the adolescent.

Background on Content

Paul and his Times: Born of a Jewish family in the flourishing hellenistic city of Tarsus, Paul was an interesting combination of Jewish faith, Greek culture, and Roman citizenship. In Paul's time the Jews of the Diaspora touched the East and the West, Asia and Europe, attracting young minds dissatisfied with obsolete myths and gods. Judaism, with its belief in the one God, with its moral code and with its unique history, was fascinating to the non-Jew.

Paul was a person of his time and his environment. The influence of Greek philosophy and culture is apparent in his writings. Nevertheless, the driving force in Paul's life was his Jewish faith (Philippians 3:5–6) and it was his Jewish past with its extreme zeal for the Law that ignited his anger with the growing Jewish Christian sect.

Paul's Conversion and Call: His extreme orthodoxy made Paul a hostile persecutor of the early Christians. As he bore down on his opponents, Paul was "grasped by Christ" (Philippians 3:12) and the thrust of his life turned radically inside out. Former values were worthless; former zeal for the Law was replaced by righteousness through faith in Jesus. Crucial to Paul's conversion experience were (1) his understanding of God's righteousness as available to all sinners, and (2) his understanding that salvation comes to all who believe in Jesus (Romans 2:16–17).

Paul understands his conversion experience in the light of his call to be an apostle to the Gentiles (Galatians 1:15–17). His message was that when God sent Christ into the world, God made salvation available to all persons who believe in Jesus Christ who suffered, died, and rose from the dead. This is central to the message which Paul drives home in his work among the Gentiles.

"Grasped by Christ" and called to be an apostle to the Gentiles, Paul reveals his overpowering missionary zeal in his letters.

Teaching Notes 1

Text Pages
20–24

Looking Into the Future

1. Before beginning ask the students to:
    ● *listen* carefully to the words of the song "Earthen Vessels" taken from 2 Corinthians 6–7 and 1 Corinthians 1:27–29 (see *Resources* for this Guide chapter).
    ● *reflect* on what they remember about Paul:
    —*events* in his life,
    —his *personality*,
    —his *role* in spreading the gospel.

Allow two or three minutes for quiet reflection on Paul and the words of the song "Earthen Vessels."

2. Divide the students into three groups, each group to concentrate on one of the above. Blackboard, newsprint, or a transparency could be used to record the summaries of each group for the others. Once this is completed, the students will have information on Paul upon which to build.

Paul the Persecutor

1. "Paul the Persecutor" (text pages 20–23) is *chosen* by God for a special work. People have been called or chosen by God for a special work throughout human history. Using this idea have the students name several figures from the Hebrew Scriptures who, like Paul, were also chosen by God. Some

examples might be:
- Abraham: Father of believers—faith
- Moses: Liberation from slavery—freedom
- Prophets: Hosea—God's forgiving love
- Isaiah: Israel must be holy as God is holy
- John the Baptist: prepares the way for the Messiah
- Mary: "Yes" to God

2. Allow the students time to brainstorm some of the common characteristics found in those who are chosen by God. Some ideas might be:
- prayerfulness: a close relationship with God
- openness: a basic desire to do what God asks of them, to please God despite any suffering or hardship involved in God's demands
- goodness: a genuine concern for others and their welfare
- generosity: always putting God first in their lives and giving themselves wholeheartedly to tasks from which they may have naturally recoiled.

3. Having looked at some prominent people in the Hebrew Scriptures and some common characteristics found among those chosen, have the students compare these people and their qualities with Paul and what they know of him as a person before he was chosen by God.

4. Possible assignments at this point could include reference to the notion that God still calls today. People like Dag Hammarskjöld, Martin Luther King, Jr., Cesar Chavez, Dorothy Day, and Mother Teresa have all responded to his unique call to them. Have students research *one* of the above (or any others who fit into this category) and prepare a brief oral report on:
- the *uniqueness* of that person's call;
- that person's *response* to God's call.

5. Have students reflect on people they know who have been called and who do witness to Jesus in their own lives. Have them write up a report about these people and their responses to God's call.

6. The exercise at the end of this section (text page 23) contains important information for understanding Paul:

a. Philippians 3:5–6: Paul considered himself faultless in obeying the commands of the law and found his righteousness in his obedience. Discuss with the students the meaning of "righteousness" for Paul (Philippians 3:2–11; *JBC* #50:23):
- How do we today consider ourselves "righteous" when obeying commands or laws?
- What more does Jesus require of us? (Inner attitude of love)

b. Galatians 1:13–14: Paul describes his zeal in living according to the Mosaic Law and to the Jewish traditions. It was this zeal that led him to persecute the early Christians. Discuss with the students:
- How can zeal be a good thing? a bad thing?
- What should be a guilding principle behind our zeal? (Jesus' law of love)

Experiences Which Transform
From Persecutor to Disciple
A Walkathon For Christ

1. With reference to these sections (text pages 23–24), have the students reflect on a special person in their lives, a person whom they admire and idealize. Then let them share their experiences on how these people have influenced their lives for the better. Students may also bring up people who have negatively influenced them and changed their lives. This can enhance the shared discussion and would be a good opportunity to stress the importance of discerning good from bad influence.

2. Returning to the list of common qualities found in those who are chosen by God (see Paul the Persecutor, #2 of this *Teaching Notes* section), have the students discuss how these qualities might predispose Paul—or anyone for that matter—for a conversion experience.

3. At this point in the chapter it might be helpful to view the filmstrip "The Road to Damascus," Episode 3 from *Paul and the Early Church* (see *Resources* for this Guide chapter). This particular filmstrip gives some background for the apostles' initial efforts to fulfill Christ's command to be his witnesses in Jerusalem and eventually to the ends of the earth (Acts 1:8). The greater part of the filmstrip covers the Damascus event, explaining in some detail the meaning of Paul's conversion experience and the role of human leaders within the Christian community. It is through Ananias that Paul's sight is restored, that he is baptized and confirmed as a follower of the Christ whom he had personally persecuted.

Teaching Notes 2

Text Pages 25–29

Life Is Christ!
In this section, "Life Is Christ!" (text pages 25–26), the exercise on people and things that make life meaningful (text page 26) can be a good tool for enabling the students to understand Paul's total interest in the person of Christ. The importance of this exercise is to have the students appreciate how Christ gave meaning to every facet of Paul's life and that without Christ there was no meaning to life at all for Paul.

Paul the Community Builder
1. By doing *Worksheet #3* the students can appreciate more the kind of leader Paul was and what talents he had for community building.

2. After reading the section "Paul the Community Builder" (text pages 26–29), the students can actually attempt to start a Christian community from scratch, using their school or parish community as a possible forum for spreading the good news. Divide the students into 5 groups:
- 2 groups of "disciples"
- 2 groups of "pagans"
- 1 group of 3 or 5 students to act as a panel of judges

Assign students as "disciples" and let them:
- discern the qualities needed for

communicating the good news;
- outline a strategy;
- actually attempt to catechize the "pagans."

The students assigned as "pagans" should:
- think of the apathy in society and how they will reflect it;
- prepare questions to challenge the "disciples";
- actually meet with the "disciples."

"Judges" should be students capable of evaluating the quality of discipleship that is evident in the students, the portrayal of their roles, and their ability to answer questions of the unbelievers. As judges they should anticipate possible questions and behavior from the "unbelievers." In the two meetings that occur they should decide which band of disciples was more effective during the actual attempt at conversion and community building and why.

Plan strategy:
- Allow 15 minutes for each group to prepare its role.
- Pair off 1 "disciple" group with 1 "pagan" group and allow each pair 10 minutes for group interaction.
- The panel of judges will determine which group of "disciples" was more effective and why.
- The judges' deliberations and conclusions will be set forth before the entire group (15 minutes).

This may require two full sessions, one for ntroduction and preparation and one for execution and discussion of the experience.

The Troublemaker
Final Arrest
The longer section, "The Troublemaker" (text pages 30–31) deals with the response Paul encountered in his enthusiastic attempt to spread the good news. For the sake of variety, divide the students into nine groups, each group responsible for a different place Paul visited. Each group should:
- read its section in the student text;
- read the corresponding text in Acts.

Paphos	Acts 13:4–12
Antioch	Acts 13:44–52
Lystra	Acts 14:8–20
Philippi	Acts 16:25–40
Ephesus	Acts 19:23–40
Troas	Acts 20:9–12
Antioch	Acts 15:36–41
Jerusalem	Acts 21:17–22; 29
Rome	Acts 28:17–31

- Give a brief oral description of the events, showing how Paul was a troublemaker there. Students may want to role play "their story."

The Warm Side of Paul
1. The students are now more familiar with Paul as a person. Suggest that they imagine themselves to be close friends of Paul from Miletus who have just learned of his death in Rome. Someone has asked that his friends draw up a profile of Paul which can

be sent to Christians throughout the lands he traveled. The profile is meant to express what his friends feel is the true St. Paul. The following points are some suggestions towards composing such a profile.

Paul of Tarsus
Raised and educated_____
In his early adult life he was a_____
and he worked diligently at_____
The turning point of his career was _____
Paul was the kind of person who_____
He died _____
He will be remembered most for _____
His greatest value in life was_____
His greatest wish was _____
Knowing Paul has made our lives more
    meaningful because_____

2. Toward the end of this chapter it would be worthwhile to have the students reflect more seriously on Paul's conversion experience. For the students, as well as for Paul, a conversion experience becomes a moment of growth in the life of a Christian. The exercise on *Worksheet #4* is meant to have the students seriously reflect on Paul's experience and their own in order to discover some painful experience which in the long run helped them to mature as a person, as a Christian.

3. The following summary of important points from this chapter should be of help to the students.
    a. *Conversion Experiences:* The sincerity and integrity of Paul's person and of his relationship with God made him receptive to an intensely personal experience of Jesus through the revelation of God.
    b. *Life in Christ:* This conversion experience redirected Paul's whole life and all his energies so that only in Christ would he find true life.
    c. *Desire to Spread the Good News:* This life in Christ could not be contained: to live in Christ for Paul means to be able to preach Christ still more.

    d. *The Person Paul:* God uses this person Paul to be his witness, as he is with all his good and bad qualities. God works through any individual who is sincere in his or her relationship with God and who allows God to act in his or her life.

Prayer Reflection
This "Prayer Reflection" (text page 35) offers the students an opportunity to internalize Paul's experience for themselves. Use a lighted candle to symbolize Christ's presence; sit in a comfortable yet respectful manner in an atmosphere of inner stillness.

Have one student read aloud the Prayer Reflection. Then allow time for application: "God calls me." Both at present and in whatever future work in which the student is involved, God calls each one to witness to him by living a life of love. Have the students reflect on their present lives and their witness value; have them reflect on one area of their lives where they can improve their witness as a Christian.

During this quiet reflection, the song "You Are My Sons" (see *Resources* for this Guide chapter) can be used as background music. Their reflection should be added to their Prayer Journals.

Prayer and Worship Experiences

1. After his experience on the road to Damascus and his stay in that city, Paul went off by himself for a while to reflect on what had happened and to give direction to his life. Encourage the students to introduce some quiet times in their lives—at home in privacy, a solitary walk, some time spent in a church or chapel. Suggest to them ways of recollecting themselves so as to enjoy and profit from such occasions.

2. Build a prayer experience on the theme of conversion or change. The emphasis should be upon persons other than the students themselves. Some examples may be from history, such as St. Justin Martyr, St. Ignatius Loyola, St. Elizabeth Seton. Others may be from the present such as Thomas Merton, Dorothy Day, or Jean Vanier. Brief readings from the lives of some such persons can be interspersed with song and scriptural readings. The service might conclude with a practical application but it should be expressed in a gentle, invitational way.

3. We can assume that Paul often prayed as he traveled on foot. Some people today find the rhythmic pattern of brisk walking or of jogging an aid to raising their hearts to God in prayer. The teacher can help by suggesting topics for reflection or meditation while walking or jogging.

Service Projects

1. St. Paul is what we have come to call "a missionary" in the life of the Church. Help the group come in personal contact with some missionary of today through their friends or relatives, through their school or parish, or through some agency in their diocese. They can find out from the missionary how they can be of practical help to him or to her.

2. Paul's travels raise the practical questions of hospitality which are true in every age. Invite volunteers to form a hospitality group to help people who are new to the school, parish, or neighborhood to feel at home and to meet some of their human and religious needs.

Independent Study Projects

1. Assist some students in designing a large map to indicate the extensiveness of Paul's many journeys. This map could serve as an aid to the group's learning.

2. Ask a small number of students to research and role play how a travel agent would describe the places which Paul visited.

3. Research such sources as the *New Catholic Encyclopedia* and the *Catholic Encyclopedia for School and Home* for futher biographical information on St. Paul.

Resources

Audiovisual

Abingdom Bible Map Transparencies. The Journeys of Paul. Item Code No. 00179X. Hammond Inc., Maplewood, NJ.

"Earthen Vessels." John Foley, S.J. Recording on the album *Earthen Vessels.* North American Liturgy Resources, 2110 W. Peoria Avenue, Phoenix, AZ 85029.

"You Are My Sons." Dan Schutte, S.J. Recording on the album *Neither Silver Nor Gold.* North American Liturgy Resources.

The Road to Damascus. sound filmstrip, Episode 3 of *Paul and the Early Church,* ROA, 1696 N. Astor St., Milwaukee, WI 53202.

Print

G. Bornkamm. *Paul.* New York: Harper and Row, 1969.

J. Fitzmyer. "Life of Paul" #46 in *The Jerome Biblical Commentary.* Englewood Cliffs: Prentice-Hall, 196.

_____. "Pauline Theology" #79 in *The Jerome Biblical Commentary.*

N. Perrin. *The New Testament, An Introduction.* New York: Harcourt Brace Jovanovich, 1974.

3

Paul, the Letter Writer

Text Pages
36–51

Objectives

Knowledge: To assist the students to understand: a) the importance of letters as a tool of communication at the time of Paul; b) that the parts of a letter used in ancient times are very similar to those we use today; and c) that he wrote his letters to meet the particular needs of the community he was addressing.

Attitude: To encourage the students to begin to appreciate Paul's affection and concern for the people whose lives he had already touched.

Practice: To motivate the students to look at the means of communication available to them today (letters, phone calls, etc.) and determine how they can show care and concern for others through these means.

Orientation

This chapter begins the serious study of the Christian Scriptures, looking for the first time at one literary form: the letter. It is a good beginning because all students have written letters (at least, it is to be hoped, in English class) by the time they begin this course. ''Getting Mail'' (text pages 36–37) is intended precisely to whet their interest. Everyone loves to receive mail, and some may even have used the postal system as a means of sending coded messages meant only for the intended recipient. The transition to the Pauline Letters can be readily made in the brief section, ''Background Information'' (text pages 38–39).

Good background for Paul's letter to Philemon is the informational section ''Slavery in the First Century'' (text page 39). The students might be familiar with slavery in the early history of the United States of America. But the fact that slavery was so widespread and so accepted in the time of Christ might be a new concept.

''The Letter to Philemon'' (text pages 39–41) is an excellent model to study Paul as a letter writer. The students will learn that letter writing has not changed much through the centuries. Other than the form, students are introduced to Paul's style of writing and the clever ways he tried to communicate his message. The Letter to Philemon is a good study case.

It is important to note that one does not always understand everything that is said in a letter for the simple reason that the writer and the addressee are aware of circumstances hidden to outside parties.

Paul's first letter to the Thessalonians is the earliest of his writings which has come down to us. "Thessalonians" (text pages 42–45) covers the early Church problems concerning the end of the world and it gives us a concise picture of Paul's manner of dealing with these problems. Remaining sections of the chapter deal with various aspects of Paul's first letter to the Thessalonians.

Life Experience Focus

There are several points at which this chapter intersects with the life experience of adolescents.

The first has to do with communication. Much of Paul's communication took the form of letter writing. For the adolescent of today communication is more by way of the telephone or direct conversation. Yet the dynamics are similar: we follow a pattern of wishing each other well; of saying good things about each other or about our topic of conversation; we find ways of pointing out what we do not like and what we think could be better; we pass on our best wishes to those who are not in on the phone call; we have a way of saying good-bye.

A second point of intersection is how we face issues which may be objectively unjust but which we are unable to change in any radical way. In St. Paul's time one such issue was slavery. Today it may be some other form of exploitation of some people by others.

A third point of intersection is the question that bothered the Thessalonians: What will the next world be like? When adolescents are asked what confuses them or frightens them or makes them think, very often they answer: death. Paul's response to the question in Thessalonica can help them explore this topic in their own terms.

Background on Content

In recent years Paul's writings have been referred to as letters rather than as epistles, and rightly so. Biblical scholars regard the epistle as a deliberate literary composition, dealing with a specific concern and intended only for the person or persons to whom it is addressed. The writings of Paul are definitely letters. Paul wrote to a particular group of people, to meet their specific needs, and to address a situation peculiar to their living out the Christ-life.

The format for ancient letters contained the same basic features of modern letters: salutation or greeting, thanksgiving or wish for health, the body containing the central message of the letter, and the conclusion. The Pauline letters share these features with slight variations. Usually his opening and thanksgiving remarks are longer than our modern ones; the body of his letters is ordinarily divided into two sections, one a doctrinal proclamation or teaching, and the other a parenesis or ethical exhortation designed to address the situation of his audience.

Since it is so short, Paul's Letter to Philemon is a perfect tool for studying the format of Paul's letters. Philemon was the owner of a runaway slave, Onesimus, who met Paul while he was in prison. There Paul converted him to Christianity and hoped to involve him in spreading the gospel. Because Roman law mandated that runaway slaves be returned to their masters, Paul was obligated to send Onesimus back to Philemon. But Paul uses this occasion not only to return Onesimus, but also to confront his "beloved fellow worker," Philemon, with the challenge of preaching Christianity by the loving manner in which he welcomes back his runaway slave.

The format of this letter contains:
- vv. 1–3: address and greeting
- vv. 4–7: thanksgiving
- vv. 8–20: message
- vv. 21–25: conclusion and final greeting

Paul's first letter to the Thessalonians follows this same basic format (in chapter and verse):
- 1:1: greeting
- 1:2–10: thanksgiving
- 2:1—5:11: body in three segments
- 2:1–16: recollection of Paul's work with Thessalonians
- 2:17—3:1–3: expression of Paul's concern
- 4:1—5:11: exhortation to holiness and love, and instruction regarding the parousia
- 5:12–28: conclusion

As the earliest writing in the Christian Scriptures, First Thessalonians addresses itself primarily to the problem of the coming of the parousia. The Thessalonians, who expected the second coming of Christ imminently, were concerned with the fate of those who died before that coming. How would these Christians share in the parousia if they had already died? Paul's response is that the parousia will come soon, but no one knows the date. The bulk of Paul's message to the Thessalonians deals with the importance of living the Christ-life so as to be prepared for the parousia when it does come. Paul's theology is clearly exposed in 4:1—5:11: Jesus died and rose for us (4:14; 5:10); all who believe in him will also rise from the dead by the power of God (4:14); there will be a second coming of Christ (4:16); in the meantime, all Christians must spend their time not only working but also living their lives within the context of holiness and love (4:9–12).

Teaching Notes 1

Text Pages
36–39

Getting Mail

1. With regard to "Getting Mail" (text pages 36–37), help the students to recognize the fact that very often the writer of the letter makes reference to people and situations that only the addressee will understand. Read the letter from John to Sam and then discuss the questions which follow the letter.

2. Have a student compose a letter to a close friend; in the letter the student should try to illustrate that a letter can be written which only the two friends would clearly understand and which would be vague to any other reader.

Early Christian Mail
Background Information

1. Have the students read through "Background Information" (text pages 38–39) and then study the map (text page 38).

2. Place the word "inspiration" on the board. After reading and discussing the meaning (text page 39), have the students write a simple definition which could be used for persons beginning a study of the Scriptures.

3. At the end of this section it would be extremely profitable to show the students the filmstrip "Letters: A Tradition" (see *Resources* for this Guide chapter). The major portion of this filmstrip deals with Paul, his life, and his letters; the accompanying Teacher's Guide offers many helpful activities to use as a preparation for or review of the filmstrip.

Slavery in the First Century

1. Since the students are familiar with the period of slavery in the early history of the United States, discuss the following questions before reading "Slavery in the First Century" (text page 39):

● Why did the early settlers find it so easy to own slaves? (Slavery was accepted in society at that time; individual human rights were not accorded to slaves since they were considered "human property.")

● The treatment of the slave depended upon the whim of the owner. In those cases when slaves ran away from their masters, what were some of the punishments upon recapture? (Whipping, mutilations, etc. Students who viewed the television production of *Roots* should have other contributions.)

● Even though Lincoln abolished slavery with the Emancipation Proclamation, more than one hundred years later "slavery" in its various forms still exists in the United States. In what ways do you agree and/or disagree with this statement? (Actual physical slavery, as it existed previously, no longer exists; however, people enslave other people in devious ways: exploitation of the poor; racial discrimination; sexism; multinational corporations' power over smaller businesses; super power nations' domination of the world's resources to the detriment of the Third World nations, etc.)

2. Slavery is the condition of enforced submission to others. Whereas physical slavery is no longer socially acceptable, there is an aspect of human nature which tries to dominate others, to put "me" first. Jesus recognized this and tried to give us a different model of behavior: "If one of you wants to be great, he must be the servant of the rest; and if one of you wants to be first, he must be the slave of all. For even the Son of Man did not come to be served; he came to serve and to give his life to redeem many people" (Mark 10:43–45).

- Divide the students into small groups and have them brainstorm practical ways in which people try to dominate others. (Someone may say an untruth about another in order to appear more righteous before the group, etc.)

- After ten or fifteen minutes, allow a recorder to list each group's findings on the board.

- Have the group react to the findings in the light of Mark 10:43–45.

Teaching Notes 2

Text Pages 39–45

The Letter to Philemon
Signing Off
What Happened
Philemon and Me

1. Have the students read the introduction presented in "The Letter to Philemon" (text page 39). Using that background have a student read aloud Paul's Letter to Philemon.

2. The next few pages of the student text analyze the format of Paul's letter (text pages 40–41). Read through these pages and then by means of discussion try to determine the students' understanding of the letter.

3. *Worksheet #5* is designed to help the students assimilate the message of Paul in his letter to Philemon.

4. Role play the situation where Paul encounters Onesimus, converts him, and writes his letter to Philemon. The students can then be creative and write their own ending to the script by describing Onesimus' return meeting with Philemon.

5. Use the Biblical Simulation, "The House Church" (see *Resources* for this Guide chapter). This activity would probably take more than one session.

Thessalonians

1. Before beginning the section "Thessalonians" (text pages 42–45), pose the following question to the group and ask for a written response:

"If science could conclusively determine that a natural disaster will occur in five years which would destroy life on earth, how would you spend the next five years?"

Allow students time to reflect and write their responses (I would . . .). These responses should be brief statements which could later be collected and read aloud to the entire group.

2. Because the Thessalonians believed that the second coming of Christ would be within their lifetime, they too were faced with a similar situation. Have the students read the material in "Thessalonians" before discussing the following questions:
- What was the Thessalonians' response to the possibility that the end of the world, the parousia, might come in a short time? (They stopped working, lived off others, etc.)
- What additional problem concerned them with regard to those who died before the parousia? (The Thessalonians thought you had to be alive at the second coming of Christ in order to be saved, thus they worried about their loved ones who had already died.)

Teaching Notes 3

**Text Pages
45–51**

A Basic Method
1 Thessalonians 1:1–10
1 Thessalonians 2:1–20
1 Thessalonians 4:1–12
1 Thessalonians 4:13–18
1 Thessalonians 5:1–28
1. "A Basic Method" (text pages 45–46) provides the students with a handy tool for understanding the Scriptures. Its method is simple and its immediate application to Paul's Letter to the Thessalonians will provide the students with the opportunity to use specifically what they have studied.

List on the board the basic parts of a Pauline letter:
- greeting and blessing
- thanksgiving
- message or body
- conclusion and final greeting

Have the students read their text section by section and indicate the parts of the letter by chapter and verse.

2. The introduction "1 Thessalonians 1:1–10" (text page 46) includes:
- greeting
- thanksgiving (vv. 2–10)
- hints about working (v. 3); about moral life (vv. 6–7); about the end of the world (v. 10).

The body of the letter is contained in 2:1—5:11 and can be divided for present purposes this way:

a. 2:1–20: Paul's recollection and interpretation of his work while in Thessalonica. Verses 9 and 10 are an indirect rebuke to those Thessalonians who are loafers; these verses should have made the loafers and high-livers feel uncomfortable about the way they were living. Discuss with the students ways in which these verses are applicable to people in our society today and to themselves as students.

b. 3:1–13: Paul's activities while visiting Thessalonica.

c. 4:2—5:22: The heart of Paul's message to the Thessalonians. In 4:13–18: The real concern of Paul's letter is contained here—verses which give instruction regarding the time of the parousia. He answers their fears about those who have died before the second coming of Christ (v. 14). Faith in Jesus is the saving factor.

Verses 16–18 of Chapter 4 are a good example of apocalyptic language (see *Resources* for this Guide chapter.)

In Chapter 5:1–11 Paul's basic message is to live each day in imitation of Christ; the day and the hour of his second coming are unknown, but all should be prepared at all times. Important for theological content, verses 9 and 10 express Paul's teaching that Jesus died that we might have life.

d. The conclusion of this letter is contained in 5:12–28.

3. *Worksheet #6* is designed to help the students to reflect on the different ways which Paul used to communicate with people and to evaluate our own means of communicating today.

4. The following summary of important points should be of help to the students:

a. The basic parts of an ancient letter should be known (see *Background on Content* for this Guide chapter).

b. These parts should be recognized in the Letter to Philemon. More important is the message of this letter:

- challenge to love as Christ did (vv. 8–11, 21);
- while accepting the social system of slavery in his day, Paul attempts to christianize it by pointing out that everyone has the same status before God (vv. 15–16);
- call to forgiveness and reconciliation (vv. 17–18).

c. The message of First Thessalonians:

- all who have died believing in Jesus will share in the resurrection and the second coming (4:13–18);
- there are no signs to indicate the exact day and time of the parousia, but it is important to live each day within the context of love.

Prayer Reflection

The Prayer Reflection (text page 51) can be used in a litany form. A Leader could introduce the litany with two other students alternating the concerns. It is important that this be read prayerfully; allow a slight pause before going on to the next concern so that the students carefully reflect on their responsibility for each concern.

Before the final prayer allow the students time to reflect on one concern in particular on which they would like to concentrate personally. They can then enter their reflections in their Prayer Journal.

This *Final Prayer* may be read by the Leader:
May our God and Father himself and our Lord Jesus prepare the way before us.
May the Lord make our love for one another and for all people grow more and more and become as great as the Lord's love for us. In this way he will strengthen us, and we will be perfect and holy in the presence of our God and Father when our Lord Jesus comes with all who belong to him. (Adaptation of First Thessalonians 3:11–13).

Prayer and Worship Experiences

1. With excerpts from the Mass of the Resurrection and the Rite for Christian Burial as a basis, help the students to construct and celebrate a Liturgy of the Word which reflects the Christian understanding of death. Do not hesitate to introduce slides, or dance, or role playing as a way of responding to the readings and the prayers.

2. "My prayer is that our fellowship with you as believers will bring about a deeper understanding of every blessing which we have in our life in union with Christ" (Philemon vs. 6). Belief for Paul was both deeply personal and broadly communal. Encourage the students to reflect privately on these two dimensions of their own faith. Help them to recognize that on the one hand no one else can make our faith-response for us and on the other it is rare that we believe in isolation from the support of our friends and family.

Service Projects

1. There are people who want to stay in touch with other people by letter or telephone but who for one reason or another find this difficult. Invite some students to explore whether people in their area have such needs and determine how they can help them.

2. All people will face death at some point in their lives. Death is fearsome for many because of the very many unknowns attached to it. Adolescents seldom think of their own death, yet they should become sensitive to the fact that there are many elderly in our society who face the possibility of death more imminently. Ask each student to think of an elderly relation or neighbor who means something special to him or her. Encourage the student to visit this person in the course of the following week to bring joy to that person.

3. Do your students know of anyone who is in a situation similar to that of Onesimus—that is, someone who is in difficulty and who needs someone to put in a good word for him or her?

Suggest that they become peacemaking intermediaries in situations where they will not be looked upon as unwelcome intruders in other peoples' problems.

Independent Study Projects

1. The concern of the people in Thessalonica for Jesus' coming and sadness over some who died before this second coming raised the question of an afterlife. Assist some students in researching what different religious traditions believe about the afterlife. Some examples might be: Buddhism, Hinduism, and Mohammedanism.

2. For the community in Thessalonica Paul gave the simple common sense advice: Those who do not work do not eat. Quite obviously he allowed for exceptions since he himself raised money in the wealthier communities to help the poor and handicapped where poverty was greater. Today the economic situation is far more complex. Help some students to research the current teaching of the Church on the rights of the poor and the handicapped for the necessities of life and the responsibility of both government and private individuals to help those in need.

Resources

Audiovisual

"Letters: A Tradition." sound filmstrip.
Episode 6 of *Understanding Scriptures.*
ROA, 1696 N. Astor St., Milwaukee,
WI 53202.

Print

J. Fitzmyer, S.J. "New Testament Epistles,"
#47 in *The Jerome Biblical
Commentary.* Englewood Cliffs, NJ:
Prentice-Hall, 1968.

_____. "The Letter to Philemon," #54 in *The
Jerome Biblical Commentary.*

J. T. Forestall, C.S.B. "The Letters to the
Thessalonians," #48 in *The Jerome
Biblical Commentary.*

J. L. McKenzie, S.J. "Apocalyptic Literature,"
in the *Dictionary of the Bible.*
Milwaukee: Bruce Publishing Co.,
1965.

D. Miller, G. Snyder, R. Neff. *Using Biblical
Simulations.* Vol II. Valley Forge, PA:
Judson Press, 1973.

N. Perrin. *The New Testament, An
Introduction.* New York: Harcourt Brace
Jovanovich, Inc., 1974.

P. Perkins. *Reading the New Testament, An
Introduction.* New York: Paulist Press,
1978.

H. Wansbrough, O.S.B. *Theology in St. Paul.*
Notre Dame, IN: Fides Publications,
1968.

4

Paul, the Trouble Shooter

Text Pages
52–67

Objectives

Knowledge: To help the students understand that spreading the good news of Christ is not always an easy task and that Paul spared no effort in order to reach others with the message of Christ.

Attitude: To encourage the students to gain some appreciation of Paul's tireless concern for helping people in their difficulties.

Practice: To assist the students in determining Christian choices in those situations where they can either help others or choose to look the other way.

Orientation

With Paul's Letters to the Corinthians, some fundamental aspects of Pauline theology comes into focus. It is through his struggle with his opponents in Corinth, that Paul formulates his key theological concepts regarding true wisdom, moral behavior, and the resurrection of the body.

"Live Issues" (text page 52) introduces the concept that crises heighten people's concern over the preservation of themselves and the world. Concern expressed today can influence the course of history for the future. In a similar manner, the crisis Paul encountered with the Corinthians

enabled him to sharpen his theological thinking and to formulate for generations to come some key theological doctrines.

While reading through "Cosmopolitan Corinth" (text pages 52–54), one can easily compare it to a modern United States city. However, Paul's teaching about Christ was to meet many challenges here, the fruit of which would be his two letters to the Corinthians.

The first of these challenges was to come via some friends. "Troubling News" (text pages 54–55) lists some of these critical problems in order to give the students some idea of what is coming. These problems are almost immediately developed in the next section "Praise and Reprimand" (text pages 55–56).

At this point the text develops the very important concept of wisdom as lived by Jesus and taught by Paul. "Logic Versus Christian Wisdom" (text page 56) unveils the problem that Jesus' death was God's wise plan to save humankind.

The real meaning of love is discussed in the section entitled "Real Teachers (1 Corinthians 3–4)" (text pages 56–57). Paul's understanding of love goes contrary to the media's portrayal of love today as narcissistic and pleasurable. The teacher will need to clearly explain this key Christian concept.

"What Is Permitted (1 Corinthians 8) (text pages 57–58) and "The Eucharist (1 Corinthians 11:17–34)" (text page 58) help the students to see the self-sacrificing aspect of Christian love. Christian love must penetrate every aspect of the Christian life, therefore, gifts and talents, in order to be fruitful for the Lord, must be based on a selfless love. This point is highlighted in "Charismatic Gifts (1 Corinthians 12–14)" (text pages 60–61).

The section on "Bodily Resurrection" (text page 62) touches upon the person's eternal search for immortality. To understand the Corinthians' problem with a resurrected body—and not with immortality—the teacher will need to explain carefully the Greek mentality dealing with the imprisonment of the soul in the body and their desire to become free from the material body. Paul's teaching that the body will rise is a difficult concept for the Greek mind to grasp.

"Try, Try Again" (2 Corinthians)" (text pages 63–64) deals with Paul's confrontation with the "Judaizers" in 2 Corinthians. Here a key concept of Paul, that salvation comes from belief in Jesus, is threatened by the Judaizers who teach that salvation comes through obeying the Mosaic Law.

The heart of this second letter to the Corinthians is treated in "Who Is Qualified?" (text pages 65–66). Here Paul describes the qualifications of a true apostle and includes as well proof that he measures up to these qualifications.

Life Experience Focus

One author on faith development, John Westerhoff III, writes that particularly important for the young adolescent is a growing and more conscious sense of affiliation in the faith community which was often taken for granted in the child's early years. This isn't always easy for the adolescent.

One reason is that the adolescent has to move out and away from his or her childhood and the Church may in many ways seem to be identified with that childhood. Secondly, the early adolescent sees much more realistically the faults and weaknesses of the adult world, including the adult faith community. Thirdly, the early adolescent has very high ideals and may have trouble with the Church because in it the adolescent sees so much mediocrity.

A study of Paul's dealing with the Christians in Corinth can help us respond to these three reasons why an early adolescent may find difficulty with the Church. First it shows Christianity as a pressing concern for adults and not just a matter for children. Second, it gives us an appreciation of how any Christian community has to come to grips with the limitations and failings of its human members. Third, the way Paul responds to the question with an appeal to self-giving love should strike a positive note in the idealism of the early adolescent.

Background on Content

True Wisdom is Found only in the Cross (1 Corinthians 1:10—2:16). Paul's first letter to the Corinthians was occasioned by Chloe's disturbing news that factions had risen in their Christian community. Some members were abandoning Paul's original message for that of other prestigious teachers. In order to answer them, Paul emphasized Christ's death. The Corinthians valued human knowledge and human wisdom as a way of knowing God. Paul rejected this and preached instead that true wisdom is found only in the cross.

This boggled the minds of the Corinthians who considered human knowledge, especially philosophy, to be real wisdom. Their whole stance toward wisdom was based on an intellectual disposition, whereas Paul's was based on a moral disposition (Philippians 2:6–11). True wisdom stems from an attitude of mind which is the same as Christ's. He emptied himself, sacrificed his life in obedience to his Father's will. It is specifically in doing the Father's will despite all cost to self that true Christian wisdom is manifested. This aspect of obedience to God's will reflects Paul's Jewish upbringing; for Jewish readers of the Hebrew Scriptures the art of living successfully and happily can only be achieved when one does God's will. Therefore, the crucified Christ becomes the model of true wisdom; through his obedience to his Father's will a person is saved. This is foolishness to the Greek mind; it is absurd because it surpasses human understanding. But God confounds human wisdom; God's ways and thoughts are very different from ours.

Conscience and Behavior (1 Corinthians 8:1–11). Paul taught that love always puts the considerations of others before self. For example, in Corinth almost all the meat sold in the markets had been previously sacrificed to idols. There were some Corinthians who *knew* that *eating* the meat was not in itself sinful. Since they *knew* gods did not exist, the common practice of the pagans around them did not touch their lives. Therefore, according to their right conscience eating that meat sacrificed to idols was not sinful. However, some Christian Corinthians did not *know* this; their behavior was based on their misinformed consciences. The problem for those with the right conscience was whether or not to eat meat sacrificed to idols in the company of those with the wrong conscience. Paul asks those with the right conscience to give up, not their freedom, but the right to follow their conscience so as not to cause the others to fall into sin (v. 13). Love for others should predominate.

This primacy of love as a motive for Christian behavior permeated Paul's theology. It appears in his teaching concerning the Eucharist (1 Corinthians 11:17–34); as a remembrance of Christ's death, the Eucharist is a celebration of the Father's love for us in Jesus. To carry out the Eucharist means to consider others before self, just as Christ gave up his life for others.

Bodily Resurrection (*1 Corinthians 15*). The issue of bodily resurrection is not confined to the Corinthian Greeks; the same issue has been continually raised even to our own day. Because the Greeks created such a dichotomy between the material body and the spiritual soul, they found it incomprehensible that their bodies—the material part of them—would rise from the dead.

Paul based his argument for a bodily resurrection on the bodily resurrection of Jesus. Because Jesus rose from the dead (Paul saw the risen Jesus in bodily form), it followed that all who believe in him will also undergo a bodily resurrection. His argument for a bodily resurrection is detailed in Chapter 15, verses 35–49: the natural body, infused with and controlled by the spirit, will rise from the dead as a spirit-dominated body. The resurrection of Jesus is the basis for the belief that all will rise from the dead (15:12–20). Because this resurrected body belongs to a new creation, Paul offers Christians the hope of immortality (vv. 35–58).

Teaching Notes 1

Text Pages
52–57

Live Issues

1. Read through the section "Live Issues" (text page 52). Have the students reflect on the sentence: "Is the use of nuclear power so critical . . . and perhaps kill a great many people?" Disuss:

- Why is there such an alarming energy crisis in the world today?
- How has this crisis forced nations to search for alternate sources of energy?
- What are some of these alternate sources of energy and why do different groups argue about which source of energy is best?

2. Invite the students to prepare their response to the following question through pictures and images rather than words. Question: Because of the energy crisis and the debate surrounding it, the people in our time will determine the course of history by the choices we make today. What are the choices available to us and how can each affect future generations?

Cosmopolitan Corinth

"Cosmopolitan Corinth" (text pages 52–54) provides the necessary background for Paul's Letters to the Corinthians. A study of the map of "Churches and Letters" should clarify the central position of Corinth as an excellent trading location in the Mediterranean. Where many people gather, there are bound to be divergent ideas. Have the students study the map (text page 38) and brainstorm about the kinds of problems such a city might have.

Troubling News

1. In preparation for "Troubling News" (text pages 54–55), have the students read the first four chapters of First Corinthians and jot down, as they read, the areas of divisions in the Church.

2. Have the students discuss the Corinthian problem as they see it at this point in their study. They should be able to pick out the basic problem: teachers have come into the community spreading different versions of the gospel message, thus dividing the community into various groups and creating disunity.

Praise and Reprimand

1. Once again the format of a Pauline letter should be placed on the board so that the students reinforce for themselves the pattern of Paul's letters. Have them read "Praise and Reprimand" (text pages 55–56) and then discuss:

- the verses which praise (vv. 4–7);
- the hints about the topics Paul will develop in his letter:
- "rich in all things, including all speech and knowledge" (1:5); later Paul will point out that "knowledge inflates" (8:2) and gifts of speech can be abused (Ch. 12 and 14).
- "have not failed to receive a single blessing as you wait for our Lord Jesus Christ to be revealed" (1:7); in chapter 15 Paul will again talk up the theme of parousia and the resurrection of the body.

2. Paul quickly gets to the heart of his message, the disunity among the Corinthians (1:10). Behind the problem of disunity lies the deeper problem of being caught up with themselves rather than being caught up with the crucified Christ. This difficulty was not peculiar to the Corinthians; Christians today struggle with the same human tendencies. In order to make this concept relevant to the teenager, use the following situation, or its equivalent, in which a person might tend to think mainly of self.

Situation: Fifteen-year-old Lisa is pregnant. In her confused state she seeks out advice from those around her; different people offer different solutions for different reasons, causing greater disunity and confusion:

- her parents urge her to have an abortion so that the family is not disgraced:
- her boyfriend urges her to give up the child for adoption so that they will not be guilty of an even greater evil;
- her closest friend encourages her to keep the baby so that Lisa can always have someone around to love and to be loved by;
- others tell her that society promotes freedom and independence for the individual: do what ever is best for you.

Paul's advice, according to 1 Corinthians 18:2–16), would be to concentrate not on self but on Jesus crucified and the message his death holds for each of us.

Application: Have the students determine how each of the above influences on Lisa would respond to Paul's teaching. Most would say that his solution was utter foolishness; only her boyfriend might see ssome wisdom in Paul's solution. Ask the students to discuss possible reasons why Lisa's boyfriend might agree with Paul. (Paul teaches that true wisdom is based on the suffering and death of Christ; because Jesus obeyed his Father's will, his sufferings and death are fruitful for our salvation. Lisa's boyfriend seems to be following Paul's line of thinking: by Lisa's going through with the pregnancy, by accepting whatever humiliations and sufferings are involved with bearing this child, she, in a similiar manner, is dying to self so that her child's life may be saved. This wisdom of life coming through death is foolishness for those who are spiritually immature).

Logic Versus Christian Wisdom

1. Recall the above situation to help clarify the controversy of "Logic Versus Christian Wisdom" (text page 56). Modern youth, not unlike the Corinthians, see as illogical the belief that suffering can lead to a deeper, richer life. Dying on the cross was not wise to a society that promoted self-gratification.

2. Have one student read aloud 1 Corinthians 1:18—2:16 and then let the group discuss the exercise at the end of this section (text page 56).

a. Paul condemns this world's wisdom as foolishness (vv. 19–20). (It is important for the teacher to clarify here the fact that Paul is not condemning knowledge or study that results in earthly wisdom; rather he is condemning that false wisdom—going back to Adam in the garden (Genesis 3:5)—whereby man sets himself in opposition to God, tries to run his own life independent of God, and actually replaces God in his life with himself. It's the old sin of pride).

b. To understand the wisdom of the cross, according to Paul, one needs faith and the power of God's Spirit who gifts a person with the mind of Christ (vv. 14–16). Through the power of the Spirit one develops the mind of Christ so that with Christ one can accept the cross in one's life (self-sacrifice), thereby doing the will of the Father. God has willed that we be saved through the obedience of his Son even unto death. This plan, carried out by Christ and continued in the lives of Christians, is wise because it leads to salvation. The statement, "Do good unto others as long as it is to your own benefit," runs counter to the wisdom of the cross because it is centered in self-aggrandizement, rather than self-sacrifice, as the motive for charity.

Real Teachers (1 Corinthians 3–4)

1. Paul develops this idea further in chapters 3 and 4 of First Corinthians. Have the students read Paul's description of "Real Teachers (1 Corinthians 3–4)" (text pages 56–57); real teachers are servants, faithful to their master, sacrificing themselves in order to build up others.

2. As the students read through 1 Corinthians 3 and 4, they should list the qualities Paul considers necessary to be a good Christian teacher:

- concerned with building up the Christian community;
- submission to God who is the real builder (1 Corinthians 3:7);
- build upon Christ, the true foundation (1 Corinthians 3:11);
- humility about the good one does to build up the community (1 Corinthians 3:21);
- service is their key function, a service that is visible in works, and not just in eloquent speech (1 Corinthians 4:2);
- marked by suffering and the cross (1 Corinthians 4:9–13).

3. *Worksheet #7* asks the students to examine the characteristics Paul looked for in one who would spread the good news and to explore ways in which people today can exhibit similar traits.

4. Have the students divide into small groups to do the exercise at the end of this section. Once they have decided on a favorite teacher, they could list his or her personal qualities, compare them with Paul's list above and then share their small group reflections with the others.

What Is Permitted? (1 Corinthians 8)

1. According to Paul it is love that builds up the community, the love manifested by Christ through his obedience to his Father's will. Love is also the solution to the next problem that Paul addresses in his letters to the Corinthians. In this section, "What Is Permitted? (1 Corinthians 8)" (text pages 57–58), Paul confronts another device people invent to put themselves before others. The apparently simple question about eating meat is really more concerned with the pride of those who know they have the right answer, but cause scandal among those who lack this knowledge (1 Corinthians 8:7). Have the students read Chapter 8 carefully, looking for the elements that distinguish a right conscience from a wrong or weak conscience.

2. After reading 8:1–13, have the students answer the questions in the text (page 58):

- Corinthians have the right to eat meat offered to idols because they know that there is only one God, that pagan gods do not exist; therefore, eating meat sacrificed to idols means nothing (1 Corinthians 8:4–6).
- Paul challenges the Corinthians to give up their right to eat this meat on the basis that the situation is not an equal one—all Corinthians do not share

this "knowledge" that other gods do not exist. Therefore, to eat meat might cause those with a weaker conscience to sin (v. 13).

● Discuss with the students the meaning of the statement: "Such knowledge, however, puffs a person up with pride; but love builds up." Their response should reflect the fact that because some people have a great deal of knowledge that in itself does not make them better people. People who think they are better or smarter than others sometimes put themselves and their interests before others; whereas, people who love do not boast about what they know but try to build up other people.

The Eucharist (1 Corinthians 11:17–34)

1. Paul's theme of love is developed even further in "The Eucharist (1 Corinthians 11:17–34)" (text page 58). Once the students have read this section have them read Paul's actual words to the Corinthians.

● How was their behavior in the direct contradiction to the whole meaning of the Eucharist? (The Corinthians were more concerned with themselves and the food they were eating. Whereas the Eucharist is a remembrance of Christ's death—an act of love whereby he gave himsef for others—the Corinthians, however, are not giving of themselves, not sacrificing themselves for others. They are thinking only of themselves).

2. Have the students share their responses to the exercise ending this section (text page 58).

3. The meal is a symbol of sharing and strengthening life. It is an occasion for expressing our trust in others, our faith in others. It is an opportunity not only to receive (eat) but to give.

The Eucharist is the meal of Christians. In the fullest sense of the word it is the Christian symbol of sharing and strengthening

life—the life that exists among Christians, and between Christians and God. Ritual sometimes hides that symbolism. Readings and music, sounds and words, sometimes obscure the reality that the Eucharist is primarily a meal.

The four main parts of the Christian meal are: *Preparation, Blessing, Breaking,* and *Eating/Drinking.* The students can appreciate these four movements by preparing a meal which symbolizes their sharing and strengthening as a group. Some suggestions for helping them gain such an appreciation follow.

● Preparation: the foods are chosen and prepared. These foods symbolize: ___
● Blessing: a prayer of thanksgiving for our unity as a group: _____
● Breaking: the food is divided and shared. Some food is put aside for members of the group who are absent. A statement of the meaning of the food is made while it is divided: _____
● Eating/Drinking: As the food is received a statement of commitment to the group is made by each member: ___

Charismatic Gifts (1 Corinthians 12–14)

1. Paul brings home his message of the importance of love once again. Have the students read "Charismatic Gifts (1 Corinthians 12–14)" (text pages 60–61), noting the significance of the six points listed.

2. Have the students read 1 Corinthians 13 and give reasons why love, as described here, is the answer for all the evils in the world. Have the students take a world problem (arms race), a national problem (energy crisis) and a local problem (existence of ghettos) and explain how 1 Corinthians 13, if *lived* by Christians, could change the world for the better.

Bodily Resurrection

1. In order to give the students an understanding as to why the Corinthians were upset about a bodily resurrection, have the students read "Bodily Resurrection" (text page 62).

2. Proceed to the exercise (text page 62) and encourage the students to express as best they can in their letters their feelings about bodily resurrection in light of Paul's teaching.

Try, Try Again (2 Corinthians)

1. In Second Corinthians Paul repeats the qualities of real teachers of Christ's message he had written about in his first letter to the Corinthians. Paul had to deal with the "Judaizers" who maintained very close ties with the Hebrew Scriptures to the point where they placed more value on the Mosaic Law than on their belief in Jesus. These Judaizers were gaining followers. Discuss with the students possible reasons why people would prefer adherence to the Law to belief in the saving power of Jesus.

2. Have the students read "Try, Try Again (2 Corinthians)" (text pages 63–64) which gives the background for the core of Paul's message to the Corinthians.

Who Is Qualified?

1. Before beginning "Who is Qualified?" (text pages 65–66), divide the students into two groups. The first group can study the scriptural passages which describe the qualities of a true disciple and then write out their definition of a true apostle according to Paul. Possible qualities are:
- 2 Corinthians 2:17: speaks in Christ's name, pure motivation, sent by God, works in God's presence;
- 2 Corinthians 4: is not perfect (earthen vessel) but the power of God is visible in him;
- 2 Corinthians 5:11–21; impelled by the love of Christ, provides a ministry of reconciliation for holiness;
- 2 Corinthians 6:1–7:1: patience, love, purity.

The second group can study 2 Corinthians 10–13 in order to show how Paul qualifies as a true apostle.

Have the first group list their findings on the board; the second group can appoint two or three representatives to use that same list to prove that Paul was a true apostle.

2. *Worksheet #8* presents the students with an opportunity to pull together what they have learned about Paul as a troubleshooter. It also helps them to appreciate how we as Christians sometimes share in this mission today.

3. Students might find helpful the following summary of important points of this chapter:

    a. *The cross is central to the Christian message.* The cross is a sign of God's love for us (John 3:16) as well as a sign of Christ's obedience to his Father's will (Philippians 2:8). Christ's death is salvific when we allow his Spirit to dominate our minds and hearts, so that we live with Christ's attitude of obedience to the Father's will.

    b. *Love, not knowledge must dominate Christian behavior.* The good of others must always be uppermost in our minds, we must be willing to sacrifice ourselves or our rights so that others will not be led into sin or be scandalized.

    c. *Our bodies will rise from the dead.* The resurrection of Jesus demonstrates that resurrection of the body is the destiny of all humankind. The resurrected body will not be like this earthly one, but will be a spirit-filled body belonging to the new creation.

    d. *The true Apostle is one who models himself or herself on Christ.* As Christ had no self-concern but gave of himself totally in order to accomplish the Father's will, so, too, the true apostle. Apostleship means loving others as Jesus did, unto death to self.

Prayer and Worship Experiences

1. The Christians at Corinth prayed and worshiped together at a get-together in which they also shared food and friendship. At this get-together special attention was given to provide for the poor. Have the students plan and celebrate a group get-together which includes these same elements: prayer, food, friendship, and special care for the poor. It may be impractical to include a Eucharist—a Liturgy of the Word would be sufficient.

2. It seems likely that the hymn on love in 1 Corinthians 13 was used in early Christian prayer and worship. Have the students use it as a basis for a prayer service on love. They may wish to illustrate its images with slides and music. Songwriters such as The Dameans and Joe Wise have incorporated all or part of this hymn into their work.

Service Projects

1. Have a group recognize some area in their school or parish in which there is friction, disharmony, or something similar to the troubles Paul faced in Corinth. Help them work out a plan for being peacemakers through Christian affirmative action, as Paul tried to do.

2. Invite some students to organize a visual presentation of Paul's hymn on love. This presentation could be displayed in a place where others, as well as group members, could profit by it.

Independent Study Projects

1. Charismatic gifts as experienced by the Christian community in Corinth which all but disappeared from the life of the Church in history seem to have returned in our day. Have the students research the current Charismatic Movement and the place of charismatic gifts within it.

2. From the hints given by St. Paul in 1 Corinthians and through library research in such books as the *New Catholic Encyclopedia,* have students reconstruct the way in which the Eucharist was celebrated in the middle of the first century. They might also compare their findings with present ways of celebrating the Eucharist.

3. In many ways recent Popes in their travels have been troubleshooters like St. Paul. Have students research one of them and prepare a report for the group on this aspect of the Pope's life.

Resources

Audiovisual

"Earthen Vessels." John Foley, S.J. Recording on the album *Earthen Vessels.* North American Liturgy Resources, 2110 W. Peoria Avenue, Phoenix, AZ 85029.

The Giving Tree. Sound filmstrip, color. Stephen Bosustow Prod., 1649 11th Street, Santa Monica, CA 90404.

Print

G. Bornkamm. *Paul.* New York: Harper and Row, 1969.

R. Moody. *Life After Life.* Harrisburg: Stockpole Books, 1976.

N. Perrin. *The New Testament, An Introduction.* New York: Harcourt Brace Jovanovich, 1974.

P. Perkins. *Reading the New Testament, An Introduction.* NJ: Paulist Press, 1977.

5

Paul, the Theologian

Text Pages
68–83

Objectives

Knowledge: To help the students to understand that salvation is a free gift of God and cannot be earned by the mere observance of laws; that it is the result of faith in Jesus Christ which expresses itself in trust of God and in loving others.

Attitude: To enable the students to appreciate the value of trusting God and the freedom which is gained by not relying solely upon their own efforts for salvation.

Practice: To encourage the students to express their faith in Jesus through specific actions of trust in God and love of others.

Orientation

The main objective of this chapter is to deepen the students' appreciation that salvation is not earned simply on human merit but that it is, first of all, a free gift of God offered in the person of Jesus Christ, especially through the events of his death and resurrection. This objective is achieved by introducing the students to this faith understanding by a study of Paul's letters to the Galatians and Romans.

"Religious Bookkeeping" (text page 68) and "The Letter to the Galatians" (text pages 69–71) place this chapter in a context with which most Christians are familiar. In response to the Judaizers, who were preaching that the "only way to be saved was to keep the Jewish law" (text page 68), Paul presents in Galatians four arguments to support "his contention that salvation is not something to be bought by observing the law but something given freely by God" (text page 69). These arguments in Galatians 1:11–24, 2:1–5, 2:6–10, and 2:11–14 comprise the opening third of this letter. "More Evidence" (text pages 71–72) further develops Paul's position that it is faith in Jesus which is the source of salvation. Indeed, this faith in Jesus renders the law superfluous. In "Freedom from/Freedom for" (text page 72), we discuss why a real Christian does not depend upon laws for motivation. The real Christian lives in such a way that she or he does all the law commands and more!

In Paul's "Letter to the Romans" (text pages 72–73) the same central point is continued. Written around 58 A.D. Romans is truly "A Theological Mount Everest" (text page 73). The text guides us to this great mountain by following the theme that faith in Jesus brings salvation. We cannot depend upon ourselves for salvation as the pagans did ("The Pagan System, Romans 1:18–32," text pages 74–76) and as the Jews did ("The Jewish System, Romans 2:1—3:20," text pages 76–77).

"Paul's System (Romans 3:21—26)" (text page 77) explains how the inadequacies of the pagan and Jewish systems are overcome. "But by the free gift of God's grace all are put right with him through Christ Jesus, who sets them free" (Romans 3:24). We can compare this faith to "The DNA Molecule" (text page 78). Without it human life is never properly, spiritually organized.

"Love, Sin, and the Law (Romans 5—8)" (text pages 78—79) addresses Paul's positive interpretation of the rejection of Jesus by the Jews. "Life in God's Service (Romans 12—16)" (text pages 81—82) presents Paul's advice on how to live the Christian life.

Life Experience Focus

The developing adolescent always seems to have to discover the limitations of pulling "yourself up by your own bootstraps" (text page 74). Life must eventually be discovered as relational—the free giving of self and the opening of self to others who freely give themselves, in whole or part, to us. This demand of life's journey is often difficult to meet. Daily we are reminded of too many persons who remain so self-oriented that loving, caring commitments to others are almost impossible for them.

For the young person this struggle with self-centeredness can be a major cause of disillusionment and frustration. Failure is often more acutely felt. But these pains are the passage to the vision that discovers interdependence as a sign that one can love and is truly lovable. This growth only occurs, however, as the young person grows in trust of self, others, and God.

Background on Content

Christianity in its roots is a "way" preached by Jesus and his disciples which was intended to fulfill and not destroy the Law and teachings of the prophets. The earliest followers of Jesus did not set out to sever their ties from their communities, nor abandon their religious customs and practices. They were Jews who saw in Jesus the fulfillment of their hopes and God's promises to their people.

This perception gave rise to many questions and conflicts as the gospel was preached to non-Jews. Over and over again a clear answer was sought to the questions: Must Gentiles first become Jews? What is the binding force of the Mosaic Law on the Gentiles?

These questions and conflicts were dividing the early Christian community founded at Antioch and resulted in a meeting of Peter, Paul, James, Barnabas and other leaders in 50 A.D. at Jerusalem. This council of the elders of the Church is described in Acts 15:1–35. Its decision, as it is recorded in Acts, reads:
"The Holy Spirit and we have agreed not to put any other burden on you besides these necessary rules: eat no food that has been offered to idols; eat no blood; eat no animal that has been strangled; and keep yourselves from sexual immorality. You will do well if you take care not to do these things" (Acts 15:28–29).

The Council of Jerusalem's decision did not receive universal acceptance. There were those Judaeo-Christians who continued to insist that Gentile converts must strictly adhere to the whole Mosaic Law. Salvation itself depended upon this adherence. The attitude of these Judaeo-Christians, known as Judaizers ("to live as a Jew") is reflected in Acts "Some men came from Judea to Antioch and started teaching the believers, 'You cannot be saved unless you are circumcised as the Law of Moses requires' " (Acts 15:1).

But adherence to the Law went far beyond circumcision and included in its extreme forms a dependence upon laws that took away true human freedom and human responsibility—an attitude challenged by Jesus in the gospels. Such an attitude is not limited to the Judaizers. Its alluring temptation was a false illusion of a security which takes away the risk and pain of making a truly human decision—a "safe feeling."

Such Judaizers were operative within the Galatian Christian community, and were challenging Paul's preaching. The Letter to the Galatians was occasioned by this historical situation. It is not surprising then that Galatians is polemical in tone.

The central message of the Letter to the Romans is similar to Galatians: "I have complete confidence in the gospel, it is God's power to save all who believe, first the Jews and also the Gentiles. For the gospel reveals how God puts people right with himself: it is through faith from beginning to end. As scripture says, 'The person who is put right with God through faith shall live' " (Romans 1:16–17).

The purpose of Romans, however, is expository, not polemical. Paul had wanted for a long time (Romans 1:13) to visit the Romans and he planned to do so on route to Spain. To prepare for his arrival, Paul wrote this letter in 58 A.D. Romans should not be considered a compendium of Pauline theology, but an exposition of the central thrust of his "gospel":
"But now God's way of putting people right with himself has been revealed. It has nothing to do with law, even though the Law of Moses and the prophets gave their witness to it. God puts people right through their faith in Jesus Christ" (Romans 3:21–22).

The message of Galatians and Romans is timeless. In many ways it was a primary contributor to the division of Christianity in the 16th century—the controversy over "faith" and "works." It is still needed today for all people who seek religious maturity.

Teaching Notes 1

Text Pages
68–72

Religious Bookkeeping

1. Allow the students time to reflect upon the value of bookkeeping or accounting in order to see its application to their growth as Christians. The teacher may have to make the following transition for the students: religious bookkeeping can be a valuable form of examining one's conscience. In making this transition the teacher should expand the concept of examining one's conscience to mean "following a method of greater self knowledge of who I am as a Christian person."

2. The students might discuss the following questions:
- What are the values of bookkeeping or accounting? Answers may include such concepts as: inventory, planning, and evaluating.
- What is the purpose of bookkeeping or accounting? Answers may include the concepts of evaluating and decision making.
- What does bookkeeping or accounting guarantee for the future? Answers should include the statement, "Nothing!"

3. The students should next be guided through three basic steps indicated in the above questions. The teacher can assist them by asking each student to draw up a "religious bookkeeping sheet" which has four account columns: God, others, self, and creation.
- Under each column have the students list all the assets or good deeds they have performed that are applicable to each column.
- Next have the students evaluate each column and make a decision on their potential for continuing growth as Christians.
- Ask the students then to state what guarantees for the future their assets give them.

The students should see that their assets are only the foundation for future growth. Much more will depend upon their response to God's free gift of himself to them in the concrete situations they will face. It is important that the students understand religious growth not as a piling up of assets but as a deepening of our relationship with God.

4. As a conclusion to the exercises suggested in items 1, 2, and 3 above, ask the students to read Matthew 25:31–40, and analyze the *attitude* of the good servant.

The Letter to the Galatians

1. This section includes four important sub-sections that are closely interwoven. Direct the students to read Galatians 1:1—2:14 before the sections are treated individually. Ask them to identify the following in both chapters:
- Paul's attitude;
- Paul's purpose;
- Paul's plan.

2. Divide the students into groups of four or five to discuss their findings. After the small group discussions, invite the groups to report their findings and try to reach a consensus regarding Paul's attitude, purpose, and plan in these chapters.

The students should have been able to identify:

- Paul's attitude as anger, or argumentative;
- Paul's purpose to convince the Galatians that salvation does not come from the law but from faith in Jesus;
- Paul's plan of presenting a series of arguments in Galatians 1:11–24; 2:1–5; 2:6–10; and 2:11–14.

More Evidence

1. Paul is certainly trying to convince the Galatians that his "gospel" and not the "teachings" of the Judaizers is the correct gospel. In the four previous arguments Paul argued that:

- he was receiving *no personal gain* in preaching the gospel;
- he had the *authority* of the council behind him;
- he had the *approval* of the community;
- he had the *living example* of Peter to support his position.

Ask the students to review Paul's arguments. Then discuss:

- Are they convincing?
- Which of the arguments do they find most convincing?

2. *Worksheet #9* helps the students to probe something which is central to Paul's argument in both Galatians and Romans. The students are asked to reflect upon the difference between what comes to us as free gift and what we earn as merited reward.

3. Invite the students to list people in their lives who have made faith in Jesus attractive to them. From that list ask them to select the one person who may have led them to think most about what it means to be a Christian. Discuss:

- Does this person act as if she or he is restricted by laws and rules?
- Or do her or his actions have a certain sense of freedom and generosity about them?

- Does this person say to them through their actions:

I do not act out of selfish reasons; but I give to you what has been given to me. (No personal gain)

My life is built on faith in Jesus which I have discovered in the Christian community. (Authority)

My life contributes to the growth of others in the community which nourishes my faith. (Approval)

Others live far better than I do. (Living example)

4. The students should now reflect more deeply on Paul's presentation of Abraham in Galatians 3:6–14. Refresh their memories concerning Abraham by asking them to retell in their own words the story of Abraham.

Teaching Notes 2

Text Pages 72–77

Freedom from/Freedom for

1. Organize the group into teams of three to five students each. The task of each team is to create a "new game" which they will explain to the other students. Each team should be able to demonstrate to the others the game's purpose, the objects to be used, and the rules and regulations that will provide the opportunity for the game to be fair and playable.

After the presentations invite the students to choose which game they are most interested in. Discuss:
- If they choose to play that game, do they consider the rules an opportunity to use their freedom, or a restriction on their freedom?
- Does following the rules of the game bring them fun, joy, a chance for friendship, etc?
- Are they forced to obey the rules, or have they chosen to accept the chance to play a game freely offered to them by others?

2. If the above suggestion does not fit your teaching situation, ask two or three students who enjoy a game which most of the others do not know how to play to explain that game to the group. Have them express:

- Why do they follow the rules?
- What does freely following the rules give them?
- Did they freely choose to learn the game?

If either of the two exercises above has been experienced, the exercise in the text on page 72 may now help the students to better understand the faith message in Galatians.

Letter to the Romans

Look at the map on text page 38 and identify the following churches:
- Thessalonica
- Corinth
- Galatia
- Rome

Note the year Paul wrote to each of these communities and the place where Paul was at its writing. Have the students read Romans 1:10–15 and 15:23–28 to discover why Paul wrote this letter.

A Theological Mount Everest

The students will be able to appreciate the complexity of the Romans by continuing the map study. Provide the students with maps of their state or country, and ask them to choose three routes to a destination that is over two hundred miles from their home. Then:

- Ask them to choose three routes, one of which is the easiest and the fastest.
- Have them compare the three routes.
- What would they see, what historic sights, or towns, or monuments, etc., would they be able to see on each route?
- Ask the group to reflect upon the following questions: Why does the selection of one route limit them to what they might clearly see? How will making the trip each time by a different route increase their ability to discover more of the details that are along the many roads that lie between their home and their destination?

Three Systems
The Pagan System (Romans 1:18–32)
The Jewish System (Romans 2:1—3:20)
Paul's System (Romans 3:21–26)
On the chalkboard or on a ditto sheet, outline for the students the plan of Paul's letter to the Romans. Point out that we are taking the major route in our study of Romans. We shall follow the theme: "The person who is put right with God through faith shall live" (Romans 1:16–17).

But first two less adequate approaches shall be studied in "The Pagan System" and "The Jewish System." Point out Paul's perception of the reason for their inadequacies— over-reliance on self. (See pages 74–77 in the text.)

Teaching Notes 3

Text Pages
78–83

The DNA Molecule
1. This section (text page 78) provides the opportunity for either a guest speaker or a research project or both. Our insights into nature provide us with deeper insights into all life—into our human life and not merely the physical dimension of our life. The discovery of the DNA molecule in the 1950s is one such example.

Have one or two students interview a member of the science department, or have the entire group research the nature and meaning of the DNA molecule. They might draw up a list of all the factors of the human person the DNA molecule influences and/or controls.

2. After the presentations suggested above have been made, ask the group to discuss the following statement on page 78 of the text: "Faith may be compared to the DNA molecule of people's spiritual life." Include in the discussion the following pivotal questions.
● In real life, can we get along by ourselves?
● How important are faith and trust in the direction of our lives?
● Do we really believe God loves us?
● Can we really trust God to be concerned about us at all times no

matter how imperfect we are or how often we may turn from him?

3. *Worksheet #10* assists the students in understanding what St. Paul means by "free" and by "faith." Galatians 5:13 and Romans 1:17 provide its context.

Love, Sin, and the Law (Romans 5–8)

1. Ask the students to write a full page advertisement for the local paper using the words "love," "sin," and "law." The purpose of the ad is to announce to the community the value of faith in Jesus. The students may use art work, photos, or whatever they judge will most effectively communicate their message.

2. Once the project outlined above is completed, these "ads" might be posted around the school. Evaluation of the other students' reactions should be made.

The Jews and Jesus (Romans 9–11)

1. As persons mature the relationships they enter into are more often of their own choosing, especially the more personal and important relationships of their lives. Allow the students quiet time to reflect upon this most important dimension of human growth.

2. Relationships are truly gifts. A relationship is the gift of one person to another and the free and respectful acceptance of that gift by the other. Relationships move in two directions. Using a slide presentation with some appropriate background music give the students the time and space to appreciate this important dimension of life.

Life in God's Service (Romans 12–16)

Have the students prepare a three-minute presentation to be given to members of the parish (e.g., eighth graders) who will be confirmed on the day after they hear the presentation. The students are to choose from one of the following themes:
- Life in God's Service (Romans 12:1–21)
- Duties Toward State Authorities (Romans 13:1–7)
- Duties Toward One Another (Romans 13:8–14)
- Do Not Judge One Another (Romans 14:1–12)
- Do Not Make One Another Fall (Romans 14:13–23)
- Please Others Not Yourself (Romans 14:14–21)

Prayer Reflection

As preparation for the "Prayer Reflection" (text page 83), assist some students in researching and reporting a brief biographical sketch of St. Augustine of Hippo. This report will help to provide a context for reflecting on the excerpt from Augustine which is cited in the text.

Prayer and Worship Experiences

1. Ask a group of students to volunteer to do a pantomime or dance expressing the theme of Galatians 1:1–2—2:14. Paul's emotions, especially his anger and anxiety, should be captured. Paul should be portrayed as a symbol of God's concern for humankind—as a Giver whose generosity is sometimes questioned and not appreciated.

2. With the assistance of a team of students rearrange the space of the room in a deliberate attempt to free it for another purpose. In this recreated space gather the whole group together for a time of prayerful reflection on the following theme: *Freedom from/Freedom for.* Suggestions:

a. Discuss the story of the singer and songwriter Johnny Cash. Student research of this personality's journey from prison to freedom to a new life may be necessary (see *Man in Black* in *Resources* for this Guide chapter).

b. Play a recording of a song by Johnny Cash which treats the theme of freedom, or the gifts enumerated in Galatians 5:22.

c. Allow the students time to reflect on rules they freely follow which provide them with the opportunity to be creative, to have the freedom for something. Begin the reflection by suggesting simple things such as the following: baking, singing, sewing, photo taking, playing an instrument or sport.

d. Read Galatians 5.

e. Closing Prayer: Eucharistic Prayer IV or a prayer composed by the students.

3. Faith, as an experience of our trust and dependence on God, can be the focus of an enriching closing reflection. This faith-trust is the source of great strength in making decisions on our life journey. It can be compared to the DNA molecule.

Mary is the model of such faith and trust in God. Invite the students to help in the preparation of a prayer service that will reflect upon Mary as "the perfect disciple"—a model of trust and faith. Suggested outline:

● Introduction (by student leader): Mary shares our humanity. She is the one person who never weakened in her trust in God.
● Reflections (by three students prepared in advance): Mary during the infancy of Jesus, Mary during Jesus' public ministry, and Mary at Calvary.
● Brief silence or song of meditation. The group might use the song "God Will Be With Me" by the Monks of Weston Priory or some selection which lends itself to quiet reflection (see *Resources* for this Guide chapter).
● Concluding Prayer: A song that either the group or an individual volunteer sings.

Service Projects

1. Within most school and parish settings there are students who are isolated from others. They are often forced to go it alone because they are afraid to reach out, or because others have refused to reach out to them. Some students may choose to reach out to these students and invite them to participate in some program or youth group.

2. Most of our communities are pluralistic. People search for God in many ways, in many different religious traditions. We are very often ignorant of these other traditions. Some students might volunteer to discuss their faith beliefs and values with young people of other religious traditions, and share their findings with the group.

3. Parishes are always in need of enthusiastic, young Paul-like Christians to help in the passing on of the Christian message. This passing on is done in many ways:

● CCD teachers' aides
● Lectors
● Members of choirs and folk groups
● Athletic coaches

Some students might wish to pass on the message of Christ in a more active way by fitting their talents to a specific form of ministry of the word in their parish.

Independent Study Projects

1. "The Letter to the Galatians" (text pages 69–71) mentions Judaizers. As Christians our heritage is deeply Judaic in origin. Yet we know little of this spiritual ancestry of ours. Some students might be interested in researching more deeply two basic dimensions of Judaism with which we are familiar, namely:

- respect for the Torah;
- annual celebration of the Exodus at the Passover.

2. "Letter to the Romans" (text pages 72–73) provides the opportunity for relating the world of early Christianity to the world of today. Some students might be encouraged to list the churches established by Paul and identify them with nations and cities that exist today. Too often we do not see the people of Paul's time as having an ongoing history. This is especially important to grasp since the Middle and Near East are playing such a significant role in world events and world politics.

Resources

Audiovisual

"God Will Be With Me," from the album *Winter's Coming Home* by the Monks of Weston Priory, Weston, VT 05161.

The Journeys of Paul. Bible Map Transparencies. Hammond, Inc., Maplewood, NJ. Item code no. 00179x.

Print

H.D. Betz. *Galatians.* Philadelphia: Fortress, 1980.

J. Cash. *Man in Black.* New York: Warner Books, 1976.

The Jerome Biblical Commentary. Englewood Cliffs, NJ: Prentice-Hall, 1968.

K. Kasemann. *Commentary on Romans.* New York: Eerdmans, 1980.

M. Norquist. *How To Read and Pray Saint Paul.* Liguori, MO: Liguori Publications, 1979.

6

Paul,
the Prisoner

Objectives

Knowledge: To help the students recognize in the living and dying of Jesus the reason for and the model of their own passage through death to new life.

Attitude: To enable the students to appreciate more fully the paschal mystery of Jesus in the sorrows and joys of their own life.

Practice: To help the students to find ways in their daily life to discover joy in those actions that *cost* them.

Orientation

This chapter completes our discussion of the Pauline letters. Fittingly the main objective of this chapter is to lead the students to value in a practical way the faith of the Christian community in resurrection. The text achieves this through a study of Paul's Letter to the Philippians, his favorite Christian community.

"A Letter From Prison" (text page 84) and "A Joyful Letter" (text page 86) situate Paul at the time of the writing of this letter, and help the students to identify the unique character of Philippians. "Death with Joy" (text page 87) explains that Philippians is a newsy thank you letter that has a definite message which reveals Paul's positive and joyful attitude toward death and dying—an attitude he wishes all to share. But dying, even for Paul, has its tensions and conflicts. He writes, "I want very much to leave this life and be with Christ, which is a far better thing; but for your sake it is much more important that I remain alive" (Philippians 1:23–24).

"The Important Things" (text pages 88–89) discusses Paul's concerns about the future when he is no longer with them, namely, (a) their preaching of the good news of Jesus, and (b) their progress in becoming more like Christ. The second concern is of particular importance to Paul. In "A Hymn to Christ Jesus" (text pages 89–92) an ancient Christian hymn is studied in order to discover how this progress is meant to occur. Assist the students to appreciate that this hymn not only says something about Jesus but also tells us that the "pattern of Jesus' life should be the pattern of our own. We too are called to go through our own deaths and resurrections" (text page 92). "What the World Could Be" (text page 93) aids the students in reflecting upon the positive consequences of patterning human life on the life of Jesus.

"Running with Christ (Philippians 3–4)" (text pages 93–95) challenges us to have Jesus as the goal of our life and never to be satisfied "being just a run-of-the-mill Christian." The students are invited to apply what has been learned about Paul and his message through the study of the seven authentic letters of Paul—Philemon, 1 Thessalonians, 1 Corinthians, 2 Corinthians, Galatians, Romans, and Philippians. It is hoped the students will have the opportunity to appreciate the timeless value of Paul's message by applying that message to contemporary world situations.

"Other Christian Scriptures" (text pages 95–96) serves as a transition to the second half of the text in which the gospels and the Acts of the Apostles are studied. The students are reminded of the totality of the Christian Scriptures.

Life Experience Focus

During adolescence young people often experience themselves as being in a prison. In their natural drive toward a greater degree of self-direction, self-discipline, and autonomy, young people often find themselves hemmed in. They sometimes feel like "breaking out" or "running away." Inside of them is the "me" few people understand. They try to communicate this "me" in many ways. Some ways are socially offensive, others are acceptable. An honest identification of this feeling can help the students acquire a sense of perspective of where they are on life's journey. They should be able to discover through others who truly listen to them that some of their "prisons" are self-made.

Background on Content

Crises are turning points in life that often lead us to seek the time and the space to reflect upon and share with others the more intimate and important values of our lives. In this sense, Philippians can be considered an example of crisis literature. Paul is in prison. We are not sure why or where but we know that he thinks he may be about to die; he says, "And my being in prison has given most of the brothers more confidence in the Lord. . . . My deep desire and hope is that I shall never fail in my duty, but that at all times, and especially right now, I shall be full of courage, so that with my whole being I shall bring honor to Christ, whether I live or die" (Philippians 1:14, 20).

There are three opinions concerning the location of Paul's imprisonment—Rome, Ephesus, and Caesarea. Those favoring Rome note the references to the "palace guard" (1:13) and "those who belong to the Emperor's Palace" (4:22) as indicating that Philippians is best dated in the early 60s while Paul was imprisoned in Rome.

Others argue for an Ephesian origin. These note the proximity of Ephesus to Philippi and the references to the false teachers which would indicate an earlier date, perhaps 56–57 A.D. They explain the references to the palace guard, etc., as being in keeping with the fact that the Emperor also had large holdings in Asia. A third opinion places the origin of the letter during a Caesarean imprisonment, sometime between the Ephesian and Roman imprisonment of Paul. Some scholars see Philippians as a composite of three different letters, namely:
- Philippians 1:1–2, and 4:10–20
- Philippians 1:3—3:1
- Philippians 3:2—4:3.

However, we shall view it as a composite of reflections revealing the personal and intimate concerns of Paul for a community with whom he wished to share, perhaps, his last thoughts concerning the driving force of his life—"For what is life? To me, it is Christ" (Philiippians 1:21).

To be like Christ was this driving force. The life of Christ was the pattern of Paul's life. In following this pattern he discovered a deep joy. It was Paul's deepest desire that the Philippians share in this joy by becoming more and more like Christ, day by day.

An ancient Christian hymn with which Paul and the Philippians were familiar is used in Philippians 2:6-11 as the basis of this soul-searching exhortation. The hymn portrays the *kenosis* or self-emptying of Christ as the key to understanding ''the Christ'' as well as the attitude that should be basic to all Christians.

An outline of the hymn reveals the following:
- 2:6 *Christ, equal to God;*
- 2:7 *empties self* and takes the status of a *slave;*
- 2:8 *empties self* even to death in obedience to Father;
- 2:9 *exalted by God,* and so is given a name greater than all others;
- 2:10 *adored by all creation;*
- 2:11 as *Kyrios* or Lord.

Such is to be the pattern of the life of the Philippians (2:1–5). It will bring Paul great joy, and bring meaning to his death: ''Perhaps my life's blood is to be poured out like an offering on the sacrifice that your faith offers to God. If that is so, I am glad and share my joy with you all. In the same way, you too must be glad and share your joy with me'' (Philippians 2:17–18).

Teaching Notes 1

Text Pages 84–88

A Letter From Prison
Guide the students to reflect upon the following statement: I am willing to die for what I believe in. Discuss:
- What are you willing to die for?
- What value(s) are you willing to make the driving force of your life—those to which you are willing to give time, energy, effort, and for which you are willing to pay a price?

Then ask them to write a brief, imagined autobiographical sketch about the next ten years of their lives depicting their life as dedicated to that value. Ask the students to include very specific details. All sketches are to have a single ending—each member of the group is to be imprisoned because of his or her efforts.

A Joyful Letter
1. Recall for the students the purpose of the letters to the Galatians and Romans and emphasize the attitude of Paul to each of those communities. Note the argumentative and angry tone of Galatians but cautious and preparatory intentions of Romans. Philippians is uniquely different.

2. Ask the students to read Philippians in its entirety. What new insights can they gain of Paul's personality? Have the students concentrate on Paul's affection for the Philippians, and write down what they discover about Paul. Then hold a brainstorming session and list the insights of the group.

Death With Joy
Experiencing Death

1. The message of Philippians relates to a current concern: death. Another book in the *Journey in Faith* Series entitled *Death and Dying* provides an in-depth study of that concern. (See *Resources* for this Guide chapter.)

Worksheet #11 can assist the students to reflect on times in our lives when we must let go of one thing in order to achieve another.

2. References suggested in *Resources* for this Guide chapter contain materials treating recent studies on "death and dying." Have the students divide into teams to discuss the following questions:
- What are some of the normal feelings and attitudes which people experience in the face of death?
- In what way are the feelings and attitudes of the survivors the same or different from those of the person who is dying?
- How has the experience of near-death persons affected views of future death?
- How has the gift of faith affected the basic attitude of people confronted with dying?

3. Ask the students to read Philippians 1:21–24, and compare Paul's statement there with the experience of Joanne Costello (text page 88). Discuss:
- In what ways are they the same? How are they different?
- In what ways do the students see themselves stepping into Paul's or Joanne's shoes?

Teaching Notes 2

The Important Things

1. The following activity can help the members of the group not only understand the nature of Philippians, but also help them more deeply appreciate the values important to their own lives.

Ask each student to imagine he or she was leaving for college and would be away from home for a four-year period. Before leaving, they want to share some thoughts with a younger sister or brother but find it difficult to talk with him or her. Things have been difficult between them, and there is fear of ridicule or rejection. But a deep love and concern does move them to share with their younger brother or sister before they leave. Have the students list the five most important thoughts they might want to share, perhaps about:

- friends
- school
- home
- tensions of growing older
- religion
- true feelings about their sister or brother

Then ask them to choose the two areas that are most important to them and to reflect "why" they wish to share those two more than the others.

2. Have the members of the group read Philippians 1:1–8, 12–14, and 2:1–4. Discuss:

- What did Paul choose to share with the Philippians?
- Are there any similarities between Paul's decision and their own as reflected on in the exercise outlined above?

A Hymn to Christ Jesus

1. Philippians 2:6–11 is a hymn about Jesus which was familiar to Paul and the early Christians. Probably of Jewish-Christian liturgical origin, the "hymn represents an early kerygmatic confession" (*The Jerome Biblical Commentary* #50–17) which had been passed on to Paul by others. Ask the students to compile a list of "hymns," confessions, or statements of belief with which they are familiar. These hymns should be taken from a variety of sources—liturgical, patriotic, "causes," etc.—and should be contemporary as well as from the past. Examples could include:

- Star Spangled Banner
- The Gloria
- School Song

A discussion of the significance of these familiar "hymns" would impress upon the members of the group the importance of

Paul's including this hymn in his letter. They might further appreciate this importance by asking the group to divide into teams, select a hymn, and rewrite the message of the hymn in prose. Next have someone from each team read the message to the whole group and then have the hymn played or sung. Discuss:
- Which approach has the greater power to communicate the message? Why?

3. This section of the chapter is central. Care and attention must be paid to the hymn as described in the text, pages 89–92. Understanding the "attitude" of Christ contained in this hymn and adopting it as the dynamic of our own lives as Christians is the basis of a truly Christian spirituality.

Worksheet #12 is designed to enable the students to reflect upon their basic attitude toward life.

Teaching Notes 3

Text Pages 93–97

What the World Could Be

The following profile of St. Thomas More should serve as a good example of one person's vision of what the world could be. *Profile:* St. Thomas More, Lord Chancellor of England, born in London on February 7, 1477, and executed for treason on July 6, 1535, because of his position against the divorce and remarriage of Henry VIII and because of his refusal to take the Oath of Supremacy. He spent the last year of his life in the Tower of London where he was allowed visits by his wife and children until two months prior to his execution when he was isolated from his family. Thomas More was decapitated but not before he asserted one last time that he was "a loyal servant of the king, but God's servant first."

More's most famous work is *Utopia* which he wrote in 1516 and in which he reflects upon the possibilities of a society built upon the insights of good reasoning. (The students may be familiar with the book *1984* by George Orwell, or *Brave New World* by Aldous Huxley, both more contemporary utopian-type writings with very different messages.)

More's life—his career and his death—certainly reveal a dedication to "what the world could be" or a search for the making of a utopia.

Divide the students into teams of five or six and have them compare Thomas More with the pattern of Philippians 2:6–11. Ask them to then draw up a list of persons similar to More. Finally they should state their opinions on the following statement: Utopias can be achieved by taking one small step today.

Running With Christ (Philippians 3–4)

1. TV and movies play a significant role in the formation of attitudes and opinions. Have the students complete a personal viewing inventory by writing down specific information about themselves:

- how much TV they watch
- how often they go to the movies
- three favorite TV shows
- three movies they have recently seen
- three favorite movie personalities
- best movie they have seen
- best TV commercial they have seen
- worst TV commercial they have seen

Invite the students to share three items with the rest of the group or in smaller groups of four. They should be encouraged to give reasons for their choices where applicable. Ask them to rate their choices with the criteria established by Paul in Philippians 4:8:

true	noble
right	pure
lovely	honorable

2. The exercises contained on pages 94–95 of the text can be given a fuller perspective by casting the elements of the exercise into a TV news production.

- The map can serve as the background for the anchor person of the news.
- A reporter can be assigned to cover the headquarters of Paul; other reporters can be assigned to be on location in the trouble spots. Their reports can be verbal or a mixture of verbal and visual.
- An audiovisual collage consisting of slides and contemporary music could be composed by other members of the group as an introduction, ending, or spotting during the broadcast.

Other Christian Scriptures

Have the students draw a timeline on which they will locate the approximate dates of the various writings of the Christian Scriptures. Through the use of the timeline the students will appreciate the time it took to complete the Christian Scriptures and the complete content of the Christian Scriptures.

    a. Title the timeline "The Writings of the Christian Scriptures."

    b. Date the extreme left of the timeline 50 A.D. and the extreme right 100 A.D.

    c. You may wish to follow the color code suggested below.

- *Blue* titles will indicate the "authentic letters of Paul" which we have studied—Philemon, 1 Corinthians, 2 Corinthians, Galatians, Romans, and Philippians, 1 Thessalonians.
- *Brown* titles will indicate "letters written by Paul's followers in his name"—2 Thessalonians, 1 and 2 Timothy, Titus, Ephesians, Colossians, and Hebrews.
- *Green* titles will indicate the "other letters"—two letters of the disciples of Peter, three by disciples of St. John, the letter attributed to St. James, the letter attributed to St. Jude.
- *Orange* title for Revelation.
- *Red* titles will indicate the four gospels and the Acts of the Apostles.

    d. Have the students date the "authentic letters of Paul."

    e. Through the use of the chalkboard or overlapping transparencies the teacher should next indicate the placement of the other writings. The students should be told to keep the timeline in an accessible place for future reference.

Prayer Reflection

The "Prayer Reflection" (text page 97) can be used as the basis for a prayer service for this chapter.

Introduction: Leader calls all to prayer and invites all to reflect on the theme: I consider my friendship with Christ the most valuable relationship of my life.

Opening Prayer: Lord, Jesus, we so often keep ourselves prisoners—prisoners to our moods, to the things we feel will make us important, to our laziness, to the opinions of others, to so many things. Now is the time to be freed, to be paroled. Help me gain that freedom.

Reading: Philippians 3:8—9. See text page 97.

Brief silence or song for meditation.

Prayer of Petitions with special emphasis on those in need of freedom from various forms of imprisonment. A slide presentation accompanying and illustrating the petitions would be helpful.

Try to involve many of the members of the group in planning and celebrating the prayer service. All volunteered talents should be incorporated insofar as possible.

Prayer and Worship Experiences

1. Ask a group of students to volunteer to make an artistic representation of Philippians 2:6—11. Their theme should be the "kenois" or "emptying" of Jesus. The representation should have three moments or movements, namely, glory-kenosis-glory. Some of the forms which the artistic expression can take are art, song, or dance.

2. Gather the students in a quiet place, either indoors or outdoors for a moment of personal reflection along the lines that follow:

- Ask the students to think of the talents that in a special way make them unique.
- While they are reflecting play softly in the background a song like "I've Gotta Be Me" which emphasizes our individuality.
- Read aloud Luke 19:11—18.
- Distribute to the students a monthly calendar and ask them to mark how and when they used their unique talent(s) up to and including the date of this session. Then ask them to finish out the month by planning possible uses of their talent(s).
- Closing Prayer: Use the prayer found in the text page 97.

Service Projects

1. Within many parish settings, the parish council has a "Social Concerns" committee—a committee which organizes the talents of the parish to meet the special needs of parishioners. The students might interview the chairperson of that committee in their own parish and discover the ways the parish reaches out to others. If any of the students have talents that can help, they should be encouraged to volunteer their time and energies.

2. True service also means being open to be served. The students might invite someone who is involved in hospice work or other forms of care for the dying to share their experience with the group. They might also help the students to understand more deeply this care as a true emptying of self which fills a person with rewards that are unspeakable. Such a sharing will be a first step in helping the students prepare for those future unknown moments when they might have to serve a dying friend or relative.

Independent Study Projects

1. Some outstanding persons of the 20th century have been, like St. Paul, imprisoned for what they believe in and again, like St. Paul, have written about their imprisonment. Examples are Dietrich Bonhoeffer, Martin Luther King, Dorothy Day, Sheila Cassidy, and Alexander Solzhenitsyn. Have some students research these or other persons and report their findings to the group.

2. Philippians 2:6–11 is both a liturgical hymn and a profession of faith. Have students research some hymns which are in use in their school or parish liturgies. Ask them to evaluate the hymns both as praise of God and as an expression of the community's belief.

Resources

Audiovisual

Death and Dying: Coping With Reality. Two part sound-slide set. The Center For Humanities, Inc., Box 1000, Mount Kisco, NY 10549.

Living With Death. Sound filmstrip. Ikonographics, Inc., P.O. Box 4454, Louisville, KY 10204.

We Belong to the Lord. Four sound filmstrips. Episode titles: "Death: Problem or Life Passage?", "We Belong to the Lord," "Through Death to Life," and "Death, Where Is Your Victory?" ROA, 1696 No. Astor St., Milwaukee, WI 53202.

Print

Eerdman's Handbook to the History of Christianity. New York: W.B. Eerdmans, 1977.

The Jerome Biblical Commentary. Englewood Cliffs, NJ: Prentice-Hall, 1968.

J.L. McKenzie. *Light on the Epistles and Light on the Gospels: A Reader's Guide.* Notre Dame, IN: Fides/Claretian.

P. Perkins. *Reading the New Testament: An Introduction.* New York: Paulist Press, 1978.

7

Introduction to the Gospels

**Text Pages
98–111**

Objectives
Knowledge: To help the students to understand the four gospels as unique presentations sharing the truth about Jesus, each of which written for a particular community with a special faith-need, and each presenting a unique faith-view of the person and mission of Jesus.
Attitude: To enable the students to feel more at home in reading the gospels and better appreciate how together they give us a wonderful many-sided picture of Jesus and his message of good news.
Practice: To assist the students in developing skills in reading the gospel as the dramatized history of the life of Jesus.

Orientation
This chapter begins an in-depth study of the gospels and the Acts of the Apostles. The main objective of Chapter 7 is to deepen the students' understanding of the gospels as *dramatized history,* and of the process which guided the evangelists in the writing of the gospels. The students will learn to appreciate that the differences as well as the basic similarities of the gospels contribute to a broader understanding of the person, message, and mission of Jesus. Chapter 7 is the basis for what follows in Chapters 8–11.

"Pyramids and Gospels" (text pages 98–99) introduces the students to the reality that the gospels are carefully constructed literary monuments. "Eyewitnesses and Authors" (text pages 100–101) establishes the evangelists as authors who composed the gospels but were dependent on others for much of their materials. Once the materials were gathered "each evangelist then chose for his gospel the stories and versions of stories he thought would best help his readers understand Jesus" (text page 101).

"Different Viewpoints" (text page 101) introduces the key to unlocking the basic reason for the differences in the four gospels, namely, each gospel was written for a specific Christian community, and the faith-needs of that community help shape the form of each evangelist's gospel.

In order to prevent confusion concerning the historicity of the gospels, "The Positive Differences" (text page 102) emphasizes that the different viewpoints enable the reader to see Jesus from many different perspectives. This is a plus. "A Living Tradition" (text pages 102–103) stresses that the basis for these differences lies in an authentic tradition and not simply in the minds of the authors. "Basics Which Are Constant" (text pages 103–104) enumerates nine basic points on which all four gospels are agreed.

"How to Read a Gospel" (text pages 104–106) provides the students with an overall approach to understanding the gospels as dramatized history. Each gospel may be viewed as the script of a play built around four categories which will help the students to "Follow the Movement" (text pages 106–108) and development of each gospel—"Credentials," "Responses," "Discipleship," and "Passion, Death, Resurrection." From Jesus' words and actions the attentive reader gains an understanding of Jesus, just as the attentive playgoer gains an understanding of the central character around whom the play revolves.

These four categories are woven together in unique ways by each of the four evangelists. A diagram is provided in subsequent chapters showing the overall structure of each gospel and its division into smaller parts and sections. This diagram will further aid the students in understanding the specific message and perspective of Mark, Matthew, Luke, and John.

Life Experience Focus

Young people, in a true sense, are gathering materials to write their own life stories. As children their first experiences of life *happened* to them. There was little understanding, a certain sense of fascination, a strong sense of what was in these experiences for "me." As young people leave childhood, they become to a greater degree participants in life. We might see them as *gatherers* of the values and *interpreters* of the experiences of the past and present. They are searching for the materials they will employ to write the stories of their own lives. Central to their search are persons—persons whose life-stories make sense. The presentation of Jesus as a person whose life made sense to the evangelists is an important challenge for the teacher. It is hoped that the students will see through faith the person of Jesus as central to the writing of their life stories.

Background on Content

Contemporary New Testament criticism has established that the gospels are *faith-histories* and that they are a unique blending of theology and history which present the faith perceptions and interpretations of the early Church concerning Jesus of Nazareth, the Christ. The question is thus validly asked: "To what degree has the Church's confession colored or shaped the history?" (*Jerome Biblical Commentary* #41:32) In other words, what elements are "history," and what elements are "faith expressions"? We refer the teacher to articles #40–41 in *The Jerome Biblical Commentary* or to Chapter One, "The Formation of the Synoptic Gospels," in Volume 3 of *Key to the Bible* for a brief and concise treatment of this problem. (See *Resources* for this Guide chapter.)

On April 21, 1964 the Pontifical Biblical Commission issued an "Instruction Concerning the Historical Truth of the Gospels" (see *Resources* for this Guide chapter). This brief instruction notes that "to judge properly concerning the reliability of what is transmitted in the Gospels, the interpreter should pay diligent attention to the three stages of tradition by which the doctrine and life of Jesus have come down to us" (#2).

Stage one: *Jesus, the historical person* who lived and fulfilled his mission among a particular people in a very specific cultural situation. This Jesus "followed the modes of reasoning and of exposition which were in vogue at the time. He accommodated himself to the mentality of His listners and saw to it that what he taught was firmly impressed on the mind and easily remembered by the disciples" (#2).

Stage two: *The proclamation by the Apostles* after the resurrection of Jesus. The experience of the resurrection gave the apostles a much deeper faith-perspective on the words and deeds of Jesus. This enabled them to explain and interpret Jesus, his words and deeds, more fully for their listeners. In doing this they too "made use of various modes of speaking which were suited to their own purpose and the mentality of their listeners" (#2). These modes included "catechesis, stories, testimonia, hymns, doxologies, prayers—and other literary forms which . . . were accustomed to be used by men of that time" (#2).

Stage three: The *writing down by the evangelists* of the traditions they had received in a specific manner and for a particular purpose in the four gospels. In each of the gospels the author "selected some things" and "reduced others to a synthesis" . . . . which were suited to the various situations of the faithful and to the purpose which they had in mind, and adapted their narration of them to the same situations and purpose" (#2).

Knowledge of the process of the formation of the gospels is very important in the presentation of the gospels to the students. Two extremes must be avoided, namely, seeing in every word and every statement in the gospels literal history, as if each gospel were a written transcript of a tape-recording, or seeing every word and every statment as the mythical interpretation of the author so that the presence of any history is denied. The words of the "Instruction" provide us with a principle. for maintaining a balance. "For the truth of the story is not at all affected by the fact that the Evangelists relate words and deeds of the Lord in a different order, and express His sayings not literally but differently, while preserving (their) sense" (#2).

74

Teaching Notes 1

Pyramids and Gospels

Using the concept of pyramids, attempt the writing of a gospel with the students. The *situation* for which the gospel is being written should be contemporary. An example would be: Look out for "number 1" for no one else will! It does not matter what you do as long as you come out on top. The purpose of writing the gospel is to present Jesus as a person who is number 1 in the eyes of God and others, but who arrived there not by stepping on people, but by serving people.

Have the students bring in six pieces of construction paper, three yellow and three green. On the yellow sheets ask them to print with a magic marker three different sayings of Jesus which they remember and which they consider important. Ask them to underline a key word in the saying. On the green sheets ask them to write down three deeds which Jesus is portrayed as doing in the gospels. On the reverse side of each sheet, ask them to write in their own words the meaning of each saying and deed.

Now gather the sheets and begin to build the pyramid. Sayings and deeds that occur only once should be used as the base of the pyramid. Build upwards so that the sayings and deeds which occur the most are towards the top of the pyramid. The saying or deed which occurs most often should be the top block.

Eyewitnesses and Authors

1. *Worksheet #13* gives the students an opportunity to reflect upon ways in which the lives of great persons who have died form part of who we are today.

2. Ask the students to analyze a major news event. Some students might volunteer to watch the TV news, others to listen to the radio news, and others to gather articles from two or more newspapers. Invite them to share their findings with the others, and compare the similarities and differences.

Different Viewpoints

1. Building upon the students' basic foundation for understanding both the similarities and differences that exist in the four gospels, carefully read this section of the text (page 101) and complete the suggested exercises.

2. The teacher might briefly outline the stages of gospel formation contained in the *Background on Content* and point out to the students the teaching of the Church on this important issue.

3. See *Independent Study Projects* in this Guide chapter for a further exercise on this topic.

The Positive Differences

1. The filmstrips "Jesus in the Gospels" and "Gospels: Portraits of Jesus" (see *Resources* for this Guide chapter), explore the nature of the gospel accounts and can help the students to read them with greater profit. The filmstrip guides contain excellent follow-up questions and activities which complement this chapter's emphasis.

2. The gospel pyramid construction suggested under "Pyramids and Gospels" can be used as the basis of a discussion to appreciate the value of different perspectives of Jesus and his work. Return to each student the six sheets he or she contributed to the pyramid. Divide the group into teams of four and invite them to share among themselves the sayings and deeds they selected. Invite those who wish to volunteer to explain the meaning of these sayings and deeds. They have already written these meanings on the reverse sides of the sheets. As a result of this sharing the students should acquire a broader appreciation of Jesus, his words and his deeds.

Teaching Notes 2

Text Pages 102–106

A Living Tradition

1. The passing on of events and meanings by word of mouth was a very common method of preserving the memory of events among people of the East. Help the students to appreciate the importance and accuracy of this method. "A Living Tradition" (text pages 102–103) alludes to this oral tradition as an important source of Paul's knowledge of the words and deeds of Jesus. Among the people of Paul's time, stories that were inaccurate or which misrepresented the facts and/or their meanings were recognized by the community. Details might have difffered, but the main line tradition was passed on accurately.

2. Have the students read 1 Corinthians 15:3–7, and 1 Corinthians 11:23–25—Paul's statements of two major parts of the tradition. Ask the students to choose one of the texts and from their own memories try to fill in the details. Then invite them to form teams of four and compare their detailed statements with the gospel accounts paying close attention to the differences of detail.

Basics Which Are Constant

1. The students should be encouraged to interview their parents(s), a relative, or someone who has had a significant role in passing onto them the tradition of the Catholic Christian community. Students need not reveal the identity of the person they have interviewed. The students might choose some of the following questions for use in the interview:

- What is the first thing you remember about Jesus?
- What is an important teaching of Jesus?
- How would you describe Jesus' attitude toward his Father?
- What was the basis of Jesus' power to influence so many persons?
- What is your favorite parable?
- How would you describe Jesus' concern for the poor and others marginated by society?
- What was Jesus' attitude toward laws?
- What was the primary reason Jesus was executed?
- What does it mean to you to believe that "Jesus is alive!"

This interview is designed to help the students deepen their appreciation of each person's growth in understanding who Jesus is. The fact that some of the answers to the above questions might be different than those the students would give should impress upon them the truly personal relationship Jesus desires to enter into with each person.

2. When the students bring the results of the interviews back to the group, encourage discussion along these lines:

- What impressed you most from the interview?
- What things about Jesus did most of those interviewed stress?
- How did the results of the interview compare with the way you would have answered the questions?

3. See *Independent Study Projects* and *Prayer and Worship Experiences* in this Guide chapter for further ideas on this topic.

Specifics Which Vary

1. Before beginning "Specifics Which Vary" (text page 104), give the group a few minutes of quiet time to reflect on these questions:

- How well do I really want to know myself?
- Others?
- Jesus?

During this period of reflection, play as a background music such as "Day by Day" from *Godspell,* or "Longer" by Dan Fogelberg.

2. Invite the students to reflect upon the sacraments as "ongoing re-tellings of the story of Jesus." On one overhead transparency list the seven sacraments on the far left of the transparency. Explain how the sacraments unite our life stories as individuals and as a community with the story of Jesus, and how the sacraments proclaim that story through ritual. Place a second transparency on top of the first. On this transparency write the following values so that they appear next to the sacraments:

Baptism	new life
Confirmation	strength-purpose
Eucharist	praise-trust
Matrimony	love for another
Orders	love for others
Reconciliation	forgiveness
Anoiting	Healing

Now place a third transparency on top of the second. This transparency contains the heading: *The Story Retold.*

The Story Retold
Baptism   New Life

Using incidents from the life of Jesus invite the students to complete the third (far right) column by explaining how these sacraments celebrate the retelling or continuing of Jesus' story today.

How to Read a Gospel
Dramatized History
Follow the Movement

1. Explain briefly that the four gospels are themselves more like dramatized histories than itemized reports of the activities of Jesus. Point out that the gospels, like dramas, contain movements and development.

Some students may be familiar with *Godspell* and *Jesus Christ Superstar.* Both are contemporary dramatized versions of the gospel. They are both interpretations of the gospel which try to make Jesus live for their viewers (listeners) by dramatizing his life.

Invite the students to brainstorm for a few moments in order to recall other dramatized versions of the life and message of Jesus, for example: *Jesus of Nazareth, The Greatest Story Ever Told,* or *The Gospel According to Matthew.* Ask them to discuss the following questions:

- What extra power does a dramatized version of the life of Jesus possess?
- How is Jesus portrayed?
- What is Jesus' main message?
- Does the author's intepretations seem to differ from their own memories of the gospel?

2. For the "Credentials" part of this section, ask the students to choose one of the following categories:

- Football quarterback
- Editor of school paper or yearbook
- Lead role in school production
- Science or Forensic award winner
- Scholarship award winner

Then have them indicate the credentials for each. Ask them to discuss in groups of four the question: Do people sometimes want the glory without the credentials?

3. For the "Response" section, provide the students with the opportunity to reflect upon whether or not they have been "booed." Don Zimmer after he had been fired by the Boston Red Sox in 1980 with only five games remaining on the schedule was asked if he had any feelings about his ordeal. He remarked, "The toughest thing I guess was winning 99 games in 1979 and getting beat by . . . Bucky Dent in the playoffs, then getting booed the next year on opening day after winning 99 games." Discuss the following questions:

- How do we feel when we "boo" or reject others?
- Why do we reject people who do not meet our expectations?
- Why do we sometimes forget all the

good someone has done or achieved and concentrate on a weakness or failure?

4. In terms of "Discipleship," have the students read Matthew 21:28–20. On a blank paper ask them to compare themselves to each of the sons in the parable. Their comparisons should include references to:
- home
- school
- friends
- work
- parish

Discuss the following questions:
- What are the signs of a true disciple?
- Are failures a sign that a person is not a true disciple?

5. For "Passion, Death, Resurrection" ask the students to read evangelists' retelling of the last days of Jesus on earth (text page 108). In addition to the directives in the text, have them analyze the attitudes, actions, or responses of the following people who witnessed and shared in the last days and moments of Jesus:
- Peter
- The Roman soldier
- Mary
- The repentant thief
- The non-repentant thief

Discuss: To what extent do you identify with any or all of these people as expressing something you feel when thinking about Jesus' death?

Know the Structure
Ready to Begin
These two sections of the text look forward to the next four chapters which will treat in turn each of the four gospels. *Worksheet #14* is designed to help the students to probe what puzzles them about different elements in the gospels. The aim of the worksheet is not to answer each of the questions it poses, but rather to bring them to the surface so that they can be answered in the next four chapters. If, however, the

teacher senses an urgency in any of these questions, he or she may lead the group in working out some preliminary response.

Prayer Reflection
The quotation of Sr. Jane Marie Richardson which is cited in the "Prayer Reflection" on text page 111 is a rich one, worthy of careful reading. The teacher may wish to have the students reflect on it line by line, helping them to grasp its meaning. By centering attention on the person of Jesus, the "Prayer Reflection" provides us with the basis from which we now begin our study of each of the gospels in more detail.

Prayer and Worship Experiences

1. Allow the students some quiet time to reflect on the quotation of Dom Helder Camara which is cited in the "Prayer Reflection" on text page 111. Invite them to express a response to this reading through some art form such as a collage, mobile, banner, or wire sculpture.

2. Assist the students in planning and celebrating a prayer service on the theme: "Jesus Still Among Us." Include some of the following elements:

    a. Introduction: A brief statement of purpose to focus everyone's attention on the theme of the prayer service and its importance in our lives.

    b. A dramatic reading of the points in "Basics Which Are Constant," text pages 103–104.

    c. Scriptural readings such as 1 Corinthians 15:3–7 (text page 102).

    d. Song selections such as "Be Not Afraid" (see *Resources* for this Guide chapter).

    e. Time for quiet reflection.

    f. A closing prayer or song.

3. If either of the two filmstrips "Jesus and the Gospels" or "Gospels: Portraits of Jesus" (see *Resources* for this Guide chapter) are available, build a time of quiet reflection around it. Invite the students to let its message speak inside of them and to respond in private prayer.

Service Projects

1. The success of the study of the gospels depends in part on the attitude of the whole group towards this study. As an expression of peer ministry, encourage the students to help one another approach this study openly and positively.

2. Invite some students to find out if there are some senior citizens in their local area who would appreciate having favorite sections of the gospels read aloud to them. Assist these students in organizing and preparing for this ministry. Encourage them to keep the group informed about the highlights of this project as it develops.

Independent Study Projects

1. Direct some students to research an excerpt from the gospels to correspond with each of the points in "Basics Which Are Constant" (text pages 103–104). Suggest that they share their work with the group by designing a two column chart showing each basic point and a corresponding scriptural reference.

2. A gospel as a literary form is something unique. In some ways it resembles biography, in some ways history, in still other ways, theology in history form. Have some students research the gospel as a literary form in such sources as those mentioned in *Background on Content* in this Guide chapter. Their report can take the form of similarities and differences between a gospel and literary forms with which the students are already familiar.

Resources

Audiovisual

"Be Not Afraid." From the album *Earthen Vessels* by the St. Louis Jesuits. North American Liturgy Resources, 2110 W. Peoria, Phoenix, AZ 85029.

"Gospels: Portraits of Jesus." Sound filmstrip, episode 7 from *Understanding Scripture.* ROA, 1696 North Astor Street, Milwaukee, WI 53202.

"Jesus in the Gospels." Sound filmstrip, episode 1 from *The Christ.* TeleKETICS, 1229 South Santee Street, Los Angeles, CA 90015.

"Day by Day" from the *Godspell* album.

"Longer" by Dan Fogelberg.

Print

E. Cuiba. *Who Do You Say That I Am?* New York: Alba House, 1974.

W.J. Harrington. *Key to the Bible,* Vol. 3. New York: Alba House.

"The Historical Truth of the Gospels." An Instruction of the Pontifical Biblical Commision (1964) as cited in R. Brown, *Crises Facing the Church.* New York: Paulist, 1975.

The Jerome Biblical Commentary, #35. Englewood Cliffs, NJ: Prentice-Hall, 1968.

J. L. McKenzie. *The New Testament Without Illusion.* Chicago: Thomas More Press, 1980.

V. Taylor. *The Life and Ministry of Jesus.* New York: Abingdon.

8

Mark:
The Realist's Gospel

Text Pages
112–127

Objectives
Knowledge: To help the students to understand the basic themes of Mark's gospel: cross and discipleship.
Attitude: To enable the students to appreciate realistically both the joys and the difficulties of discipleship.
Practice: To help the students to face the reality of their own life situations and to find practical ways to give of themselves to others.

Orientation
Mark may have been the first evangelist to set down the gospel traditions in writing, but that does not make him the easiest to understand. The content and message of Mark is difficult for the mature Christian; it is even more so for today's adolescent. "The Challenge of Reality" (text page 112) introduces the students to the very difficult mature behavior of facing reality and making choices that are responsible and constructive for personal growth. The exercise in this section is designed to tap the students' personal experiences in order to clarify their understanding of the challenge Mark presents.

To really live the gospel message in today's world is sometimes tantamount to opening oneself to criticism and ridicule. The gospel message is still foolishness. "The Realist's Gospel" (text pages 112–115) is intended to introduce the students to Mark's challenge of facing reality; to live as a Christian brings not only joy but suffering as well. The outline highlights the key themes and the clear organization of the gospel. "Motivation" (text page 116) gives value to the choices made in life. "Mark's Motivation" (text page 116) for embracing suffering is his acceptance of the suffering Jesus; reality for Mark is following Jesus along the way of the cross. Because he is convinced of the greatness of Jesus, Mark uses a good part of his gospel to prove Jesus' messiahship (1:14—8:30).

"It Takes Time" (text page 116) points out the very realistic fact that the disciples were slow to believe in Jesus and to trust his message. People do not necessarily "see" the evidence before their eyes; faith is needed. Mark presents the parable of "The Good Soil (Mark 4:1–20)" (text page 117) to indicate the attitude of heart necessary to "see." The exercise in this section is intended to have the students search out this attitude in 4:1–20.

Because people shun pain and rejection, Mark challenges us with the reality of true discipleship. "Facing Challenges" (text pages 117–118) introduces the students to the heart of Mark's message on discipleship. Mark develops this message in three stages:

1. "God's Way (Mark 8:31–9:29)" (text page 118) deals with the necessity of suffering and death; the exercise allows the students the opportunity to clarify this message. "Joy In the End (Mark 9:2–13)" (text pages 118–120) treats the hope-filled interlude of the Transfiguration which gives the disciples courage and strength to follow Jesus along this way.

2. Ordinarily, one does not seek to be a servant; but in "The Serving Disciple (Mark 9:30–47)" (text page 121) the students are confronted with a second important element of discipleship: servanthood. Faith is the crucial element for the loyal servant of Christ. The exercise dealing with the rich young man, "Three Points (Mark 10:17–31)" (text page 122) reinforces the fact that sacrifice and faith in Jesus are essential to discipleship.

3. Servanthood by way of the cross is presented in "A Hard Pill to Swallow (Mark 10:32–52)" (text page 122); here the cup offered is the way of the cross. All of this is a difficult message for adolescents to absorb.

The story of "Damien the Leper" (text pages 122–123) concretizes the message of discipleship in the life of an extraordinary Christian. The exercise at the end of this story allows the students to apply the message of Mark to the life of Damien.

The concluding chapters of Mark deal with "The Last Week (Mark 11–16)" of Jesus' life (text pages 124–125). This section should be the most familiar to the students. Important for the teacher to stress is that these chapters show Jesus living out his own teaching of discipleship as an example to be followed. "A Meditation" (text pages 125–126) at the end of this chapter provides the students with the opportunity to internalize this central teaching of Jesus in their own lives.

Life Experience Focus

There are some values and some perplexities for early adolescents which parallel the concerns of this chapter.

First, adolescents appreciate and admire people who "tell it like it is." They suspect people who dodge the facts and offer a rosy but ultimately unsatisfying view of the world. They can be very critical, for example, of advertising or political slogans when these latter present easy half truths. Here a word of caution may be in order. In "telling it like it is" adolescents often tend to use superlatives. For example, it isn't only cold; it's freezing. I'm not just hungry; I'm starving. This school isn't merely strict; it's a prison. The teacher should help them to nuance their descriptions of reality.

Second, adolescents are troubled by the question which bothered Mark's audience: Why do people who are basically good experience persecution, suffering, even painful death? Mark's answer is one which calls for faith rather than satisfies reason. We can't expect that it is going to put our students totally at ease in their minds and hearts. However, it will help them to explore both realistically and religiously why suffering forms part of human life.

Background on Content

As one of the synoptic writers, Mark is sharing his faith experience of the risen Jesus with the community he is addressing. His Jesus is speaking to the members of the church for which Mark writes; they are Christians somewhere in between the resurrection and the parousia, living in a state of heightened apocalyptic expectation. As Paul had to deal with the false teachings of the Judaizers in Corinth, so Mark deals here with the false Christs and false prophets who are leading the people astray. His gospel exhorts and instructs his readers to face the sufferings of the day—it was the time of the destruction of the Jerusalem Temple—as they await the parousia. Mark deals with the reality of following Jesus along the way of the cross; apocalyptic literature is deceptive whereas the cross cannot deceive.

Mark first deals with the *authority of Jesus.* Jesus is recognized for the authority with which he speaks, not like that of the scribes and pharisees. Jesus' authority is seen not only in his words but more importantly in his actions: he calls and people follow; he teaches and heals; he places love above the Sabbath law. The miracle stories underplay the power of Jesus and stress instead the authority of the divine Son who teaches by his life, who takes a stance toward the way of the cross (1:16–3:12).

The rejection of Jesus by his own people is Mark's next important theme. For Mark, Jesus is rejected by some of his own people because they think he belongs to the devil; their rejection limited his power to do miracles. Mark introduces the theme of rejection which weaves throughout the entire gospel: Jesus has to be rejected, otherwise people would have thought him to be simply the powerful one, the miracle worker. In rejection Jesus couldn't be powerful, therefore you can see him for who he really is. It is the paradox of rejection; a prophet cannot function in his own country. The successful prophet is not the real prophet.

Jesus is rejected *by the leaders of the synagogue,* not because of his miracles but because of their lack of faith in him. In the days prior to the Passion, Jesus comes to Jerusalem lowly, riding on an ass, and is rejected. Thus rejected by the political and theological groups of his time, Jesus stands alone, a man for others, ready for the cross.

Mark uses *parable* in a unique way; Jesus not only teaches by means of parables, but he also teaches by his life which is a living parable. Mark teaches that the heart of all living is a deep interiority—an inner purity manifesting itself in outward behavior; that alone matters. This interiority and depth cannot be reached by signs (miracles) but only by faith (7:1–23; 8:11–12). It is only at this point of interiority that you can understand the mystery that is Jesus.

Discipleship is the heart of Mark's gospel (8:31–10:52). Mark is interested in the crucified Jesus and for him discipleship is simply gradually understanding who Jesus really is and standing with Jesus in his suffering and death.

For Mark, misunderstanding is part of the growth process of every Christian who seriously attempts to live the Christian life. Mark uses the format of a journey to Jerusalem to teach his audience about discipleship. He has Jesus *predict the passion* three times (8:21; 9:31; 10:33–34). Each of the three times the disciples misunderstand Jesus (8:32–33; 9:32; 10:35–41). This allows Mark to have Jesus respond with teaching about *true discipleship:* take up your cross and follow Jesus (8:34–9:1); the necessity of servanthood and childhood (9:33–37); servanthood in terms of the cross (10:42–45). Mark then links *parable and discipleship.* At this point Jesus no longer speaks parables but becomes a living parable. Jesus lives his teaching and invites his followers to a fuller discipleship: to live with him the mystery of the cross, of littleness and of servanthood. Discipleship means following Jesus in *his way.*

The Apocalyptic Discourse and the Passion end Mark's story; they go together because they parallel each other. For Mark, the apocalyptic discourse of Jesus (ch. 13)—the coming of the Son of Man in glory—can be fully understood only in the light of the Passion.

The Challenge of Reality

1. As an introduction to "The Challenge of Reality" (text page 112), you might want to play "I Will Try" (see *Resources* for this Guide chapter). The song speaks of openness, releasing gifts, trusting and emptying self in love. Ask the group to listen carefully to its message:

You ask me will you open your hands
    Clinging to dreams you hold inside
You ask again can you release the gifts you
    have
    And all I can say is I will try.

Why do I think holding will make something
    mine
    Even the people in my life
Knowing that captive love like grabbing a
    butterfly
    Will only make the beauty die.

You ask me will you open your hands
    Clinging to dreams you hold inside
You ask again can you release the gifts you
    have
    And all I can say is I will try.

So what does it profit to gain everything
    Possessing the treasures of the world
And lose the gift that can never be destroyed
    Your love which sets us free to live.

I don't know why I can't put all my trust in you
    I fear that I may lose
And yet your Son emptied himself in total love
    Believing his life would be renewed.

You ask me. . . . and all I can say is I will try.

2. Ask the students to write a paragraph or two explaining their understanding of the song cited above. Encourage them to share their reflections with the others. The song deals with the Father's call to each of us to follow his Son. At this early stage in the chapter, it would be important to emphasize the willingness to try: "I will try."

Before moving on, summarize the Father's request as stated in the song:
- to open self to possibilities which might be better than the dreams we hold;
- to release the gifts we have, not to use them selfishly, but make them available for others;
- to resist grasping people tightly, but rather to hold them gently in love;
- to seek God's love as the one true treasure that sets people free;
- to trust in the Father as Jesus did, so that the total gift of self in love becomes fruitful for the life of others.

3. Once the summary is completed and understood, have the students read "The Challenge of Reality" (text page 112). Following the gospel challenge is not easy; by doing the exercise the students will have concrete situations from their own life upon which to build the idea of discipleship in Mark's Gospel.

The Realist's Gospel

1. "The Realist's Gospel" (text pages 112–115) is an introduction to Mark's challenge of discipleship. Discuss what is meant by the following:

- credentials: the fact that Jesus teaches and acts with authority; his performance of miracles;
- response: some accept him, others reject him.

2. Assist the students in studying the Structural Outline of Mark's Gospel (text page 115); clarify any question they may have; note the three main sections to be studied; emphasize the part on discipleship.

3. *Worksheet #15* may help to focus the students' attention on a key element in their study of Mark's Gospel. The worksheet offers an opportunity to keep the discussion of suffering in concrete examples rather than abstractions.

Motivation
Mark's Motivation

It is the motive behind our words and actions which gives value to them. Suffering for the sake of suffering has no value, but suffering embraced in imitation of Jesus becomes extremely valuable in the eyes of God. In the section "Mark's Motivation" (text page 116) the students are asked to read Mark 1:14—8:30 and look for episodes that show:

- Jesus as Messiah and Son of God;
- those who accept Jesus' credentials;
- those who reject Jesus' credentials.

Divide the students into three groups, one researching evidence for each of the above. Either allow time during the session for

this or assign it as homework. The results, however, should be shared and discussed together.

It Takes Time
Beginning to Believe

The exercise at the conclusion of "Beginning to Believe" (text page 117) is intended to reinforce the fact that after all Jesus had said and done to reveal himself, the apostles, his closest friends, were only beginning to believe in him.

The Good Soil

1. Belief in God requires openness to the possibility of his existence; belief in Jesus as the long-awaited Messiah requires openness to God's idea of the Messiah. "The Good Soil" (text page 117) is a parable about the various possibilities of openness to God's Word. Have the students read Mark 4:1–20 and then do the exercise provided.

2. Once the students have grasped the message of Mark 4:1–20, divide them into groups and allow each group time to create a modern version of this parable, which would convey the same basic message. After the groups have created their "modern" parable, invite them to role play their parable for one another; the observers should be able to interpret the parable.

Facing Challenges

Facing the reality of suffering in life is a difficult process; most people seek ways to avoid it. "Facing Challenges" (text pages 117–118) introduces this very basic notion. Mark's response, however, encompasses some of the richest spiritual values as lived by Jesus and offered to others who will follow him. Mark's teaching on discipleship—the heart of his gospel—follows.

God's Way (Mark 8:31—9:29)

1. The basic pattern Mark uses to teach discipleship should be explained to the students (see *Background on Content* for this Guide chapter). Have the students read Mark 8:31—9:29 as a whole in order to distinguish the prediction of suffering (8:31–32), the misunderstanding (8:33), and the teaching on discipleship (8:34—9:1). Once the students have clarified the above, have them read "God's Way" (text page 118).

2. Before moving on it would be good to have the students express their feelings about Jesus' teaching on discipleship:

- What is their gut reaction to forgetting themselves, carrying the cross (embracing suffering) and following Jesus?

- How do Americans today respond to such an invitation?
- Do you think Jesus' invitation is too much for us? Explain.

Joy in the End (Mark 9:2–13)

1. God never asks for more than we can do. He no sooner challenges us with the cross when he holds out to us a joy that is greater. "Joy in the End" (text pages 118–120) offers the encouragement of the Transfiguration experience. Read this section with the students, emphasizing for them the two meanings provided in the text.

2. The episode of the boy with the evil spirit is recounted in Mark 9:14–29. Students should be able to locate the two criteria necessary for imitation of Jesus along the way of the cross: faith and prayer.

The Serving Disciple (Mark 9:30–47)

1. In preparation for "The Serving Disciple" (text page 121), have the students read Mark 9:30–37 and identify:

- the prediction of suffering (9:30–31);
- the misunderstanding (9:32–34);
- the teaching about discipleship (9:35–37).

2. Concerning the first exercise at the end of this section, encourage the students to react to Jesus' statement: "Whoever wants to be first must place himself last of all and be the servant of all."
- What did Jesus mean? (love serves others' needs at the expense of self)
- In the context of American society how is this "foolishness," as Paul would say? How is it wisdom?

3. Have the students read Mark 9:42–47 and 10:13–16 and explain how faith and childhood are related. Most children implicity trust their parents from whom they receive all good things; Jesus asks that we have a similar childlike trust in God who will bring good out of suffering.

Three Points

1. The story of The Rich Man is brought out in "Three Points" (text page 122) to reinforce the message in the Parable of the Sower (Mark 4:1–20). Discipleship is offered but we must rid ourselves of our false securities and willingly follow in faith. Read this section and have the students respond to the question.

2. *Worksheet #16* may help the students to gain a new understanding of the story of the Rich Young Man. Note that the worksheet asks that the passage be read in three ways: literally, symbolically, and practically.

A Hard Pill to Swallow

Once again have the students read Mark 10:32–52 before reading "A Hard Pill to Swallow" (text page 122). James and John ask for places of honor; Jesus offers them the cup of suffering. Have the students discuss:
- How must Jesus have felt at this third misunderstanding?
- Why were the disciples, why are we, so slow to understand?

Damien the Leper

1. The story of "Damien the Leper" (text pages 122–123) is a story about discipleship. A comparison is made in the text to Mark's account of the cure of Bartimaeus. Direct the students to read Mark 10:46–52. Note the following:
- Mark's teaching on discipleship, the heart of his gospel, begins (8:22–26) and ends (10:46–52) with the cure of a blind man;
- Mark seems to be comparing the physical blindness of the blind man to the spiritual blindness of the disciples. The blind Bartimaeus "sees" Jesus for who he is: "Son of David, have mercy on me!" (10:48);
- Mark reiterates the necessity of *faith* in Jesus' response: "Go, your faith has made you well."

2. Ask the students to explain how people can be spiritually blind with regard to God's action in their lives. (They lack faith which "sees" God in all things [Romans 8:28]).

3. Return to Damien; once the students have finished reading this section, ask them to explain how Damien is a modern model of discipleship. Some possible responses are:
- he served God's people, suffered and died for them;
- he had faith in God and trusted in his ways;
- his reward was the joy of doing God's will by serving others.

4. A good review of the whole teaching of Christian discipleship would be helpful at this point. Show the filmstrip "To Be a Disciple" (see *Resources* for this Guide chapter) to help the students grasp the meaning of discipleship in their own lives.

Teaching
Notes 3

The Last Week (Mark 11–16)
The material in this final section on Mark, "The Last Week" (text pages 124–125), is probably the most familiar to the students. Divide them into six groups with the following tasks:

- read one chapter;
- discuss the meaning of the incidents recorded there;
- one member for each group report its findings to the others.

A Meditation
1.   With the above as background, have the students do "A Meditation" (text pages 125–126); they can share in an open discussion how Jesus might have felt in each of the experiences listed.

2.   It might be beneficial to discuss the trust that Jesus had in his Father while undergoing the worst of sufferings. Read Psalm 22 to note that Jesus uses the first verse when hé cries out in anguish on the cross (Mark 15:34): "My God, my God, why have you abandoned me?" Discuss:

- How does this psalm lead one to believe that Jesus trusted in his Father in his darkest moment?

This psalm, often applied to the suffering Jesus, is most appropriate. Jesus knew the Hebrew Scriptures well; so, too, he would have known that while the beginning verses expressed his feelings of abandonment on the cross, the ending (vv. 22–31) also revealed his deep trust in his Father.

3.   The filmstrip "The Son of God—Mark" is an excellent summary of Mark's Gospel. (See *Resources* for this Guide chapter.)

4.   The following summary of important points from this chapter could be discussed:

   a. *The authority of Jesus is manifested in both his words and actions.* He calls others, teaches new ways, heals both body and spirit.

   b. *Jesus was not accepted by all.* Those reject him who refuse to believe in him. Acceptance of Jesus is connected with openness and faith.

   c. *Jesus is the living Parable.* The One who speaks parables becomes the Parable. Jesus not only uses the parable to convey his message; he also lives out that message so that his life, death, and resurrection become the Parable.

   d. *Discipleship is demanding but possible for those who trust in God.* Basically, discipleship means putting others first, sacrificing self, no matter what the cost, for others. Discipleship is living love.

e. *Mark does not accept the apocalyptic without the passion.* Jesus is glorified because of the passion. He is revealed as Son, not because of his miracles, but because of his suffering, dying, and rising from the dead.

Prayer Reflection

You may want to try some shared prayer with this "Prayer Reflection" (text page 127). The following is a suggested procedure:

- Create a prayerful atmosphere, recalling the presence of God.
- Ask for stillness of heart, openness to God's message, faith in his power in us.
- Before prayer assign each of the four truths to four students who will read them in a prayerful manner for the whole group.
- Allow quiet time for reflection after each reading; those who may wish to share their reflections should be encouraged to do so; it helps if the teacher also participates in this sharing.
- At the end play the song "Peace Prayer" by John Foley, S.J., or some similar selection (see *Resources* for this Guide chapter).

Prayer and Worship Experiences

1. "A Meditation" (text page 125) invites the students to reflect prayerfully on what Jesus was experiencing during his passion. Help the students to build a prayer service around this meditation. If any of them have done the first project outlined in *Independent Study Projects* in this Guide chapter, their findings might make a rich complement to the prayer service. Allow for quiet time during which the students can read some of Mark's retelling of Jesus' passion, death, and resurrection. Use appropriate music.

2. Assist the students to compose their own way of doing the Stations of the Cross. One possibility is to recall at each station someone today who is undergoing suffering or oppression similar to that of Jesus. In keeping with the Scriptures, suggest that the students conclude with a final station called the Resurrection.

3. Suggest that the students form a daily habit of recognizing God's active presence in their lives. This recognition can take the form of a brief prayer, a few moments' silent recollection, or spending some time reading the Scriptures.

Service Projects

1. Suggest that some students become involved with handicapped persons for a twofold purpose. First that they may positively help the handicapped person in some way. Second that they may learn from the handicapped person how suffering can be turned into a positive good by people who accept it and deal with it in faith.

2. People who are suffering sometimes feel like outcasts because others are uncomfortable in their presence. Have volunteers spend time with people in difficulty and for whom the only help they seem to offer is a concerned and understanding presence. This would be especially helpful in the case of family members and friends who have experienced setbacks.

Independent Study Projects

1. Jesus' passion, death, and resurrection are central to Mark's Gospel. Assist some students in researching artistic representations of these events—in music, picture, or slide collections. Direct them to keep Mark's account in mind as they select items which say in music or image what Mark has expressed in word. Invite the students to share their findings with the others.

2. In "Beginning to Believe" (text page 117), Jesus asks his apostles: "Who do you say I am?" Assist some students in organizing a report on how some of Jesus' followers today might answer that same question. Research the lives of persons such as Dom Helder Camara, John Paul II, Helen Hayes, Archbishop Oscar Romero, and Mother Teresa of Calcutta for excerpts in which they express in part their understanding of Christ in their lives. Combine these reports with some live interviews of persons whom the students respect. Share the results of this work with the group.

Resources

Audiovisual

"I Will Try." Recording from *Day of the Son* by the Dameans. TeleKETICS, 1229 South Santee St., Los Angeles, CA 90015.

"Peace Prayer." Recording by John Foley, S.J. from *A Dwelling Place.* North American Liturgy Resources, 2110 W. Peoria, Phoenix, AZ 85029.

"The Son of God—Mark." Sound filmstrip from the series *In the Light of the Resurrection: The New Testament.* Our Sunday Visitor, 200 Noll Plaza, Huntington, IN 46750.

"To Be a Disciple." Sound filmstrip from the series *God the Son* by Donald Senior. Argus, 7440 Natchez, Niles, IL 60648.

Print

P. Achtemeier. *Mark.* Philadelphia: Fortress Press, 1975.

G. Bornkmamm. *Jesus of Nazareth.* New York: Harper and Row, 1960.

S. Freyne and H. Wansbrough. *Mark and Matthew.* Chicago: ACTA Foundation, 1971.

X. Leon-Dufour, S.J. *The Gospels and the Jesus of History.* Garden City: Doubleday and Co., 1970.

E.J. Maly, S.J. "The Gospel According to Mark" in *The Jerome Biblical Commentary.* Englewood Cliffs, NJ: Prentice-Hall, 1968.

P. Perkins. *Reading the New Testament: An Introduction.* New York: Paulist Press, 1977.

N. Perrin. *The New Testament, An Introduction.* New York: Harcourt Brace Jovanovich, 1974.

J. Rohde. *Rediscovering the Teaching of the Evangelists.* Philadelphia: The Westminster Press, 1968.

9

Matthew: Idealist's Gospel

Objectives
Knowledge: To help the students to develop an understanding of the structure and purpose of Matthew's Gospel.
Attitude: To encourage the students to appreciate the struggle of reaching for the ideal of Christian living despite the impulse to settle for less.
Practice: To assist the students in finding practical means for living out discipleship according to Matthew and communicating those means to others.

Orientation
The mood for this chapter is set very aptly by the story of Jill Kinmont who, despite tremendous odds, clings to her ideals and achieves what appeared impossible. "Idealists" (text pages 128–129) sets this theme of striving for the ideal despite obstacles and thereby introduces the central motif of Matthew's Gospel.

In order to understand a writer it is important to understand the pattern that forms the core of his or her message. "A Grand Staircase" (text pages 129–130) does just that. By studying the structure of Matthew's Gospel beforehand, the student should have a clearer idea of where Matthew is likely to lead them and the technique he uses. "The

First Narrative (Matthew 1—4)" (text pages 130–131) sets up the obvious comparison of Jesus with Moses. Since the Jews were familiar with Moses, Matthew uses their respect and admiration for this great Israelite prophet to encourage their respect and admiration for Jesus who is greater than Moses.

The Sermon on the Mount contains Matthew's core teaching on discipleship. "The First Instruction (Matthew 5—7)" (text page 131) introduces the students to this very idealistic way of following Jesus. "God's Will (Matthew 5:21–48)" (text page 132) gets right to the heart of Matthew's idealistic approach in his gospel. This section portrays Jesus as demanding the more perfect mode of behavior, a life motivated by love no matter what the cost to self.

Jesus' credentials are detailed in "The Second Narrative (Matthew 8—9)" (text page 132). His ability to heal, call, and teach others provides the proof that Jesus comes from God. This section prepares the disciples to be more receptive to his message in "The Second Instruction (Matthew 10)" (text pages 132–133) to be of service to others regardless of personal sufferings.

The students are introduced to the turning point of Matthew's Gospel in "The Third Narrative (Matthew 11—12)" (text pages 133–134). This section exposes them to the reality of disbelief in Jesus despite the credentials he presented, and to the hardness of heart of some of the Jewish leaders in relation to Jesus and the observance of the Sabbath. The "Turning Point (Matthew 13)" (text pages 136–137) has faith as its pivot: the disciples hear and obey Jesus and thereby become the true Israel; the Jewish leaders do not hear and do not obey and they represent the pseudo-Israel. It is important for the teacher to emphasize that faith and openness are crucial for hearing and obeying the Word of God. The use of the parable in Matthew 13:1–8 reinforces the message behind the turning point: the Kingdom of God is for those who hear and understand.

"The Fourth Instruction (Matthew 18)" (text page 138) deals with yet another idealistic approach to discipleship. In chapter 18 Matthew presents the essence of discipleship as a childlike trust and dependence upon God and as a love for others that seeks out the lost and forgives the sinful brother. While Matthew presents the ideal, he is not unaware of the reality of following Jesus.

The students are provided with an opportunity to clarify the positive qualities of Christian living by following the directions in "The Fifth Instruction (Matthew 23—25)" (text page 138). By asking the students to identify the negative qualities condemned by Jesus, the teacher can elicit from them the opposite positive qualities lived by Jesus. The phrase "In the End" (text pages 138–139) outlines the basic message of this highly symbolic 24th chapter. The message behind the apocalyptic language should be stressed.

"More About Active Faith (Matthew 24:32—25:46)" (text page 139) deals with the underlying theme of Jesus' life: words or teaching must be supported by living what one teaches. "The Conclusion of the Gospel (Matthew 28:18–20)" (text pages 140–141) appropriately summarizes the major themes of Matthew's Gospel. The disciple can be idealistic because Jesus has promised to be with him always to strengthen him along the way (28:20).

Life Experience Focus

The life experience of the early adolescent which corresponds to Matthew's Gospel is the other side of the coin from what was said about Mark's realistic approach. Adolescents want to know things not only as they are but also as they can and ought to be. As are all human persons, adolescents are born believers, born hopers, born lovers, and born dreamers. They need help in giving shape to their beliefs, their hopes, their loves, and their dreams. Matthew's Gospel provides us with a vocabulary for this.

On the other hand, without in any way subtracting from the fullness of Matthew's Christian vision, we have to keep in mind the developmental stage of most of the adolescents with whom we are ministering. The Sermon on the Mount, in particular, presents a motivation for human action and relationships which most developmentalists would put at the top of the scale and which most individuals may not reach until well into adulthood, if at all. Thus we have to take pains to present the teaching of Jesus in a way which respects the fact that most of our adolescents are still too self-centered or peer-centered or convention-centered to understand or live this teaching in its fullness.

The treatment of law in this chapter calls for a similar sensitivity. We have to recognize that we are trying to present a post-conventional mentality to young people who are still trying to find their way on the conventional level.

Background on Content

Matthew's Gospel is a series of narratives and sermons, neatly woven together to invite committed Jewish Christians who have settled somewhere north of Palestine to follow Jesus by doing the "more perfect" thing with love. His gospel is catechetical in purpose. Matthew presents the ethics of Christian conduct: love Christ in one another, love the Jesus mystery in one another ("As often as you did it. . . ."). Using their familiarity with the Hebrew Scriptures as his foundation, Matthew presents the Church community as the true Israel, Jesus as the Messiah and Son of God, and love as the law of laws.

Central to Matthew is his invitation to follow Jesus in love all the way to all those who would be true leaders in the community. Therefore, his gospel is idealistic; he invites Church leaders to be witnesses who will lead others in the ethics of the Sermon on the Mount; he challenges Christians to go out and make disciples of others by living all that Jesus taught. This would be an impossible task were it not for the presence of Jesus who is with us all days making the impossible possible.

Discipleship is taught specifically in the five instructions of Matthew:
The Sermon on the Mount (Matthew 5—7) outlines three major things to do to live an ethical life. (1) *The true Torah* is basically living the will of God—love—in utter simplicity flowing from the depths of one's heart (5:17–48). (2) *The true temple service* is not found in public expressions but rather in a life that has no ostentation, in a life that is ordinary and normal, true and simple (6:1–18). (3) *The true works* are those done with loving kindness, with a genuine open helpfulness to others which manipulates neither self nor others (6:19—7:12). In the Sermon on the Mount, Matthew presents a new way of life made possible by Jesus who lived it unto death; it is a simple life, an interior life where love matures, and Matthew challenges his readers to follow Jesus in this way of love.

The Instruction on the Apostolate (Matthew 10) confronts its readers with the reality of living the mystery of Jesus' passion in their own history; it invites Christians to become witnesses to the values of the Sermon on the Mount through their own self-emptying and dying to self so that others may be touched by the life of Jesus in them. The task is enormous, the ideal beyond human achievement; yet Jesus tells those who will try "Do not be afraid" (10:26–31), "I will be with you" (10:32–33).

The Third Narrative (Matthew 11—12) prepares for the third *Instruction on Parables.* Both the narrative and the instruction will be discussed together for both form the turning point of Matthew's Gospel. Faith in Jesus becomes the pivotal force which enables Christ's followers to do the impossible. This faith is revealed in those who are little children (11:25), in those who are gentle (11:18–21), and in those who do the will of the Father (12:46–50). The person who is little, gentle, and obedient to the will of the Father is disposed to hear the message of the parables in the sermon that follows.

The Instruction of Parables (Matthew 13) marks the turning point in Jesus' ministry. He no longer addresses those who do not believe in him and therefore do not "hear" his message. Jesus turns to those who believe and speaks to them in parables; their faith enables them to "hear" this special language and to "see" the meaning behind all he does. Matthew uses these seven parables on the kingdom to emphasize the distinction between the unhearing and unrepentant Israel and the disciples who hear and obey. The parables present the kingdom as the existing reality; believers and unbelievers, good and bad, make up the imperfect community of the Church.

The Fourth Instruction (Matthew 18) very significantly deals with life in the Christian community. Childlike trust characterizes the community of faith. Both the littleness of the child and his or her trusting dependence upon God become the source of strength enabling individuals to seek out those who are lost and to forgive those who have wronged them. Continual conversion within a person's heart is necessary if there is to be growth in mature Christian love which seeks out others and forgives no matter what the cost to self.

The Fifth Instruction (Matthew 23–25) echoes the idealism of the Sermon on the Mount. All depends upon the quality of one's love for others. Matthew exhorts Christians to do something for the littlest and the least; however it is not what one does for the least but how one does it that makes the special difference for Christians. By living this way Christians witness to Jesus and bring others into his way of love.

Teaching Notes 1

Text Pages 128–133

Idealists

1. As an introduction to the idealism of Matthew's Gospel, have the students begin with *Worksheet #17.* Have the students divide into groups in order to create a charter for an ideal society in the 21st century. The questions for consideration may spark some ideas, but their creativity should be encouraged to go beyond the questions. Once each group has completed the worksheet, have the groups share their ideal society with the others. Then discuss reasons why idealism is important for human progress.

2. Have the students read "Idealist" (text pages 128–129) and then discuss what qualities in Jill Kinmont's character enabled her to achieve the seemingly impossible.

3. Using the above as background, introduce the students to Matthew's Gospel which presents to all of us the ideal way of living the Christian life by doing God's will perfectly.

A Grand Staircase

"A Grand Staircase" (text pages 129–130) presents the totality of Matthew's Gospel in picture form. Have the students study this "picture" before reading the text and let them share all that they notice in this grand staircase. They should be able to pick out:

- the narrative/instruction pattern
- discipleship teaching in the instruction
- importance of chapter 13

This section in the text should then be read for confirmation of their feelings.

The First Narrative (Matthew 1—4)
1. Begin the study of Matthew by showing the filmstrip "The Reign of God—Matthew" (see *Resources* for this Guide chapter). This viewing should acquaint the students with the general thrust of Matthew so that they will know what to look for as they read the student text. A good technique would be to reshow this filmstrip at the end of their study of Matthew for a deeper clarification.

2. "The First Narrative" (text pages 130—131) highlights the parallels between Moses and Jesus, thus preparing the students to *listen* to Jesus who speaks with the authority of God. Have two students alternately read the scriptural passages referring to Moses and Jesus.

The First Instruction (Matthew 5—7)
1. The idealism of Matthew is clearly evident in his Sermon on the Mount. This "First Instruction" (text pages 131) introduces the students to the heart of Matthew's idealism. Have them read Matthew 5:21—48 and indicate the behavior Jesus challenges us to if we are to "be perfect" as our heavenly Father is perfect. Gentleness should characterize such behavior:
- not to react in anger but to be reconciled and to respond with generosity (5:20—26);
- not to lust in your heart, but to be pure and calm (5:27—30);
- not to run out on those who belong to you, but to be commmitted and faithful (5:31—32);
- not to be shallow and talk big, but to be simple, sincere, and reverent both in your heart as well as in you words (5:33—37);

- not to retaliate with physical violence (5:38—42);
- not to cut out those you can't stand, but to stand up for them (5:43—48).

2. Have the students react to Matthew's idealism and reflect on the feasibility of striving to live this idealism in everyday life. Discuss with the group what ways they might attempt to live this way and what might be the possible reactions of others to this behavior.

God's Will (Matthew 5:21—48)
1. Jesus' way is gentler than Moses' in one's outward behavior with others; it is more demanding in that it reaches to the interior of one's life. In "God's Will" (text page 132) the will of God as manifested through Moses is compared with its manifestation through Jesus. Have the students read through the comparison and discuss how Jesus' way goes to the "roots of moral behavior."

2. The exercise which follows (text pages 132) can be used as a group discussion of Matthew's statement in 5:48.

The Second Narrative (Matthew 8—9)
In "The Second Narrative" (text page 132) Matthew interweaves vocation stories and healing stories. Have the students read Matthew 8 and 9.

Discuss:
- how Jesus speaks and acts with authority, (miracles and cures);
- how Jesus' healing made disciples of those cured (healing inspires faith);
- how Jesus calls the outcasts to follow him (Matthew is a hated tax-collector, the leper is a danger to people, the centurion is not a Jew).

The Second Instruction (Matthew 10)

1. Have the students read "The Second Instruction" (text pages 132–133) and Matthew 10:1–42. Once the reading is complete, group the students and have them list (1) the kind of *behavior* expected by Jesus from his disciples, (2) what disciples should expect as possible *reactions* of their preaching and (3) what their *response* should be.

- Behavior: Matthew 10:5–15
- Reactions: Matthew 10:10–26
- Response: Matthew 10:26–33

2. Discuss with the students their responses to the statements concluding this section (text page 133).

Teaching Notes 2

Text Pages 133–138

The Third Narrative (Matthew 11—12)

1. With "The Third Narrative" (text page 133–134) we come to the center of Matthew's Gospel and his preparation for his teaching on discipleship. Divide the students into three groups, each group reading the Scriptures and the material under each subheading:

- The Unbelievers
- Jesus and the Law
- Once More the Unbelievers

Each group should then summarize for the whole class its understanding of its section.

2. The exercise (text page 134) provides the opportunity to discuss with the students a very important concept: if we don't want to believe, no one, God included, can make us believe. Ask the students to describe modern "unbelievers" from among the peers and adults they know.

The Turning Point

1. With reference to "The Turning Point" (text pages 136–137), the key concept presented is that faith is crucial in order to "hear" and "see" the message of the parables. Jesus uses parables so that only those who believe in him will learn the secrets of the Kingdom of God (13:13–15). Have the students read Matthew 13 and then do the exercise (text page 137) dealing with moral beliefs and religious principles.

2. Using these same moral principles, either divide the students into four groups, each group creating a modern parable based on one of the above; or assign each student the task of writing and illustrating a modern parable based on one of the four principles.

The Fourth Instruction (Matthew 18)

1. Before beginning "The Fourth Instruction" (text page 138), discuss with the students those childlike qualities Jesus would demand of those who follow him: *dependence,* because they acknowledge their need of God; *trust,* because they know he loves them and cares for them; *simplicity,* because they want only to please their Father.

2. The two parables which follow upon this key concept of childhood deal with seeking out those who are lost and with forgiveness. Show the filmstrip "The Unforgiving Debtor" (see *Resources* of this Guide chapter). This filmstrip uniquely communicates the idealism of Matthew's Gospel: forgiveness is a beautiful way to show one's love for others.

3. Between this filmstrip and a reading of the scriptural passage itself, the exercise (text page 138) can spark a meaningful discussion on practical applications for contemporary Christians.

Teaching Notes 3

Text Pages 138–143

The Fifth Instruction (Matthew 23—25)

In preparation for the material contained in "The Fifth Instruction" (text page 138), use *Worksheet #18.* The purpose behind this worksheet is to provide an opportunity for the students to sketch a portrait of themselves which represents the type of person they would like to be. See *Prayer and Worship Experiences* in this Guide chapter for another use of *Worksheet #18.*

Have the students read Matthew 23:1–36 and do the exercise suggested (text page 138). Discuss with them the qualities Jesus condemns in the Pharisees and list them on the board. Then allow the students time to compare themselves as they are now with the Pharisees who were criticized by Jesus.

In the End (Matthew 24:1–31)

"In the End" (text pages 138–139) deals with Matthew's apocalyptic message. Have the students read both the text and the corresponding scriptural passage. The teacher should stress the message behind the apocalyptic language as outlined in the students' text.

More About Active Faith (Matthew 24:32–25:46)

This final parable section by Matthew deals once more with the basics for discipleship:

faith in Jesus and love for one another despite the inevitable trials. Read "More About Active Faith" (text page 139) as well as Matthew 24:32—25:46.

The Conclusion of the Gospel (Matthew 28:18—20)

1. "The Conclusion of the Gospel" (text pages 140–141) illustrates how the last three verses summarize the major themes in Matthew's Gospel. Read and discuss the significance of these verses with the students.

2. Assist the students in the creation of a collage using each of the three verses for a separate panel or section of the collage (for example, one on the transmission of authority, one on the love commandment, and one on Jesus' presence in our world).

3. Students might be helped by the following summmary of important points from this chapter:

a. The core message of Matthew is idealistic: to follow Jesus all the way in love; this seemingly impossible task becomes possible through faith in Jesus who enables one to do the impossible.

b. To follow Jesus in love one should seek to do the will of God—love—with a sincere heart and genuine concern for others.

c. Faith is crucial to "hearing" and "seeing" what Jesus is all about.

d. Faith is characterized by a childlike trust and dependence upon God, both of which become enabling forces for continual growth in Christian love.

e. In the end, it is the depth of our love which witnesses to Jesus and draws others to him.

Prayer Reflection

Play the song "Impossible Dream" from the album *Man of La Mancha;* words are printed in the student text on page 143.
Reading: Matthew 5:43—48 (read by one student).
Reflection: quiet time to make Jesus' words a personal challenge. If the teacher wishes, the students can share their reflections.

Our Father: prayed by all.
Final Prayer:
Lord Jesus,
your kingdom is here within our hearts—
there are people all around us who
    hunger for our love;
those who love us and those who hate us, both
    need us to care for them;
your will is that we give of ourselves to others
    no matter what the cost.
We pray, Lord, for your help to live out this
    "impossible dream"

Amen.

Prayer and Worship Experiences

1. *Worksheet #18* can be a source of prayer as well as reflection. It can serve as an occasion to instruct the students in private prayer. They should first clear their minds from distracting thoughts by concentrating on some one thought or object. Then let their minds review the items on the worksheet. There is no need to follow any particular order, and they can give full rein to their imaginations. Help them to come back to such thoughts as "nothing is impossible with God," "God gives to those who ask," and "God is calling them and enabling them to become their best selves."

2. Matthew 6:5–15 has several observations of Jesus on simple spontaneous prayer. Through some brainstorming, help the students recognize how this teaching of Jesus can become part of their own prayer life. Remind them, however, that Matthew was writing for people who prayed often and regularly. To guard against their giving too much importance to length and structure in prayer, he quotes words of Jesus which emphasize brevity and informality.

Service Projects

1. Jesus in Matthew's Gospel is very much a teacher. This may be the time to suggest that some students may want also to be teachers even now. Possibilities are: offering their service within a parish religious education program, a school tutoring program, or helping younger members of one's family.

2. Using Matthew 25:31–46 as background, ask the students to list those people who might be considered "the least" in their neighborhood or school. Have them devise ways in which they can go out to these people with sincere love of Christ. Some examples might be: they could visit the elderly, shop for them, help them with lawn or garden chores.

Independent Study Projects

1. "Anyone who is not for me is really against me; anyone who does not help me gather is really scattering" (Matthew 12:30). Assist some students in expressing their understanding of this passage either verbally or visually. Encourage them to share their work with the others.

2. Matthew, writing for converts from Judaism, and Paul, writing for Gentile Christians, take different approaches to the Mosaic Law. From such texts in Matthew as 5:17–20 and from what Paul wrote to the Galatians, have students compare Matthew's and Paul's estimation of the Mosaic Law.

Resources

Audiovisual

Beatitudes: A Call to Discipleship. Sound filmstrip. Ramsey, NJ: Paulist Press.

"Jesus and the Kingdom." Sound filmstrip by Donald Senior, from the series *God the Son.* Niles IL: Argus Communications.

"Matthew: Discipleship." Sound filmstrip from the series on the *Evangelists.* Ramsey, NJ: Paulist Press.

"The Impossible Dream." Song from the album *Man of La Mancha.*

"The Reign of God." Sound filmstrip #3 from the series *In the Light of the Resurrection: the New Testament.* Our Sunday Visitor. 200 Noll Plaza, Huntington, IN 46750.

The Unforgiving Debtor. Sound filmstrip. St. Anthony Messenger Press.

Print

G. Bornkamn. *Jesus of Nazareth.* New York: Harper and Row, 1960, pp. 64–95.

P. Ellis. *Matthew: His Mind and His Message.* Collegeville, MN: The Liturgical Press, 1974.

A. Gelin, P.S.S. *The Poor of Yahweh.* Collegeville, MN: The Liturgical Press, 1963.

J. Jeremias. *The Parables of Jesus.* New York: Scribner's, 1963.

J.L. McKenzie, S.J. *The Dictionary of the Bible.* New York: Macmillan, 1965, pp. 41–42 on "Apocalyptic Literature" and pp. 635–636 on "Parable."

N. Perrin. *The New Testament: An Introduction.* New York: Harcourt Brace Jovanovich, 1974.

10

Luke: Joyful Gospel

**Text Pages
144–159**

Objectives

Knowledge: To help the students' recognize the themes and message of the Gospel of Luke with its emphasis on the joy and liberation of the truly "poor in spirit."

Attitude: To help the students to appreciate that God's love for them is real, personal, and unqualified.

Practice: To encourage the students to share this message of joy by making their love for others real, personal, and unselfish.

Orientation

Joy is a major theme running throughout Luke's Gospel. The "Journey of a Pope" (text page 144) sets off on this theme by comparing Pope John Paul's message of joy with Luke's same message. The journey motif is another theme basic to Luke who uses it in parallel form in both his gospel and in Acts. "A Travelogue" (text page 146) introduces this concept of Luke-Acts as a continuous story of his joyful message.

The Infancy Narratives are included by Luke to set the tone for his gospel. "Joy to the World" (text page 147) extends the good news of salvation beyond the Jewish community to the Gentile world, especially to the poor everywhere. Acceptance and rejection of Jesus has been studied

already in Mark and Matthew. The exercise connected with "Part One: Credentials and Responses (Luke 1:1—9:50)" (text page 148) allows the students to reinforce their understanding of this concept of acceptance and rejection. "Part Two: Discipleship (Luke 9:51—19:27)" (text pages 148–149) introduces Luke's message on discipleship. Luke uses the journey motif to convey Jesus' teaching on discipleship.

"Call to Commitment" (text pages 149–150) highlights Pope John Paul II's message to American youth: a challenge to be disciples for Christ in today's world. This section leads into the following one, "Luke's Call" (text page 150), which presents the real facts about discipleship: difficulties as well as joys will be encountered. The Pharisees are used as an example of how not to follow Christ. "How Terrible for You Pharisees! (Luke 11:37–54)" (text page 150) reveals Jesus' condemnation of the Pharisees' behavior. "More About Discipleship" (text page 152) lists the positive qualities of those who follow Christ, and asks the students to recognize these same qualities in people they know.

Luke has a special message of liberation for the poor; in "Wealth and Worry" (text pages 152–153) Luke's ideas on discipleship are discussed: childlike trust, dependence, poverty, renunciation, and self-sacrificing love. Luke's message of joy continues in this last section, "Part Three: The Last Week in Jerusalem (Luke 19:28—24:53)" (text page 154). Even in this suffering, Jesus shows concern and compassion for others; this is Luke's joyful message freeing all who will listen. Jesus' ascension is "The Ultimate Journey (Luke 24:36—53)" (text page 154) and Luke uses this journey to link his gospel with Acts which begins the journey of the Church.

"The Acts of the Apostles" (text page 155) continues the Lucan themes of journey and joy. Although the Acts are not treated in detail, the connection with these themes is an important aspect to be stressed by the teacher. The exercise included in "The Birth of the Church (Acts 1—2)" (text page 155) is designed to carry the joyfulness of the good news into the early days of the Church. By the presence of Jesus' Spirit among the early Christians, their joy is increased and that in turn sparks their witnessing to Jesus.

The concluding sections give an account of this witnessing. "The Church in Jerusalem (Acts 3:1—8:3)" (text page 156) describes the core Christian-Jewish community: their life with one another, the joys and trials experienced as disciples. "The Journeys and Witness of Paul (Acts 12:1—28:31)" (text page 157) carries the theme of joy and journey beyond the Palestinian scene into the Graeco-Roman world Luke is addressing.

Life Experience Focus

There are several reasons why, of the four gospels, the one according to Luke often holds most appeal for adolescents.

First, it was written for a non-Jewish audience. It speaks more directly to people, such as our students, who are not well-versed in the culture and thought patterns of first-century Palestine. Its themes are more universal: peace, reconciliation, joy, simplicity of lifestyle, concern for the outcast.

Second, these themes respond to what many adolescents either are experiencing or would like to experience. Four of the needs described by sociologist Merton Strommen in *Five Cries of Youth* apply very directly here. He hears from 20% of youth the cry of self-hatred, that is, a debilitating poor image of oneself. Luke's message of peace can help them accept and love themselves. One out of five youth also feel themselves to be psychological orphans because of troubling family conditions. Luke's stories of reconciliation can show them the way to a better understanding of God our Father and hopefully to improved relationships within the family. One out of ten youth are strongly concerned for action on social issues. Luke's Gospel above all shows Jesus sharing their prophetic ardor. Finally, the largest group identified by Strommen, about me out of three, are joyful in their relationships with God, with their Church, and with the people in their lives. Luke's spirit of joy gives them reason to reflect upon and celebrate the grace from God which they enjoy.

Third, the journey framework of Luke suits the mood of many high school students. Although adolescence has its own integrity and is more than just a passage from childhood to adulthood, the four years of high school do have a transitional character to them. There is a sense of moving on to something or some place else. They can see the value of setting one's life in a certain direction, as Jesus did toward Jerusalem (Luke 9:51) or as Paul did so often until finally he arrived in Rome.

103

Background on Content

The author of Luke/Acts is a non-Jewish evangelist, companion to Paul, who writes for a Gentile-Greek audience around the year 85 A.D. His main concern was the transposition of Jewish-Christian images and symbols into the culture of the Greek humanistic mind. Luke uses Mark's Gospel, and, while remaining faithful to the Jewish-Christian tradition, cleverly extracts the core message from its very Jewish overtones and incorporates the good news into an atmosphere of liberation and joy for the non-Jewish mind.

Luke structures his gospel and Acts in parallel form using Luke 24 and Acts 1:4–11 as the interim time. The parallelism begins with Jesus' baptism in the Jordan (Luke. 3) and the Church's Baptism in the Spirit (Acts 2). The literary technique of the journey continues the parallelism: Jesus journeys to Jerusalem (Luke 9—19); Paul journeys to Rome (Acts 19—28); Jesus has four trials (Luke 21—26); Jesus' death (Luke 23) is vindicated by his resurrection (Luke 24); Paul's death is vindicated by the growth of the Church.

Jesus' mission to the poor is one of the characteristics of Luke's Gospel. The infancy narratives abound with the *anawim:* Mary, Joseph, Elizabeth, the shepherds. The "power" of God's Spirit is operative in the "weakness" of these *anawim* who are very aware of their need for God. In this Luke reminds us very much of Paul (Romans 8:26–28). Luke has Jesus specifically state his mission (4:18–19) and promise of joy to these poor (6:20–23). Only those who are truly poor—materially and spiritually—can follow Christ.

The boundlessness of God's loving kindness for all people through Jesus and the Holy Spirit is a source of *great joy.* It is this joy which Luke tries to covey to his Greek audience. This joy will be theirs if they, like God, are generous to the poor regardless of personal cost. Luke challenges his readers to a generosity that is noted for its hospitality and bounty, its forgiveness and peace. Joy is a specific aim of Jesus' mission: "The Spirit of the Lord is upon me because he has chosen me to bring *good news* . . . to proclaim *liberty* . . . to *set free* . . ." (4:18–19). This joy is evident in Luke's section on discipleship as well: the disciples return from their missionary journey "in great joy" (10:17): Jesus himself rejoices in his Father's work (10:21). The resurrection accounts are replete with expressions of joy: the disciples on the road to Emmaus (24:32), the disciples in Jerusalem (24:41), and after the ascension (24:52). Joy cannot be contained, and so the disciples must tell the good news and witness to the world the love and mercy of God.

Luke's Gospel has also been called the "Gospel of Mercy" for he stresses in a unique way the *mercy and forgiveness of the Father* as manifested in Jesus. Jesus' forgiveness reaches out to touch all (3:6), and Luke weaves a repentance theme throughout the gospel pericopes and sayings of Jesus in order to reinforce this idea. Peter begins his following of Jesus by confessing he is a sinner (5:8); the sinful woman is forgiven and praised in the home of Simon the Pharisee (7:36–50); the lost sheep, the lost coin and the lost son (15) are stories that reveal the Father's personal concern for each of us and his tremendous joy at our return to him. The repentance of the thief on the cross (23:39–43) is unique to Luke and repeats the theme of the Father's faithful love and forgiveness to all who turn to him.

Discipleship in Luke means following Jesus precisely in his generosity and hospitality to the poor, in his poverty of spirit which trusted totally in his Father, in his endurance of suffering for love of his Father and all people, and finally in his prayer and joy which witness to the Father's love and call to intimacy to each of his sons and daughters.

Journey of a Pope

1. Once the students have read this section on the pope, let them discuss their recollections of his visit from TV coverage, or from those who actually saw and heard John Paul II in person. The joy and enthusiasm of the experience should be highlighted by the teacher in order to facilitate the transition to Luke whose gospel is one of joy and enthusiasm for Jesus.

2. If an audio recording of John Paul's visit is available play a selection to help recall the experience. The filmstrip set, *Pathways of Peace,* can also help to recreate this event (see *Resources* in this Guide chapter).

A Travelogue
Luke: The Joyful Gospel—A Structural Outline
The Acts of the Apostles

1. In order to have the students discern Luke's use of the ascension as the turning point of Luke-Acts, have them read Luke 24 and Acts 1. Ask them to look for a passage that is common to both readings. Once they have discovered the ascension passage, discuss with them Luke's use of this passage to indicate the interim time between the journey of Jesus to the Father and the journey of his Church influenced by his Spirit.

2. Have the students read these three sections (text pages 146–147) and familiarize themselves with the outline of Luke-Acts.

Joy to the World
Joy to the Poor! (Luke 1:46—4:21)

1. The students are probably very familiar with Luke's Infancy narrative and the joy it enkindles in hearts at Christmastime. Have them read "Joy to the Poor!" (text page 148) and discuss ways in which people give joy to each other at this time of the year.

2. Divide the students into small groups and have each group read Luke 1:1—2:20 and compare it with the words of Rosalyn Carter and Pope John Paul II, as suggested in the exercise on text page 147. Allow each group to share the similarities found with the others.

3. *Worksheet #19* is designed to help the students reflect on the theme of peace which is a key part of Luke's Gospel.

4. Luke 1:46—4:21 continues in a special way the message of joy to the poor. Have the students read this passage and find the many references to the poor before they read the summary of these points in the student text (page 148).

Part One: Credentials and Responses (Luke 1:1—9:50)

1. "Part One: Credentials and Responses" (text page 148) presents Luke's account of people's acceptance or rejection of Jesus. Divide the scriptural assignment into four sections and then assign a group of students to each section.

Ask them to read the chapters assigned and express in their own words Jesus' presentation of his credentials and the various responses given to him.

2. The parable of the sower (8:4–15) summarizes in the story form the actual responses to Jesus by the people he encounters. Try to determine from the students the relationship of this parable to all that has preceded it in Luke's Gospel. Then point out how this becomes a turning point after which Jesus focuses his attention and teaching on his disciples.

Teaching Notes 2

Text Pages 148–154

Part Two: Discipleship (Luke 9:51—19:27)

The Journey section is Luke's way of teaching others how to follow Jesus. "Part Two: Discipleship" (text pages 148–149) introduces the students to Luke's message about following Jesus. Show the filmstrip "Lord Teach Us—Luke" (see *Resources* of this Guide chapter). Emphasize discipleship as:

- associating with the "wrong people," with the outcasts of society, with sinners (spiritually poor—Luke 7:36–50; 19:1–10);
- becoming childlike in one's relationship to God and to others (spiritually dependent—Luke 18:16–18);
- selling all and following Christ (actual material poverty—Luke 18:18–25);
- trusting in God and not worrying about material goods (poverty of spirit—Luke 12:22–28);
- recognizing all people as poor in one way or another, and therefore, reaching out to all as neighbors (Luke 10:25–37).

Call to Commitment

1. "Call to Commitment" (text pages 149–150) recalls once again the joy experienced by the pope's message to the youth of America. After the students have read this section ask them to indicate the call to discipleship as expressed by the pope:

- "Heed the call of Christ . . ."
- ". . . a choice for Christ and his way of life and his commandment of love."
- ". . . reveal the true meaning of life in your world."
- "If you really accept that love from Christ, it will lead you to God, to the service of love. . ."

2. Play the recording of the pope's message to youth at Madison Square Garden (see *Resources* of this Guide chapter). Ask the students to listen to the pope's challenge to them, to hear his words of challenge, and to express their reactions to this challenge.

Luke's Call

1. "Luke's Call" (text page 150) deals with the joys and difficulties encountered by those who respond positively to the call to discipleship. Have the students read 9:51—10:37 and discuss the difficulties mentioned by Luke (9:51–62) within the context of the motive of love (10:25–37).

2. The exercise dealing with 10:21–24, provides an opportunity to become practical and real in the service of God and neighbor. Small groups allow for greater interaction and freedom of expression; a recorder from each group could report suggestions about service to the others. The teacher may want to act upon one or two of these suggestions.

How Terrible for You Pharisees! (Luke 11:37–54)

1. A description of how not to be a disciple of Jesus is given in "How Terrible for You Pharisees" (text page 150). Invite the students to compose a "blessing of praise" as a positive side of the negative condemnation.

2. Lest there be a general condemnation of all pharisees in the minds of the students, it is important to give some background on the Pharisaic Movement. Read John Pawlikowski's article "Our Jewish Roots" (see *Resources* for this Guide chapter).

More About Discipleship

In "More About Discipleship" (text page 152) the positive qualities of discipleship are listed. After reading the scriptural reference for each quality of discipleship, the students should explain how each reference exemplifies a particular quality.

Wealth and Worry

1. "Wealth and Worry" (text pages 152–153) highlights the necessity of setting one's heart on lasting values. Have the students read Luke 12:1–53 and discuss the values of the rich man as compared with the values found in 10:38–42, 11:1–4, and 11:28.

2. Luke sets up a choice for all who would be true disciples of Jesus: God or wealth. Divide the students into four groups to focus in on each of the following:

a. Luke 16:1–15. Read the story and discuss how people in today's society attempt to serve both God and money.

b. Luke 16:19–31. Read the parable and discuss how we in America might be considered the rich man and the poor of the third world are Lazarus. How would Luke have us treat the poor? How can we as individuals try to live according to Luke's message?

c. Luke 18:18–29. Read the parable and discuss each student's personal response to Jesus' invitation (v. 22); discuss the very real difficulty of trying to live as Christ in our consumer society.

d. Luke 19:1–19. Read the story and discuss how Zacchaeus rose above the "sneers of his peers" in order to see Jesus. What are ways in which Christians today can rise above the false values in society in order to help others to see Jesus in their lives?

3. To summarize this important section, show the filmstrip "Luke, Prayer and Social Apostolate" (see *Resources* of this Guide chapter).

Part Three: The Last Week in Jerusalem (Luke 19:28—24:53)

1. With reference to "Part Three: The Last Week in Jerusalem" (text page 154) have the students read the text and note the passages peculiar to Luke. Discuss with them how these passages support the theme of joy which runs throughout the gospel.

2. *Worksheet #20* leads the students through a study of prayer as we see it exemplified in Jesus during the last week of his public ministry.

The Ultimate Journey (Luke 24:36—53)
"The Ultimate Journey" (text page 154) concludes the gospel account and at the same time provides the link to the Acts of the Apostles. Ask the students to explain how the ultimate journey of Jesus is not an ending but a beginning.

Teaching Notes 3

Text Pages 155—159

The Acts of the Apostles
Have the students read "The Acts of the Apostles" (text page 155) which gives an overview of Luke's second work. The Acts are treated briefly in the student text but the teacher should decide how much reading of the twenty-eight chapters would be profitable. The decision may be to summarize certain important events from this section with the students.

The Birth of the Church (Acts 1—2)
1. "The Birth of the Church" (text page 155) deals with the coming of the Holy Spirit and the effect this coming has on the infant Church. Ask the students to discuss what they know about the Charismatic Movement in the Church. Assign some of them to research this growing phenomenon and have others interview someone they know to be a Charismatic about his or her experience of being "born again" in the Spirit.

2. The exercise (text page 155) of this section allows the students to concretize some essential aspects of Church: its universal mission and its empowerment by the Holy Spirit.

The Church in Jerusalem (Acts 3:1—8:3)
The next section deals with "The Church in Jerusalem" (text page 156). The teacher

should stress the main topics presented and compare the lives of the early Christians with the Christ whom they followed.

The Growth of the Church (Acts 8:14—12:25)

1. The paradox of the seed dying in order to bring forth new life symbolizes the mystery of "The Growth of the Church" (text pages 156–157) through the death of the martyrs. The teacher should point out that "death" reaches beyond the physical to all those selfish aspects of human nature which are obstacles to spiritual growth. Have the students discuss ways in which they can "die" to themselves, to their selfishness, in order to promote life in others and to grow in Christ's life.

2. The exercise (text pages 156–157) for this section enables the students to search out those events which contributed to the growth of the Church.

The Journeys and Witness of Paul (Acts 12:1—28:31)

1. Luke focuses once more on his journey theme in the second part of Acts. "The Journeys and Witness of Paul" (text page 157) tells of the rapid spread of the gospel of joy to the Gentile world.

2. If the teacher wishes to cover this section in detail, it might prove benefical to divide the students into three groups, each group concentrating on one of the three journeys of Paul (13:1—14:27; 15:36—18:22; 18:23—20:38). Each group should:
- read the appropriate scriptural passage;
- draw its journey on a transparency, indicating specific places visited;
- using its transparency, report to the others the central events of the journey and people Paul met, converted, had trouble with, etc.

3. The students might be helped by the following summary of important points from this chapter:

a. *The Journey Theme* is the literary technique used by Luke to convey his *Gospel of Joy.* This joyful news extends beyond the Jewish-Christian community to include all people who believe in Jesus as the human embodiment of the Father's faithful love.

b. *Discipleship* according to Luke means following Jesus in *childlike trust in the Father* and in *reaching out to the poor and the outcasts* of society. Following Jesus' love means following Jesus in his concern and compassion for others to the point of self-sacrifice.

c. The *Ascension event* links Luke's Gospel and the Acts so that the journey of Jesus on earth is continued by the journey of the Church—Christ's body—on earth. The Ascension event records Jesus' commission to spread the good news throughout the earth and is followed by the Pentecost event which provides the power of Jesus' Spirit to continue his work in and through his Church.

Prayer Reflection

Assemble the students in a special place in order to create a climate of prayer. Put a candle in the center of the group and explain to them that the candle represents Christ's presence in their midst. Play the song, "Looking for Space" by John Denver (see *Resources* for this Guide chapter) asking the students to reflect on the repeating refrain, "I'm looking for space and to find out who I am."

All persons search for identity; ideals challenge most people, youth in particular. Ask a student to read the "Prayer Reflection" (text page 159) which deals with Pope John Paul II's challenge to American youth. Taking the sentence, "Real love is demanding," ask the students to share ways in which living Christ's love makes demands on their lives. After this sharing, use the song, "The Cry of the Poor" by John Foley, S.J. (see *Resources* for this Guide chapter) as the closing prayer.

Prayer and Worship Experiences

1. Have the students illustrate the teaching and example of Jesus about prayer which they have researched through *Worksheet #20.* It can be done by way of slides, posters, or music. With these ingredients, plus selected texts from Luke's Gospel, have them put together a prayer reflection on prayer itself.

2. Luke's Gospel shows great concern for the poor, the oppressed, and the outcast. Have the students compose a litany of petitions based upon the present needs of people. Encourage them to recall these petitions in prayers at quiet moments in their daily lives.

3. Encourage the students to structure a prayer service centered around the theme of discipleship. They can use readings from Luke's Gospel that are referred to in this chapter. It would be beneficial to include a period of quiet reflection on the meaning of discipleship in their lives as they journey together in growing in faith.

Service Projects

1. Building upon the litany suggested in #2 of *Prayer and Worship Experiences* in this Guide chapter, have the students brainstorm ways in which its petitions can flow into practical action.

2. Two themes in Luke's Gospel are rejection and reconciliation. Perhaps in the group there has been some instance of rejection and some need for reconciliation. With a small group of students explore to what extent rejection may be happening and how reconciliation may be achieved without embarrassing anyone.

Independent Study Projects

1. The framework of a journey which gives structure both to Luke's Gospel and to the Acts of the Apostles, is a common device for literature, for films, and for music. Have some students research instances of this journey theme. Invite them to report their findings to the group and to explain why authors and artists so often choose the journey framework.

2. *Worksheet #19* gives some recent quotations on peace. Have the students research other statements on this topic. Some sources can be: the Scriptures, history, literature, music, and recent Church documents, especially those from Pope John XXIII to the present. Suggest that they devise some creative way of presenting their findings to the group.

Resources

Audiovisual

John Paul II's Major Talks in America. 6 cassettes. National Catholic Reporter, P.O. Box 281, Kansas City, MO 64141.

"Looking for Space." Sound recording by John Denver from his album, *Windsong.* RCA Records, New York.

"Lord Teach Us—Luke." Sound filmstrip 4 from the series *In The Light of the Resurrection: The New Testament.* Our Sunday Visitor, 200 Noll Plaza, Huntington, IN 46750.

"Luke—Prayer and Social Apostolate." Sound filmstrip from the series *Service Filmstrips.* Paulist Press, 545 Island Ave., Pamsey, NJ 07446.

"The Cry of the Poor." Sound recording by John Foley, S.J. from the album *Wood Hath Hope.* North American Liturgy Resources, 2110 W. Peoria Ave., Phoenix, AZ 85029.

Pathways of Peace. Sound filmstrip set. W.H. Sadlier, 11 Park Place, New York, NY 10007.

Print

F. Danker. *Jesus and the New Age, According to Luke.* St. Louis: Clayton Publishing House, 1972.

L. Fox. *Youth in Concert with Pope John Paul II.* Morristown, NJ: Silver Burdett, 1980.

R.J. Karras, O.F.M. *What Are They Saying About Luke and Acts?* New York: Paulist Press, 1979.

J. Pawlickowski. "Our Jewish Roots." *Sign.* October, 1980.

N. Perrin. *The New Testament: An Introduction.* New York: Harcourt Brace Jovanovich, 1974.

J. Rohde. *Rediscovering the Teaching of the Evangelists.* Philadelphia: The Westminster Press, 1968.

C. Stuhlmueller, C.P. "The Gospel According to Luke," *The Jerome Biblical Commentary.* Englewood Cliffs, NJ: Prentice-Hall, 1968.

11

John:
New Life Gospel

Text Pages
160–175

Objectives

Knowledge: To help the students to an initial understanding of the Christology of John's gospel with its central message of the Christian's passage to new life through Jesus.
Attitude: To enable the students to appreciate more fully the gift of new life which is offered to them, and to be willing to open themselves to growth in this life.
Practice: To encourage the students to try to live in love with others in obedience to Jesus' command: "Love one another as I love you."

Orientation

The introductory section of this chapter, "New Life" (text page 160), attempts to give the students a deeper understanding and appreciation of this phrase by comparing it to the rebirth of nature after the long winter months. The main concept is one of transformation which enables all peoples to share in the life of God.

"John's Audience and Style" (text pages 160–161) points out that John writes for a Jewish audience which, at the end of the first century, had difficulty deciding whether to accept Jesus and join the Christian Church or to remain with the Jewish synagogue.

"The Structure" (text pages 161–162) of John's Gospel brings out the difference between John and the synoptics. The five acts of John's Gospel have Chapter 6:16–21 as their center point, thus revealing John's emphasis on the divinity of Jesus: "Do not be afraid, it is I."

The structure of John's Gospel begins to unfold with "Act One: Credentials" (text pages 162–163). In order to convince his audience of the divinity of Jesus and his messiahship, John presents a host of divine and human witnesses who testify to that divinity.

The term "reborn" may be familiar to many students. "Being Reborn" (text page 163) uses this familiarity to lead into the theological thrust of John's Gospel: one must believe in Jesus in order to be reborn into the newness of the divine life he offers all people.

"Act Two: Response" (text pages 163–164) covers both positive and negative responses to Jesus. Belief and acceptance come not from the chosen people, the Jews, but rather from the outcasts—the Samaritans—and from the pagan Gentiles. John's "Monologues for Unbelievers" (text pages 164–165) argue for

Jesus by pointing out the hardness of heart of those Jews who refuse to believe in Jesus' divine powers because they were revealed on the Sabbath.

The heart of John's Gospel is revealed in "Act Three: The Turning Point" (text page 165). Jesus walks on the water, reveals himself to his frightened disciples as the "I Am" who will deliver them to safety. All of this is meant to remind the Jews of Yahweh who delivered his people to safety by using Moses to lead them through the waters of the Reed Sea.

"Waters of Life" (text pages 165–166) continues to develop the comparison of Jesus with Moses, showing how Jesus leads the new people of God to a new and richer life in God. The parallelism is striking and John's Jewish audience should have clearly seen the reference to Jesus as the new Moses and the promised Messiah.

The drama continues to unfold as the tension mounts in "Act Four: Defense" (text pages 168–170). Jesus refutes the indictments of the Jewish leaders by declaring his relationship with his Father as the cornerstone of his authority. The drama closes with "Act Five: Discipleship, Passion, Death, and Resurrection" (text pages 170–171), which deals with the themes of life, death and new life at this crucial moment in Jesus' journey on earth. The text deals with those elements of John's Gospel which support John's thesis of new life: the farewell discourse in chapters 13—17 and the resurrection account in chapters 20—21.

"The Farewell Discourse" (text page 171) introduces the students to John's exposition on discipleship which is given in this discourse on the night before Jesus died. The tone is set by "The Washing of the Feet" (text pages 171–172) which reveals Jesus' actions as much more than humility. The washing of the feet symbolizes a love that is unto death: the Father's love for us which allows Jesus to give his life for us, and the Son's love for his Father and for us which strengthens him to give up his very life.

"Encouragement and Support" (text pages 172–173) exposes the students to Jesus' promise to send the Holy Spirit. Finally, "The Resurrection" (text pages 173–174) covers that section in John which is unique to him: Peter's vocation as a leader of all those who have received the new life brought by Jesus.

Life Experience Focus

Several reasons make the Gospel of John a special challenge to adolescents. First, its Christology is descending, that is, it begins with the divinity of Jesus and then leads to his humanity. Most adolescents seem more at home with an ascending Christology, that is, one which begins with Jesus' humanity and then leads to a realization of the fullness of divinity present within him. Second, the mode of development is more cyclic than linear. Adolescents can think more easily when the development is more sequential in its logic. Third, John's use of symbols is highly sophisticated for early adolescents to appreciate. They tend to see things in a literal, one-dimensional way. In John there are often several layers of meaning to a symbol such as water or light.

On the other hand, there is something happening among adolescents today that opens them to John's Gospel. It is a renewed interest in the transcendent, in prayer, in personal spirituality. This still may not be true for the majority, yet the number seems to be increasing. A recent work of sociologist Andrew Greeley documents this phenomenon. With this in mind, the teacher should approach John's Gospel with the same attitude as its author, that is, with an unembarrassed faith in Jesus as the eternal Word, God's own Son. This includes an invitation that the students begin to make this faith their own and begin to live the kind of discipleship described in John's Gospel.

Background on Content

Writing to those who could not make up their minds about following Jesus, John arranges his good news to show that Jesus is the divine Son who brings new life to the world. Faith is the force needed to be reborn; faith is the force needed to accept the new life offered. This central message becomes the heart of John's Gospel.

It is contained in six short verses (6:16–21). As Moses led the chosen people from slavery across the waters of the Reed Sea to a new land and a new life, so Jesus leads those who believe in him across the waters of · life to a new home and to a new life with his Father. The disciples are in fear of the storm; Jesus walking upon the water reveals himself as "I Am": "Don't be afraid, it is I!" (6:20). What John is basically saying is that when you touch the "I Am" point of Jesus, you have gone beyond all possibility of fear. It is by grasping what Jesus is all about, what Christianity is all about in the mystery of Jesus, that one discovers what life is all about, the new and richer life offered to all by the Father. Jesus tells all of us: I am the one who is with you so do not be afraid. This is John's message to those would-be disciples; it is a message to believe in Jesus who offers new life.

The *defense* of Jesus contains a series of "I AM" statements:

a. *"I am the bread of life"* (6:35): The Bread of Life discourse is connected with Moses because Moses had promised them the bread of life in the desert—manna. Here the important thing is that Jesus says "I am the Bread of Life." He is not saying "I am bread", but he reveals the mystery of "I AM."

b. *I am the Living Water:* Water in the Hebrew mind always meant life. John presents Jesus as present at the Temple at the time of Tabernacles when the water is carried back to the Temple by the Jewish priest. Then Jesus says: "Whoever is thirsty should come to me and drink" (7:37).

c. *"I am the light of the world"* (8:12): John proceeds to the ceremony of the lighting of the lamps in the Temple court and has Jesus say there "I am the light of the world."

d. *I am He!:* "You have already seen him, and he is the one who is talking with you now" (9:37). The man born blind is yet another disciple who believes.

e. *"I am the good shepherd,* who is willing to die for the sheep" (10:11). Jesus represents the Father's love for all people (3:16), a love which he expresses by giving up his life for others.

f. *I am one with the Father:* "The Father and I are one" (10:20). On this Feast of the Dedication of the Temple, Jesus proclaims that he is the one whom the Father consecrated and sent so that all people may have life through him.

g. *"I am the resurrection and the life"* (11:25). Lazarus is a disciple of Jesus and his death and resurrection is a sign of the new life Jesus will attain for all people through his own death and resurrection.

John teaches *discipleship* in the Farewell Discourse of Jesus (13—17). The washing of the feet is more than the obvious cleansing, more than the apparent lesson in humility. The washing of the feet symbolizes the greatest act of love: love unto death. Jesus challenges his disciples to follow his example (13:15), to love as he loves)13:34). The disciples cannot do this on their own and Jesus tells them not to worry because he will give them a Helper who will stay with them forever (14:16). The Spirit will support and strengthen them to live this love command so long as they remain united to Jesus (15:5).

Teaching Notes 1

Text Pages
160–165

New Life

1. Introduce the theme of Chapter 11 by reading to the students a section from *Hope for the Flowers* which deals also with dying and being reborn to new life (see *Resources* for this Guide chapter). Ask them to listen to the reading and then restate in their own words the underlying message: one must let go and die to former securities if one is to grow into a new and richer life.

2. The introductory section, "New Life" (text page 160) uses the change of seasons from winter into spring as an example of transformation into new life which John talks about.

John's Audience and Style

"John's Audience and Style" (text pages 160–161) presents important information for understanding John's message. The teacher should clearly explain the three points which reveal John's purpose in writing his gospel and the drama he creates.

The Structure

Similar to Matthew, John uses the staircase for "The Structure" (text pages 161–162) of his gospel. Unique to John, however, are the long dialogues and monologues he uses to convince his audience of the divinity of Jesus who offers new life to all who believe in him.

Act One: Credentials (John 1:1—4:3)

With reference to "Act One: Credentials" (text pages 162–163), have the students read John 1:1—4:3 and identify those verses which witness to Jesus' divinity:

- John 1:1–2,18
- John the Baptist 1:29–34
- Holy Spirit 1:32
- apostles 1:41,49
- Jesus' first miracle 2:1–11
- Jesus' authority 2:18–22
- Jesus' power over death 2:19–21
- Nicodemus 3:5–21
- John the Baptist 3:27–30

115

Being Reborn

1. Once the students have read "Being Reborn" (text page 163) invite them to discuss some prominent people who have been reborn and how this has changed their lives. If some students know personally anyone who has experienced this transformation, it might be helpful to have that person talk to the group either in person or on tape.

2. Before being reborn it is necessary to believe in Jesus and to be open to accept the "new life" he offers. Discuss "openness"—its signs, its importance for growth and development in every area of life, especially the spiritual.

Act Two: Response (John 4:4—6:15)

1. Each of the evangelists has recorded the different reactions to Jesus. In "Act Two: Responses" (text pages 163–164) those who accept and reject Jesus are discussed. Divide the students into three groups:

- the Samaritans 4:4–45;
- the Gentiles 4:46–54;
- the Jews 5:1—6:15.

Have three students study the part of Jesus in each encounter and prepare to play his role with each group. Once the groups have read and understood their roles, encourage them to role play Jesus' interaction with each.

2. After all three groups have completed their reenactment, help the students to discuss their feelings as they played the different roles: the three who took the part of Jesus, the Samaritan woman, the government official, and the Jewish people.

Monolgues for Unbelievers (John 3:10–21; 5:19–47)

"Monologues for Unbelievers" (text pages 164–165) exposes the students for the first time to John's literary use of monologues as a technique for expounding his theology. Have the students read the two monologues and determine for each one: 1) the audience to which it is directed, and 2) the message John wishes to convey to them.

a. Nicodemus 3:10–21
● audience: those Jews wavering in their belief in Jesus.
● message: God loves us so much he gave us his Son that whoever believe in him may have eternal life.

b. Following the healing of the paralytic 5:19–47
● audience: those Jews who would not believe in Jesus.
● message: The Son loves his Father so much that he willingly gives up his life so that all who believe in him will be saved.

Teaching Notes 2

Text Pages 165–170

Act Three: The Turning Point (John 6:16–21)

1. That Jesus is the promised savior is John's main thesis in "Act Three: The Turning Point" (text page 165). John presents Jesus as the new Moses leading the Jewish people through a second Exodus to eternal life. The teacher should stress the connection with the Hebrew Scriptures made by John for this gives a clearer insight into the importance of this scriptural passage beyond the obvious miracle story.

2. Explore with the students the meaning of the turning points in people's lives. Ask them to describe particular turning points in the lives of people they may have read about (for example, St. Paul, St. Elizabeth Seton, Danny Thomas, George Foreman).

Waters of Life

"Exodus: Waters of Life" (text pages 165–166) focuses in on the Exodus connection between Jesus and Moses. Have the students read aloud Exodus 3:1–15 and 14; then highlight the points made under "Exodus" (text page 166). Proceed to John 6:16–21 and ask the students to pick out the similarities before reading them under "John" (text page 166). Emphasize the very important point John is making at this central part of his gospel: Jesus is divine ("I AM"); those who believe in him will be led by him through the sea of life to a new and richer life as the people of God.

Act Four: Defense (John 6:22—12:11)

1. Because of the tension between Judaism and Christianity at the end of the first century, John writes the next section of his gospel to refute the false accusations against Jesus. "Act Four: Defense" (text pages 168—170) clearly outlines both the accusations made by the Jews and Jesus' statements of defense.

Have the students read "The Indictment" (text page 169) and explain why these accusations are very logical and very human.

Using the Scriptures as well as the student text, have the students study each of Jesus' rebuttals in "The Refutation" (text page 170). Ask the students to explain how faith in Jesus is the essential element in each of these statements.

2. *Worksheet #21* can help the students to understand this section better through a study of the story "Jesus Heals a Man Born Blind," in Luke's ninth chapter.

Act Five: Discipleship, Passion, Death and Resurrection (John 12:12—21:25)

1. This final section of John's Gospel (12:12—21:25) is perhaps the most poetic and most mystical of all the gospels. "Act Five: Discipleship, Passion, Death and Resurrection" (text pages 170—171), while presenting an overview of Jesus' last week on earth, highlights John's themes of life, death, and new life.

2. *Worksheet #22* asks the students to reflect upon Christian discipleship in terms of images used by Jesus about himself here and earlier in John's Gospel.

The Farewell Discourse (John 13—17)

The student text deliberately concentrates on "The Farewell Discourse" (text page 171) which explains discipleship as entering into Christ's life and death in order to share in the new life he offers to all people. This section serves as an introduction to a more detailed explanation of discipleship.

The Washing of the Feet (John 13:1—17)

1. "The Washing of the Feet" (text pages 171—172) gets to the heart of discipleship immediately. Have the students read John 13:1—17 carefully noting:
- the obvious lesson in humility.

- references to Jesus' death in verses 1, 3 and 7.
- the challenge of Jesus to follow his example in verse 15.

2. The exercise (text page 172) attempts to pull together the above aspects with John's key idea on discipleship (13:34). Jesus challenges all who would follow him to love others as he loves: unto death. It is important that death be explained not only as physically dying for another (which is rare) but more importantly as a dying to the selfishness hidden within human nature which prevents the expression of true love for others.

Encouragement and Support (John 14—16)

1. Discipleship is not easy. "Encouragement and Support" (text pages 172–173) is designed to explain the source of strength available to those who attempt to follow Christ's call to discipleship. Divide the students into three groups; each group should carefully read one chapter, discuss among its members the support offered, and then report its findings to the others.

2. Once the groups have reported their findings, ask the students to illustrate how each chapter relates to John's theme of a new life:

    a. Chapter 14 describes the new life that will be theirs and promises the Holy Spirit as support for that life.

    b. Chapter 15 reveals the importance of developing a real relationship with Jesus through prayer; by remaining united to Jesus through love, this new life will be fruitful.

    c. Chapter 16 promises the Holy Spirit as a support through the turbulence of this life which becomes fruitful for a new and richer life in God.

The Resurrection (John 20—21)

1. "The Resurrection" (text pages 173–174) focuses on Jesus' appearance at the Lake of Galilee, reported only by John. Peter, as head of the Church, is the main character here.

Read 21:1–19 with different students taking the parts of the narrator, Peter, Jesus, group of three apostles, and one student as John, the disciple whom Jesus loved.

2. After the reading have both the readers and the listeners ponder and react to Jesus' dialogue with Peter. Discuss with the students the manifestations of love, trust, and forgiveness contained in this dialogue and its ramifications for living Christ's life today.

3. A good summary of this final section would be a viewing of the filmstrip "Death and Victory" by Donald Senior (see *Resources* for this Guide chapter). This filmstrip presents modern biblical scholarship on the very theme covered in the student text on John: life, death, and new life.

4. Having read the text and viewed the filmstrip, have the students list the events from John's Gospel which strengthen belief in Jesus as God's Son.

5. The following summary statements may be of help in summarizing this chapter:

    a. Faith in Jesus as God's Son is essential for anyone who wishes to participate in eternal life. It is this faith which enables us to be reborn.

    b. John presents Jesus as the New Moses who leads all who believe in him to a new life in God.

    c. Jesus reveals himself as divine through a series of "I AM" statements; this is John's way of trying to convince those Jews who hesitate to believe in the divinity of Jesus.

    d. Discipleship for John means remaining one with Jesus so as to share his life and to love all as he does, no matter what the cost to self.

Prayer Reflection

Begin the "Prayer Reflection" (text page 175) by playing the song, "New Life, New Creation" (see *Resources* for this Guide chapter). Before reading John 17 prepare the students to listen to this reading as Jesus' personal prayer for each one of them. Have a student prayerfully read this chapter and allow time for quiet reflection and personal application. The students can then share those parts of Chapter 17 that had special meaning to them. After the sharing, all read the concluding prayer (text page 175).

Prayer and Worship Experiences

1. The sixth chapter of John's Gospel speaks of Jesus as bread from both a sapiential and a sacramental point of view. Jesus nourishes those who believe in him both by the wisdom of his teaching and by the quality of his whole person. This parallels our Christian Eucharistic liturgy in which Jesus nourishes us both in the Liturgy of the Word and in the Eucharist proper. A prayer composed with these thoughts in mind applies this to the way we should be Eucharist to one another. Its source is *Bread For the World* (see *Resources* for this Guide chapter).

"I believe that bread comes from grain that grows in the wind and the rain with the farmer's help far from the eyes of the city folk.

I believe that bread comes from love, the love of the Father, the love of the farmer, the love of the baker's hands, the love of those who bring it to me.

I believe that bread can be and should be broken and shared and given to all persons until all have enough and then some. I believe that Jesus loved bread and took it and blessed it and fed his disciples and asked them to feed us forever.

I believe enough in bread to want it from Jesus, to want it to nurture me, to want his life through it.

I believe that his body as bread feeds me and as part of his body I want to be bread for others.

I believe that the Spirit will help me as will Jesus' people. Amen.

2. Good prayer blends together awe and ease, reverence and relaxation. Perhaps in approaching the Jesus of the synoptic gospels we have emphasized ease by concentrating upon Jesus in his humanity. In John's Gospel we can shift the emphases to awe in the presence of Jesus as divine. Here we may get help by drawing upon the prayer forms and traditions of Eastern Christianity. This can be done by a visit to one of their churches, by having one of their clergy speak with the students, or by research in the library. One important dimension is that the students not only learn about this tradition but also experience it as part of their own prayer.

Service Projects

1. Brainstorm ways in which we can imitate the example Jesus gave us when he washed his disciples' feet. Some acts of service might be: helping around the house, running an errand for a neighbor, cutting the lawn or shoveling snow off the sidewalk for a senior citizen.

2. In John's Gospel we find explicit witness to Jesus Christ as God's own Son. Have the students figure out realistic ways in which they can witness to each other and to others this same kind of faith in Jesus Christ. Possibilities are: participation in the Liturgy of the Word, reception of the Eucharist, helping to prepare someone younger for the reception of the sacraments, praying with the family.

Independent Study Projects

1. John's account of Jesus' resurrection differs in a number of ways from those of Matthew, Mark, and Luke. The chapter in the text looked at one of these differences, the way John describes a meeting of Jesus with his apostles at the Lake of Galilee. Assist some students in researching some of the other ways in which John's account of Jesus' resurrection differs from those of the other evangelists.

2. St. John's Gospel uses signs and symbols as ways of sharing new life. This parallels what happens in the sacramental life of the Church. Have the students read through St. John's Gospel with attention to parallels with the sacraments of Baptism, Eucharist, and Reconciliation. Suggest that they share their work with the group.

3. Invite some students to rework the story "Jesus Heals a Man Born Blind," (John 9) into a script for a group dramatization. Tell them to feel free to fill out the story as they think it may have happened. They can present the dramatization to the others or, if video equipment is available, they might videotape it and play it back for the total group. This project could serve to complement the student's completion of *Worksheet #21.*

4. Encourage the students to explore the meaning of the suffering and death of Jesus in John's Gospel as compared to the synoptic gospels.

Resources

Audiovisual

"New Life, New Creation." Sound recording from the album *Listen* by the Monks of Weston Priory.

"Death and Victory." Sound filmstrip from the series *God the Son* by Donald Senior. Argus Communications, 7440 Natchez, Niles, IL 60648.

"John: Spirituality and Sacrament." Sound filmstrip from the *Service Filmstrip: The Evangelists.* Paulist Press.

Print

W. Harrington. *Explaining the Gospels.* Glen Rock, NJ: Paulist Press, 1963.

Lord Make Us Hungry . . . Make Us Bread. Bread for the World, 32 Union Square East, N.Y., N.Y. 10003.

T. Paulis. *Hope for the Flowers.* New York: Paulist Press, 1972.

P. Perkins. *Reading the New Testament.* New York: Paulist Press, 1977.

N. Perrin. *The New Testament, An Introduction.* Harcourt Brace Jovanovich, Inc., 1974.

B. Vawter, C.M. "The Gospel According to John," and "Johannine Theology," in the *The Jerome Biblical Commentary.* Englewood Cliffs, NJ: Prentice-Hall, Inc., 1968.

12

Conclusion: A Discussion

Text Pages
176–191

Objectives

Knowledge: To help the students learn that the many dimensions of the person Jesus conveyed to us in the Christian Scriptures are due in part to the different faith experiences of those who wrote about him.

Attitude: To enable the students to appreciate the different emphases on Jesus as different facets on a diamond, each side reflecting the total beauty and richness of Jesus.

Practice: To encourage the students to incorporate the messages of Paul and the evangelists into their world today by serious attempts to live as Christ.

Orientation

The main thrust of the round table discussion is to recall and synthesize the key teachings of Paul and the evangelists in the Christian Scriptures. Each writer adds his faith experience to the image of Jesus as portrayed in the Christian Scriptures. Alone each has a special message; together, the message embraces the spiritual richness and depth of Jesus as God's Son sent to save all people. Though the message is clarified today by the work of biblical scholars, total understanding of who Jesus is will be complete only when "... we shall see face-to-face" (1 Corinthians 13:12).

Life Experience Focus

Two of the strongest conflicting drives within adolescents are first of all to be one's own self, a unique individual, and secondly to be accepted as part of a group, to be part of something larger than oneself. This chapter illustrates how the authors of New Testament kept these two values in a kind of dynamic tension. Each writer preserved his individuality yet each writer formed part of a larger organic whole. An understanding of this can help adolescents to see that the tension between individual and community is not an either/or polarity but a both/and complementarity.

A second point in favor of the approach in this chapter is that it meets one of the most frequent complaints of adolescents with regard to religion: that it is boring. The round table discussion format has life, conflict, and humor. It can serve as a model for their own presentation of what Christianity means today.

Finally, the diversity of scriptural accounts that appear in the Christian Scriptures can speak to the adolescent of the gradual unfolding of the meaning of Jesus in the student's life. Supported by their study of the Christian Scriptures the students can come to view their life process as an inexhaustible journey in faith.

Background on Content

The theological background for this chapter is cumulative; it synthesizes the theology of all the previous chapters, revealing a clearer picture of Jesus.

Briefly, *Paul* preaches the good news that Jesus has saved all peoples, that faith in him is indispensable to salvation, and that all those who follow Christ are to be Christ to the people they meet wherever life leads and in all the complexities of that life.

Mark writes the first gospel to impress his readers with the total gift of self Jesus made on the cross and to encourage all to follow Jesus specifically in that aspect of total self-giving.

Matthew stresses not the dying but the living of Jesus. He challenges Jesus' followers to imitate this living love towards all people and in all the circumstances of their daily lives so that like Jesus they, too, will enter a kingdom where God's will reigns in the hearts of all.

Luke portrays a gentle and kind Jesus who is approachable and loving. He asks all who follow Jesus to preach by their lives the message of the good news: like Jesus to be gentle and kind, approachable and loving.

John's Jesus is the Son of God, given to us by the Father and sent to show his love by doing the will of the Father in all things. Followers of John's Jesus must believe in him and live a life of love even unto death. Thus we have a Jesus who calls to faith in himself, a Jesus who challenges his followers to be joyful witnesses of a self-giving and constant love with all people in the everyday circumstances of life.

Teaching Notes 1

Text Page 176

123

Perspectives

The "Round Table Discussion" can be carried out very effectively by inviting some students to do a dramatic reading of the discussion. Have the students read the chapter on their own. Choose several of them to do the dramatic reading around a round table (or in a circle) for the whole group to see. After the reading have the students share their feelings as Paul, Mark, etc. Discuss the many aspects of Jesus portrayed (see *Background on Content* for this Guide chapter), and encourage the students to share their own faith experiences of Jesus to add to the "diamond" image of Jesus.

**Text Pages
178–191**

**Scriptural
Simulation**

Christian Scriptures Review
Worksheets #23 and *#24* represent alternate ways of recapitulating our study of the Christian Scriptures. Both worksheets while cognitive in substance also imply an affective dimension. By using them for prayer and reflection, as well as for discussion, the teacher can help the students experience them as more than just a cognitive restatement of the text.

Prayer Reflection
The "Prayer Reflection" (text page 191) is written in the first-person singular so that it can be used directly by teacher or student as a personal prayer response to the study of the Christian Scriptures. The quotation from 1 Corinthians reminds us that this response is still unfinished and that we are called to translate it into practical Christian living.

Will The Real Christians Please Stand Up!
(A Futuristic Simulation Based on the Gospel Message)

Instructions To The Teacher
This simulation is modeled after a conference which might concern itself with any world crisis. There is no definite outcome to be achieved other than to have the students apply gospel principles to their lives today and to have them realize that they do make a difference. Much of the outcome will depend upon the creativity and the dynamics within the small groups and their interaction with each other. Time will be required for this simulation to become a meaningful experience. The following time schedule is suggested:

Explanation and assignments	20 min.
Reading of assigned passages	45 min.
Planning of group position	60 min.
Conference simulation	90 min.
Reviewing session	45 min.

The time schedule should be adjusted to meet the different lengths of sessions in each program.

Grouping: all the students should be participants in the conference. They will be needed to fill the following roles:
- Chairperson of the conference (and two advisors if the group is large)

- The remainder of the students should be divided equally into five groups: Pauline, Markan, Matthean, Lucan, and Johannine.
- Each group should select from among its members a group leader, a group recorder, and an outside witness (someone who will bolster their group view by giving examples of past solutions that did not work).

Atmosphere: Allow the students to be creative both in their use of space and in designing costumes and props in order to create an atmosphere resembling a real situation. Their imaginations should devise interesting clothing and furniture for the year 2033.

Explanation: The teacher should introduce the simulation as a creative and interesting way to summarize all that the students have learned and to apply it to real life situations. It is important that the simulation and its situation be understood, that the group activities and procedures be carefully followed, and that the conference action steps be clearly articulated in the final session.

Reviewing Session: This final session is important for gospel value assimilation by the whole group. The atmosphere is not that of the conference but rather that of a group discussion of serious applications of specific ideas and suggestions for present day living. (See "Procedures for Reviewing Session" in the actual simulation.)

Simulation: Will the Real Christians Please Stand Up!

The Situation: It is the year 2033, two thousand years after the Death and Resurrection of Jesus. The world community of nations stands at the brink of disaster: *hunger* has reached into all parts of the globe, partly as a result of peoples' misuse of resources and partly as a result of selfishness and greed; the *energy* crisis has radically changed the lives of those in the developed nations; the world *economy* has suffered greatly because of the arms race; nuclear *war* is a constant and very real threat; *family life* is threatened by

scientific advances which can produce babies in test tubes and develop them in artificial wombs, as well as by a moral decadence which fosters sexual gratification rather than a selfless love; *human rights* are violated among nations which exploit one another and among individuals who make crime and violence a way of life.

A group of dedicated Christians from around the globe attend a conference in Rome to plan a strategy for summoning forth Christian leaders who will turn the tide from impending disaster to a real hope for new life for all peoples. These Christian leaders reflect the theology of Paul, Mark, Matthew, Luke, and John.

Activities for Group Presentations:
Each group should:

1. Assign a chairperson for the entire conference who will call the meeting to order and who will acknowledge the different speakers.

2. Assign students into groups: Pauline, Markan, Matthean, Lucan, and Johannine.

3. Name a leader for each group who will conduct the preparation period and who will lead his or her group in the simulation.

4. Appoint group recorders who will note the process of each group as well as the process of the simulation as seen from the group's perspective.

5. Examine those texts in the Christian Scriptures which support the identity of a particular group.

6. Identify your position to the entire assembly by use of a song, gesture, or banner.

7. Given your group identity, describe your reaction and solution to the situation as presented.

8. Help the recorder to outline your strategy by spelling out your position clearly before the simulation conference begins.

Procedures to be followed:
1. Each group will be allowed five representatives at the conference. Extra

members may sit with the group and offer suggestions on occasion.

2. Each person in a group may speak when recognized by the chairperson.

3. The conference begins as the chairperson *calls* the meeting to order, *clarifies* the procedures to the entire assembly, and *presents the problem:* How can we summon forth Christians from around the globe to become world leaders in a new era where gospel principles and values become a vital force for behavior among all peoples?

4. An open discussion follows during which the chairperson presides.

5. Each group will be given an opportunity to express its views on which aspects of the gospel to promote and, more importantly, on how to promote gospel values in a world which has apparently rejected them.

6. The groups will cooperate with the chairperson in formulating a strategy for action; possible solutions will be presented by each group; possible difficulties for implementation will be raised by others; compromises and joint effort should create realistic action steps.

7. Finally, the conference will draw up a strategy for immediate action.

Decisions to be made by the simulation conference:

1. How can Christians work together to effect a radical change in global events?

2. Who should be involved in this effort and to what extent?

Procedures for the reviewing session:

1. Students form a large circle.

2. Students discuss with the total group their feelings during the simulation.

3. Group recorders discuss the intention of the group as well as its point of view.

4. Discuss:

● In what practical ways can we as Christians help our society today become more just, peaceful, selfless, and concerned?

● What will we have to change in our personal lives in order to reflect more truly Christ to our world?

Instructions for Small Group #1: The Pauline Christian
Your group will identify itself with Paul's theology and you will stress his ways of being Christian in the modern world. Read the passages noted below and determine how you can apply them as solutions to the specific problems facing the Christian conference.

Philemon: v. 9: love makes demands; vv. 10–20: forgiveness;

1 Thessalonians: 2:9–10: example of work; 4:1–12: do the more, be holy;

Galatians: 2:11–14: salvation based on faith in Jesus;
5:13–15: freedom from Law for higher purpose: love and service;
5:16–26: Spirit of Jesus gives new life;

Philippians: 1:21: life is Christ;
2:1–11: attitude to imitate;
3:7–11: Jesus the supreme value;

1 Corinthians: 1:18—2:16: Christian wisdom;
3–4: real teachers of Christ live love;
8:1–13: conscience;
13: importance of love;

2 Corinthians: 4:1–18: signs of true disciple;
5:11–21: place of Christ in our lives;

Romans: 1:16–17: God saves all who believe and trust in him;
3:21–26: all are sinners; all can be saved through faith in Jesus who saves through his death on the cross;
5:1–11: God's love for us even while we were sinners; no one is righteous;
8:1–17: Spirit brings life and freedom;
8:18–39: relationship with God our hope for the future;
12–16: how to live a truly Christian life.

Instruction for Small Group #2: The Markan Christian
Your group will identify itself with Mark's theology and you will stress his ways of being a disciple of Christ in the modern world. Read the passages noted below and determine how you can apply them as solutions to the specific problems facing Christian Conference.

Mark, The Realist

4:35–41	need for absolute confidence in Jesus
7:1–23	need for sincerity of heart
8:1–9	Jesus feeds 4000 people
8:31–38	Jesus did not run away from suffering and death; disciples should follow Jesus in the way of suffering
9:33–50	qualities of a child—dependence, trust, service—are important for building a relationship with God
10:32–45	disciples must have faith in God in order to serve others as Jesus did
11:15–25	power of prayer, importance of forgiveness
12:41–44	giving, not out of one's surplus, but out of one's need
13:5–37	need for trust and watchfulness
14:32–42	acceptance of God's will

Instructions for Small Group #3: The Matthean Christian
Your group will identify itself with Matthew's theology and you will stress his ways of being a disciple of Christ in the modern world. Read the passages below and determine how you can apply them as solutions to the specific problems facing the Christian Conference.

Matthew, The Idealist

4:1–10	temptation of Jesus
5:1–12	true happiness
5:13–16	living by word and example
5:21–48	be perfect as God is perfect
6:1–4	true charity
6:9–13	importance of prayer
10:8	give freely of all received
10:16–27	preaching the gospel will bring hardships
10:28–33	encouragement
10:34–42	deciding for Christ
13:1–52	accepting and living God's word is passage into the kingdom
18:1–9	childlike trust is the kind of faith God wants
10:10–14	seeking out sinners
18:21–35	forgiveness knows no limit
23:3–39	live the truth; do not be hypocrites
24:32– 25:30	use every opportunity to do good

25:31–46	salvation depends upon what we do for others—active love

Instructions for Small Group #4: The Lucan Christian
Your group will identify itself with Luke's theology and you will stress his ways of being a disciple of Christ in the modern world. Read the passages noted below and determine how you can apply them as solutions to the specific problems facing the Christian Conference.

Luke, the bearer of joy to the poor

3:7–11	obligation to help those in need
4:6–21	imitate Jesus' mission to the poor
6:20–23	Christians should be distinctive for their poverty
24–26	Christians should be careful of the dangers of wealth
27–28	Christians should be loving towards enemies
39–45	Christians should be critical of self
46–49	Christians should be obedient to teachings of Jesus
9:57–62	hardships and joys of discipleship
11:37–46	hypocrisy verses justice and love
12:13–21	trust in God, not in possessions
12:32–34	true treasure
14:12–14	true charity
14:25–35	Christ demands all live high values
15:1–7	forgiveness
16:13–15	caution against avarice
19:1–10	repaying for injustices

Instructions for Small Group #5: The Johannine Christian
Your group will identify itself with John's theology and you will stress his way of being a disciple of Christ in the modern world. Read the passages below and determine how you can apply them as solutions to the specific problems facing the Christian Conference.

John, the messenger of new life

2:13–16	Christian zeal
3:16–21	belief in Jesus brings eternal life
6:16–21	trust in Jesus through the storms of life
6:25–59	the "bread" Jesus offers is his teaching which leads to new life
10:1–21	care and compassion
12:6	abuse of rights
12:12–19	new commandment
13:1–17	service and love unto death to self
13:29	giving to the poor
13:34–35	we follow Jesus when we live his love for all peoples
14:1–31	strength to live the new life
15:1–8	how to be a productive Christian
15:9–17	a disciple's love
15:18–27	world's reactions to Jesus' disciples
16:20–24	power of prayer

Prayer and Worship Experiences

1. After the students have completed the simulations suggested in this Guide chapter, invite them to compose a prayer service to share with others. Some suggestions follow:

Topic: a prayer for our planet

Earth Readings: one or two selections from the Christian Scriptures chosen by the students to convey a message which they deem important.

Petitions: taken from the headlines of the daily newspaper. After each headline which is chosen, the students can form a petition to complement it. These petitions can be spontaneous but may be more on target if prepared beforehand.

Closing prayer: a spontaneous or prepared response by a small group of the students.

2. Invite the students to put aside time for some quiet reflection on the highlights of their study of the Christian Scriptures. If they have kept a journal or a notebook they can leaf through it, pausing when something special strikes them. They can page through the student text in the same way. Hopefully they will have a sense, as they close something and prepare to move on to something else, that they have something worthwhile to bring with them from this study.

Service Projects

1. Perhaps from the group discussion which the simulation will occasion, suggestions will emerge for specific service projects within the scope and ability of the group's members.

2. If there were service projects which resulted from this study of the Christian Scriptures, it would be wise to review and evaluate them as the course comes to a close. These projects should also be assessed as to what should be continued and how this can be accomplished.

Independent Study Projects

1. The process of the first century that produced complementary portraits of Jesus has continued in Church history, in art, in music, in literature, etc. Different artists give different understandings of the person of Jesus. Have some students research how they have done this. Help them evaluate these presentations of Jesus in terms of the different New Testament authors.

2. A creative way to engage the students in a summary of their study of the Christian Scriptures might be to have them compose a slide and cassette program on the theme: "Jesus' Message for All Peoples." Divide those working on this project into five groups: Paul, Mark, Matthew, Luke, and John. Each individual or group is responsible for creating a script and slides to accompany it. Blank write-on slides and pens are available from local audiovisual or photography stores. Teacher guidance is essential so that the message of each author is authentically conveyed and form a unified whole with the others.

Resources

Print

J.T. Burtchaell, C.S.C. *Philemon's Problem.* Chicago: ACTA Foundation, 1973.

R. Schnackenburg. *The Moral Teaching of the New Testament.* New York: Seabury Press, 1965.

R. Sider, ed. *Cry Justice! The Bible on Hunger and Poverty.* New York: Paulist Press, 1980.

Justice/Peace Themes in the High School Curriculum. New York: Office for World Justice and Peace, 1011 First Ave., 1977.

A set of twenty-five worksheets is an important component of each Guide of the *Journey in Faith Series*. These worksheets include an attitudinal and informational survey to be used at the beginning of the course and at least two worksheets per chapter. These resources are designed as alternative ways of teaching to encourage reflection and dialogue about the themes of the chapter and as a more dynamic way of facilitating the student's journey in faith.

These worksheets are reproduced in individual form here for the teacher's use. They are available as a *Spirit Master Pak* in reproducible form for student use from William H. Sadlier, Inc., 11 Park Place, New York, NY 10007.

Name: _____

Survey

1. It is often said that the Christian Scriptures are "the most important book for Christians." Why?

2. Circle the best description of the gospels:
   Biographies of Jesus   Testaments of faith in Jesus
   Histories of Jesus   Stories made up about Jesus

3. List some important facts we know about Jesus from the gospels.

4. In St. Mark's Gospel, chapter 1, verse 15, Jesus says, "The time has come and the kingdom of God is close at hand. Have a change of heart and believe the Good News." What is this "Good News"?

5. Read chapter 5 of St. Matthew's Gospel. How do you feel about what Jesus has to say? (Check one.)
   ____ Jesus meant every word of it just as it is.
   ____ It is a noble but impossible ideal.
   ____ It "makes sense" only if you accept the Good News.
   ____ Jesus is giving his followers a new set of rules.

6. Choose a favorite story from the Gospel of St. Luke and say why you like it.

7. Select a story from St. John's Gospel that shows Jesus giving new life to someone and mention how he does it.

8. The event that changed St. Paul's life radically was _____

9. How did Paul respond to the event?

10. Choose one passage from any of St. Paul's letters. Describe what you think it means. Does it tell you anything about the personality of St. Paul?

From *Spirit Master Pak for New Testament: Christian Scriptures.*
Copyright © 1981 by W.H. Sadlier, Inc.

Name: _____

Worksheet #1

A Journey

Directions:
As you begin your study of the Christian Scriptures, you are in a way beginning a journey. People are usually wiser at the end of a journey because of the people they have met and the experiences they have encountered. Imagine you are on a journey. You first pass through an open green meadow with many wild flowers. Pause there a while and experience the meadow. What are your feelings as you leave the meadow?

_____

Your journey takes you into a wooded area. You walk beneath the coolness of the trees. After a time you come upon a clearing. Jesus is there talking to a small group of people; you approach and stand at the edge of the group listening to his words. When he finishes you leave to continue your journey. What are your feelings at this point?

_____

At the end of the wooded area you begin to climb a mountain. At first it goes easily, but then it becomes difficult and sometimes your foot slips and you fall. However, you keep struggling to reach the top of the mountain. What are your feelings as you reach for the top?

_____

You finally get to the top of the mountain. Your view of the world and life is greatly changed by both the journey's experiences and what you are now able to see. You have a new perspective on life. What in your personality would you like to have changed? Explain.

_____

What in your personality would you like to have changed? Explain.

_____

From the vantage point at the top of the mountain what place would you give to Jesus and his words in your life if you were starting the journey over? Explain your response.

_____

From *Spirit Master Pak for New Testament: Christian Scriptures.*
Copyright © 1981 by W.H. Sadlier, Inc.

Name: _____

Worksheet #2

Asking the Right Questions

Directions:
Someone has said a sign that indicates we are learning is not that we give the right answers but that we ask the right questions. In faith we Christians believe that our Scriptures answer some of life's most basic questions. List what you consider to be some of life's basic questions, ones for which you hope to find answers as you study the Scriptures. It may help to group your questions according to the following headings.

myself

_____

other persons

_____

God in my life

_____

suffering

_____

evil

_____

death and what comes after

_____

Christian community

_____

meaning

_____

From *Spirit Master Pak for New Testament: Christian Scriptures.*
Copyright © 1981 by W.H. Sadlier, Inc.

134

Worksheet #4

Name: _____

A Moment Difficult to Treasure
Acts 9:1–19

Directions:
As a help in understanding Paul's experience on the road to Damascus, read Acts 9:1–19 and answer the questions which follow.

In what sense was Paul's experience on the road to Damascus a moment difficult to treasure?

_____
_____
_____

Yet Paul did treasure it—he frequently retold it to others. Why?

_____
_____
_____

Name an experience in your own life which was difficult at the time but which you have come to treasure.

_____
_____
_____

Explain how through this experience you may have grown as a person, learned more about life, or matured as a Christian.

_____
_____
_____

Explain in terms of Paul's experience or your own the extent to which faith is necessary to turn a moment difficult to treasure into a source of growth.

_____
_____
_____

Worksheet #3

Name: _____

Vote for Paul

Directions:
Let us presume that someone like Paul of Tarsus were to come upon the scene today. Let us presume also that his friends put him forward as a candidate for some special position in civil or church life. Examples could be: Secretary General of the United Nations, Bishop of Rome, city mayor, school principal, pastor of a parish, television preacher. How would you complete the following statements?

I would back Paul for the position of: _____

My reasons for supporting him are:

_____
_____
_____
_____

Those who oppose him for this position would probably say:

_____
_____
_____

I would not like to see Paul in the position of: _____

My reasons for this stand are:

_____
_____
_____
_____

His friends would say in support of or opposition to me:

_____
_____
_____

Worksheet #6

Name: _____

Keeping In Touch

Directions:
Paul touched people and kept in touch with them through many ways, some of which are listed below. Rank the present effectiveness of these ways of personal contact (**1** for **most** effective, **5** for **least** effective).

Paul's ways of touching and keeping in touch	Present effectiveness
speaking with people directly	___
writing letters when distant	___
sending someone in his place to meet the people	___
revisiting the people himself	___
praying to God for the people	___

List other ways which were not available to Paul but which can help us today to touch and keep in touch with one another.

_____

_____

Which two ways of touching and keeping in touch with others do you use most often and why?

_____

_____

Name two means by which members of the Christian community keep in touch with one another.

_____

_____

Suggest one way by which we can improve communication within the Church.

_____

_____

Worksheet #5

Name: _____

Getting Rich by Giving

Directions:
There are some things in life which if given to others leave us poorer. There are other things in life which if given to others leave us richer. Read St. Paul's Letter to Philemon, and answer the questions which follow.

What was Paul asking Philemon to give up which would make Philemon poorer?

_____

In sending Onesimus back to Philemon, in what way was Paul becoming both poorer and richer?

_____

In what way had all three—Paul, Philemon, and Onesimus—enriched each other through sharing something of themselves?

_____

What are some things in life which become greater even for the giver when shared with others?

_____

Describe an experience in your own life in which you have become richer when you have given something to someone else.

_____

Describe an example of when you became poorer because you held on to something which you could have shared.

_____

Worksheet #7

Name: _____

Being Teachers
1 Corinthians 3–4

Directions:
In 1 Corinthians 3–4 Paul discusses characteristics which should be possessed by those who would spread the Christian message. Read these two chapters and indicate ways in which people today can exhibit the following qualities.

Humility about our accomplishments

_____
_____
_____

Concern about strengthening the Christian community

_____
_____
_____

Trust in Christ

_____
_____
_____

Appreciation of suffering

_____
_____
_____

From *Spirit Master Pak for New Testament: Christian Scriptures.*
Copyright © 1981 by W.H. Sadlier, Inc.

Worksheet #8

Name: _____

Troubleshooting

Directions:
As a troubleshooter, Paul responded to practical problems in a local community. He did two things: he first suggested a solution, and he then explained his position in terms of faith in Jesus Christ. Read the following problem situations and in terms of *one* of them, reply to the items which follow.

Situation #1: Requiring Service
A parish has a Confirmation program for young people aged 14 and 15. Those in charge have decided that one of the conditions for receiving Confirmation should be to take an active part in a service program for a period of at least six months. Some adolescents find this too demanding; some parents claim that school work, duties at home, etc. do not leave the young people time enough for service programs.

Situation #2: A Parish Youth Mass
A youth group in a parish would like to have, on a regular basis, a Mass styled for young people. The parish council thinks it more important that young people worship together with their families at the regular parish liturgies.

1. The situation I choose to respond to is:

2. I think that Paul would have resolved the problem in this way:

3. The reasons he would have given are:

4. My own response to the problem is:

5. My reasons are:

From *Spirit Master Pak for New Testament: Christian Scriptures.*
Copyright © 1981 by W.H. Sadlier, Inc.

Worksheet #9

Name: _____

Gifts and Rewards

Directions:
Central to St. Paul's argument in Galatians and Romans is the difference between what comes to us as free gift and what we earn as merited reward. Check the extent to which the following items are free gift or merited reward.

	Totally gift	Mostly gift	Mostly reward	Totally reward
Winning first prize in a lottery				
Getting paid for babysitting				
Being born				
Staying healthy				
Getting high grades				
Being loved by parents				
Having some very close friends				
Winning at gin rummy				
Finishing first in a footrace				
Enjoying good music				

What pattern do you note in your answers? _____

Use this same checking system for some aspects of our relationship with God:

Living in God's grace				
Being forgiven for sin				
Getting to heaven				
Being a member of the Church				
Being united with God and one another in the Eucharist				

What pattern do you note in your answers? _____

How does this pattern compare with your first set of replies? _____

How does this exercise apply to what St. Paul was trying to tell Christians in Galatia and in Rome? _____

Worksheet #10

Name: _____

Paul, Freedom and Faith
Galatians 5:13; Romans 1:17

Directions:
Read Galatians 5:13 and Romans 1:17. To show your understanding of what St. Paul means by "free" and by "faith," react to each statement according to how closely related it is to the freedom or faith (believing and trusting) that Paul speaks of. For several of these items there can be a legitimate difference of opinions.

	Identical to Paul's meaning	More similar than different	More different than similar	Totally different
Free				
People not in jail are free.				
I'm free to stay out late on Friday nights.				
I'm free to aid people who can use my help.				
Democratic countries constitute the free world.				
Freestyle dancing makes me feel free.				
I'm free from guilt because God accepts me and I accept myself.				
When I get out of high school I'll really be free.				
The best things in life are free.				
When offered drugs, I am free to say yes or say no.				
To be a Christian is to be free.				
Faith				
We can believe as true the television nightly news.				
My parents believe in my ability to do well.				
I can trust that the food from the store is not poisoned.				
I believe that my friends will stand by me.				
I have faith in promises my parents make to me.				
We can rely upon airline pilots to be competent.				
I believe that people are basically good.				
Seeing is believing.				

In your own words, state what St. Paul means by "free" and by "faith." _____

138

Name: _____

Worksheet #12

Reasons to Live
Philippians 2:5

Directions:
Read Philippians 2:5. Take the opportunity now to reflect upon some basic attitudes in terms of what the attitude is, where it comes from, and in whom we find it expressed.

What:
Of the following basic attitudes about life, first check which ones you try to make your own, then rank them from **1** to **3** in descending order of their importance to you.

	Check	Rank
God is the center of my life.	___	___
I believe in myself.	___	___
I value the life and well-being of other persons.	___	___
Truth is what I seek.	___	___
My heart reaches out for beauty and goodness.	___	___

From where:
In a similar way, of the following possible sources for your basic attitudes toward life, first check which ones apply to you, then rank them according to their influence upon you.

	Check	Rank
What my parents have taught me.	___	___
What my friends believe in.	___	___
What my religion holds as valuable.	___	___
What I have figured out for myself.	___	___
What has made my life happy and meaningful.	___	___

In whom:
Perhaps you have noted your ideals embodied in someone else, as Paul saw his ideal in Jesus Christ. Fill in the name of such a person and explain his or her influence upon your own basic attitudes toward life.

From my family and relatives: _____

From my friends and acquaintances: _____

From my church or school: _____

From the world of sports, entertainment, politics, etc.: _____

From the Scriptures and history: _____

Name: _____

Worksheet #11

Moving On

Directions:
St. Paul in prison was thinking of moving on. This time it was not to a new town but, through death, to fuller union with Christ. To appreciate how a person feels at such a time, reflect on some of the lesser "movings on" which we all go through in life. Name three situations in which, to some extent, we leave behind our past, turn toward our future, and are very conscious of the moving from one thing to another (for example, to a new school).

1.

2.

3.

Describe one of these "movings on" which you personally have experienced by responding to these questions:

What from the past did you take with you?

What did you leave behind?

How did you feel toward the part or period of your life which was closing?

To what extent was the future unknown or unfamiliar?

What were your expectations of it, both positive and negative?

At the time of transition, how did you feel—joyful, sad, excited, apprehensive, open, empty, etc.? Please explain.

In terms of these same six questions, describe Paul's attitude toward his life, his death, his union with Christ.

**I Wonder . . .
About the Gospels**

Name: _____

Directions:
Before studying the gospels systematically, it may help to surface some questions, difficulties, doubts, etc. that we may have about them. Below are some questions about the gospels which have puzzled others. Indicate to what extent they are also your questions. Then add what else may cause you to wonder about the gospels.

	I really wonder about that . . .	That has occurred to me . . .	That has never occurred to me . . .	That is not my concern at all . . .
If Jesus is God's own Son, why did he suffer and die?				
Was Jesus really serious when he told us to turn the other cheek?				
If Jesus was able to heal some of the sick and crippled, why did he not cure them all?				
If Jesus was such a good person, why did some people hate him enough to have him killed?				
Why did Jesus teach in parables?				
Why did Jesus not take a clear stand on such issues as the oppression of the poor, slavery, warfare, the status of women, etc.?				
Did Jesus think that the end of the world was about to happen?				
How can Jesus be a model for us if he knew everything and never made a mistake, if he did not sin, if he had power to work miracles—in brief, if he was the Son of God?				

Choose one of the questions above and give a *preliminary* answer to it now.

_____
_____
_____

Still Among Us

Name: _____

Directions:
When someone with a following dies, especially if he or she is young and the death is violent, people try in various ways to keep alive his or her memory. Something similar happened with regard to Jesus, but with major differences. To appreciate the similarities and the differences answer the following.

Today when someone with a following dies suddenly (such as John F. Kennedy in 1963 and John Lennon in 1980), *five things* people do to continue his or her presence among them are:

1. _____
2. _____
3. _____
4. _____
5. _____

In the first century, after the Ascension of Jesus, *five things* Jesus' disciples did to continue his presence among them were:

1. _____
2. _____
3. _____
4. _____
5. _____

One big similarity in these two cases is:
_____
_____

One major difference is:
_____
_____

The main reason for the difference is:
_____
_____

Name: _____

Worksheet #16

Money in the Bank
Mark 10:17–29

Directions:
Read carefully what Jesus had to say about riches when a man asked him what he should do to receive eternal life (Mark 10:17–29).

Explain how you understand this passage *literally* (that is, taking the words to mean exactly what they say).

_____
_____

Explain how this passage can be understood *symbolically* (that is, seeing the words as figures of speech which stand for something else).

_____
_____

Explain how a believer can apply this passage *practically* (that is, what would be different in his or her life by following Jesus' advice).

_____
_____

Give three examples of persons from history or the present who have followed this invitation of Jesus literally or symbolically or practically or some combination of the three).

_____
_____
_____

In this passage, what might Jesus be saying to you about your own life-style?

_____
_____
_____

From *Spirit Master Pak for New Testament: Christian Scriptures.*
Copyright © 1981 by W.H. Sadlier, Inc.

Name: _____

Worksheet #15

The Why of Suffering

Directions:
Through suffering comes joy and victory—we cannot argue the truth of this mystery. To live by it calls for faith which goes beyond evidence. Yet some evidence from experience can help us make such a faith-commitment. Explain how someone from the Scriptures grew through suffering (for example, Job in the Old Testament, Paul in the New Testament).

_____
_____

Cite persons from Church history who, like Damien of Molokai, lived out their faith in part through suffering.

_____
_____

Give examples from secular history where hardship forms part of the path to victory (for example, the Continental Army at Valley Forge).

_____
_____

Describe from everyday experience how the acceptance of what is difficult or painful implies the facing of reality, while the avoidance of what is difficult or painful implies running away from reality (for example: rehearsing for a play or practicing for an athletic event).

_____
_____

From *Spirit Master Pak for New Testament: Christian Scriptures.*
Copyright © 1981 by W.H. Sadlier, Inc.

Name: _____

21 Century Utopia

Directions:
Your group has the unique opportunity to create a charter for an ideal society in the 21st century. You are familiar with the ills in today's society, using this knowledge and the questions below, draw up your charter for the ideal society. Make up a motto which describes this ideal society. It should be brief enough to be stamped on coins (if you intend to have money).

Phrase a 25–50 word preamble describing the society's goal.

_____
_____
_____

Frame five laws which will help achieve this goal (if you intend to have laws).

1. _____
2. _____
3. _____
4. _____
5. _____

Outline how those who violate the laws would be handled.

_____
_____

Explain the chances that your ideal society has of surviving into the 22nd century.

_____
_____

How does your society compare with the ideals expressed by Jesus in the Sermon on the Mount (see especially Matthew 5:17–48)?

_____
_____

Name: _____

Aiming High

Directions:
Someone has said a person's reach should exceed his or her grasp, that is, we should keep our ideals or goals high, even though we know realistically that we shall never quite attain all of them. In terms of the following items, sketch your own ideal self.

1. I am happiest about myself when:
_____

2. Things in my life I'd like to change are:
_____

3. Ideals which I accept from my family are:
_____

4. The kind of friendship I most want in my life is:
_____

5. I would like others to know me as:
_____

6. Faith in God influences my ideals in this way:
_____

7. My ideals compare with those expressed in Matthew's Gospel as follows:
_____
_____
_____

Name: _____

Worksheet #20

Lord, Teach Us to Pray

Directions:
Jesus gave a direct answer when his followers asked him to teach them how to pray. He taught them the Lord's Prayer. In addition, throughout St. Luke's Gospel, we find many clues about how, when, and where Jesus prayed. We also learn what his attitude toward prayer was. Search out the following passages in Luke's Gospel. After each grouping summarize what you have learned about the when, where, how, or what of prayer.

"When" of prayer

3:21–22   At Jesus' baptism   _____
6:12   A night in prayer
18:1–5   Persevering in prayer   _____
21:36   Vigilant and constant prayer   _____

"Where" of prayer

4:16–19   Jesus in the synagogue   _____
5:16   Away to lonely places
19:45–4   The Temple as a house of prayer   _____

"How" of prayer

9:18   Alone at prayer   _____
9:28–31   Praying with Peter, John, and James
11:1–13   Instruction prayer   _____
18:9–14   Prayer of the Pharisee and the Publican
22:39–46   Praying on the Mount of Olives   _____

"What" of prayer

6:28   For whom we should pray   _____
10:2   Prayer for workers in the harvest
10:21–24   Speaking with the Father   _____
22:19–20   Giving thanks and breaking bread
22:31–34   Prayer for Simon and Peter   _____
23:34   Prayer for mercy
23:46   Final prayer to the Father   _____
24:30   Blessing and breaking bread at Emmaus

From *Spirit Master Pak for New Testament: Christian Scriptures.*
Copyright © 1981 by W.H. Sadlier, Inc.

Name: _____

Worksheet #19

Peace Be with You

Directions:
When Jesus spoke of peace he had in mind particularly a disposition and attitude within the heart of each person. Below are some 20th century statements on peace. Read them and answer the questions which follow.

1. "The world will never have lasting peace so long as men reserve for war the finest human qualities. Peace, no less than war, requires idealism and self-sacrifice and a righteous and dynamic faith."   John Foster Dulles

  a. Some claim that most countries budget more money, material, and personnel for war than for peace. Do you judge this to be true? Explain.

  b. Please explain what can be done to make peace a priority in our society.

2. "The worst sin toward our fellow creatures is not to hate them, but to be indifferent to them; that's the essence of inhumanity."   George Bernard Shaw

  a. What is one area of injustice or oppression in society today?

  b. To what extent is this the result of indifference rather than hatred?

3. "Peace is a daily, a weekly, a monthly process, gradually changing opinions, slowly eroding old barriers, quietly building new structures. And however undramatic the pursuit of peace, the pursuit must go on."   John Fitzgerald Kennedy

  a. What are the opinions and the barriers which President Kennedy most likely had in mind in the above quotation?

  b. What progress in these areas has been made since the early 1960s?

4. "When the world seems large and complex, we need to remember that great world ideals all begin in some home neighborhood."   Konrad Adenauer

  a. How is this true in your family, neighborhood, or parish?

  b. Does this quotation reflect the meaning of peace as found in St. Luke's Gospel?

From *Spirit Master Pak for New Testament: Christian Scriptures.*
Copyright © 1981 by W.H. Sadlier, Inc.

Name: _____

Believing Is Seeing
John 9:1-41

Directions:
Chapter Nine, "Jesus Heals a Man Born Blind," illustrates many of the dimensions of the Gospel according to St. John. Read it carefully, then explain the following elements within it.

1. A dramatized trial story

a. the accusers:

b. the indictment:

c. the testimony of the man's parents:

d. the testimony of the cured blind man:

e. the refutation by Jesus:

2. A call to discipleship

a. credentials of Jesus:

b. response of different persons and groups:

3. Use of words and gestures with symbolic meaning

a. darkness and light:

b. mud, spittle, washing:

c. blindness and seeing:

4. In terms of 20th century life, what does the one who believes in Jesus Christ "see" and to what are those who reject him "blind"?

_____

From *Spirit Master Pak for New Testament: Christian Scriptures.*
Copyright © 1981 by W.H. Sadlier, Inc.

Name: _____

Christ to One Another

Directions:
When Jesus says simply "I Am" (John 8:58), he shows his relationship with Yahweh, the God of Israel. When he expands it to "I am the light of the world" (John 8:12), etc., he tells us more about his relationship to us. The expressions he uses are figurative or symbolic. In the first column below please explain what Jesus is saying about his place in your life through the following statements. In the second column, indicate how the same images and symbols can explain what Christians are called to be in the world in which they live.

	Jesus present in my life	Christians present in the world
"I am the bread of life. He who comes to me will never be hungry; he who believes in me will never be thirsty" (John 6:35).		
"I am the light of the world. Whoever follows me will have the light of life and will never walk in darkness'" (John 8:12).		
"I am the good shepherd, who is willing to die for the sheep" (John 10:11).		
"I am the resurrection and the life. Whoever believes in me will live, even though he dies; and whoever lives and believes in me will never die" (John 11:25–26).		
"I am the way, the truth, and the life, no one goes to the Father except by me" (John 14:6).		
"I am the vine, and you are the branches. Whoever remains in me, and I in him, will bear much fruit; for you can do nothing without me" (John 15:5).		

From *Spirit Master Pak for New Testament: Christian Scriptures.*
Copyright © 1981 by W.H. Sadlier, Inc.

144

Name: _____

Worksheet #23

Discipleship

Directions:
As the different New Testament authors present varying and complementary portraits of Jesus, so they each place a different emphasis on what it means to be a disciple. If, in a second imaginary round-table discussion, Peter were to ask Paul, Mark, Matthew, Luke, and John their thoughts on discipleship, what would they say? Suggested below are selected passages for your starting point, but feel free to build on other texts of your own choosing.

1. Paul: "It is no longer I who live, but it is Christ who lives in me. This life that I live now, I live by faith in the Son of God, who loved me and gave his life for me" (Galatians 2:20). For Paul, a disciple is a person who:

_____
_____

2. Mark: "If anyone wants to come with me, he must forget himself, carry his cross, and follow me" (Mark 8:34). For Mark, a disciple is a person who:

_____
_____

3. Matthew: "Go, then, to all peoples everywhere and make them my disciples: baptize them in the name of the Father, the Son, and the Holy Spirit, and teach them to obey everything I have commanded you" (Matthew 28:19–20). For Matthew, a disciple is a person who:

_____
_____

4. Luke: "When the Holy Spirit comes upon you, you will be filled with power, and you will be witnesses for me in Jerusalem, in all of Judea and Samaria, and to the ends of the earth" (Acts 1:8). For Luke, a disciple is a person who:

_____
_____

5. John: "And now I give you a new commandment: love one another. As I have loved you, so you must love one another. If you have love for one another, then everyone will know that you are my disciples" (John 13:34–35). For John, a disciple is a person who:

_____
_____

From *Spirit Master Pak for New Testament: Christian Scriptures.*
Copyright © 1981 by W.H. Sadlier, Inc.

Name: _____

Worksheet #24

Lovely in Eyes Not His

Directions:
The poet Gerard Manley Hopkins writes:

For Christ plays in ten thousand places,
Lovely in limbs, and lovely in eyes not his
To the Father through the features of men's faces.

This means not only that many people share the new life brought by Jesus Christ, but also that they live in imitation of him and that people find in them resemblances and echoes of Jesus himself. According to the following categories, name persons whom you would in that respect consider to be Christ-like. For each one also name the New Testament author who describes Jesus in this way and cite a passage where he does so.

	Christ-like person	New Testament author	Scriptural passage
1. is concerned for the poor	___	___	___
2. is close to God in prayer	___	___	___
3. teaches others God's way	___	___	___
4. heals the suffering	___	___	___
5. speaks out for justice	___	___	___
6. respects all persons as equal	___	___	___
7. helps form the Christian community	___	___	___
8. gives one's life for others	___	___	___
9. announces God's presence among us	___	___	___
10. reconciles persons who are in conflict	___	___	___

From *Spirit Master Pak for New Testament: Christian Scriptures.*
Copyright © 1981 by W.H. Sadlier, Inc.

Journey in Faith Series

New Testament: Christian Scriptures

by
Peter Francis Ellis, S.S.L.
Judith Monahan Ellis

General Editors
John S. Nelson, Ph.D.
Catherine Zates Nelson

Special Consultants
Rev. James T. Mahoney, Ph.D.
Rev. Peter Mann
Sr. Ruth McDonell, I.H.M.
Sr. Rosemary Muckerman,
S.S.N.D.
Rev. Samuel Natale, S.J., Ph.D.
June O'Connor, Ph.D.

Contributors
Elinor R. Ford, Ed.D.
Eileen E. Anderson
Eleanor Ann Brownell
Joyce A. Crider
Mary Ellen McCarthy
William M. McDonald
Joan McGinnis-Knorr
William J. Reedy
Joseph F. Sweeney

The content of this program
reflects the goals of *Sharing
the Light of Faith* (NCD).

Sadlier
A Division of
William H. Sadlier, Inc.
New York
Chicago
Los Angeles

Contents

Nihil Obstat
Joseph P. Penna, J.C.D.
Censor Liborum

Imprimatur
✠Joseph T. O'Keefe, Vicar-General
Archdiocese of New York
October 25, 1980

The nihil obstat and imprimatur are
official declarations that a book or
pamphlet is free of doctrinal or moral
error. No implication is contained therein
that those who have granted the nihil
obstat and imprimatur agree with the
contents, opinions, or statements
expressed.

Printed in the United States of America.
Home Office:
11 Park Place,
New York, NY 10007
ISBN: 0-8215-2907-2
ISBN: 0-8215-2917-X
123456789/987654321

Project Director: William M. McDonald
Project Editors: Joseph Curran,
Moya Gullage, S.H.C.J.
Managing Editor: Gerald A. Johannsen
Design Director: Willi Kunz
Designer: Grace Kao
Photo Editor: Lenore Weber
Photo Researcher: Mary Brandimarte
Photo Coordinator: Martha Hill Newell

Introduction

The *Journey in Faith Series* is offered to contemporary Catholic youth and to those who minister with them as they work through faith questions together and share faith experiences as a Christian community. The team of authors, consultants, and editors for this Series believe that they have put together fresh and useful materials to respond to these needs.

The team hopes that this Series will serve as a useful instrument for such wider goals as these:
● That those who use it come to know more and more that they are a ministering community, that is, people who help each other along the way.
● That in this shared journey all of us find our own way of believing, praying, serving, becoming our own best self.
● That all of us become more literate and at home with the community's symbols, doctrines, values, and great persons.

The *Journey in Faith Series* reflects the spirit and goals of *Sharing the Light of Faith*. The Series' catechetical team members have welcomed the Directory as normative for their catechetical thinking. They are confident that this Series applies practically the wisdom of *Sharing the Light of Faith*.

This book brings you into contact with the earliest writings about Jesus—St. Paul's letters, the four gospels, and the Acts of the Apostles.

It brings Paul alive for you as "the traveling apostle" in the Acts of the Apostles, as "the letter writer" in the letters to Philemon and the Thessalonians, as "the trouble shooter" in 1 and 2 Corinthians, as "the theologian" in Romans and Galatians, and as "the prisoner" in the letter to the Philippians.

The gospels help us understand Christ and Christianity. This text, therefore, explains what the gospels are, how they came to be written, and how the inspired authors composed them. From your reading of the gospels, you come to know each gospel author as a distinct personality with a unique understanding of Jesus.

The aim of this book is to make the Christian Scriptures the most important book in your life. St. Jerome said, "Ignorance of the Scriptures is ignorance of Christ." Our hope is that this book will help you develop a deeper and more active knowledge and love of Christ.

1

Christianity's Most Important Book

Future and Past

New Year's Eve 2000! People are already imagining it!

- T.V. telephones in every room!
- Jetliners that whoosh through the air at 5000 miles per hour!
- Pills that cure cancer and halt muscular dystrophy!

Will even half the marvelous things scientists dream about and science fiction movies show begin to come true? Writers in these fields are not the only ones pondering the future. People down the centuries have always wondered what the days to come would bring.

The future is alluring, but so is the past. Archeologists spend millions of hours and dollars digging up the remains of ancient civilizations. Historians haunt libraries searching for documents that reveal the events of ages past. Scholars are convinced that the past not only helps to explain what is happening in our present but also helps us to chart our way into the unknown future.

In this book we will be concerned with the Christian Scriptures to see how they influence our present and future.

The Historical Me

We are history more than we might suspect. The way we think, the way we speak, the way we live depend very much on the past: on our family backgrounds, on our cultural traditions, on the history of the country in which we live.

Stop and think for a moment how different your life might be if England instead of the United States had won the Revolutionary War, or if Japan instead of the United States had won World War II. Even in your personal life, the past greatly influences your present way of thinking and acting. Let us say you were born in the mountains of Vermont and you were your school's champion downhill skier. However, when you were thirteen years old, your parents moved to Florida. Your career as a skier would have been greatly affected. You might now decide to become a golfer, a surfer, or perhaps even a beachcomber.

■ Recall some past events in your family's life or your country's development that influence what you think and do today and what you might think and do in the future. Discuss in groups these events and their significance for you.

Year	Events
1700	**1797** Cheops' Pyramid
1600	
1500	
1400	
1300	
1200	
1100	
1000	
900	c. **977** Abraham c. **927** Isaac
800	c. **867** Jacob
700	**797** Israel in Egypt
600	
500	
400	**487** Exodus
300	
200	**222** King Solomon **247** King David
100	**182** Kingdom Splits **122** Elijah
B.A.U.C.	
A.U.C.	**15** Isaiah **72** Money Invented
100	**156** Jeremiah **167** Babylonian Exile
200	**244** Roman Republic
300	
400	**413** Aristotle **421** Alexander the Great
500	
600	
700	**716** Herod the Great **726** Caesar Augustus **754** Jesus **767** Tiberius **785** St. Paul Converted
800	**823** Rome Destroys Jerusalem
900	**919** Great Plague Hits Rome
1000	**1066** Christianity Legalized **1077** Constantine
1100	**1163** Rome Falls
1200	**1278** Dionyius Exiguus Invents Calendar

Calendars

Fairly soon we'll reach the year 2000. How did it get to be numbered that way on our calendar? From history we learn that at different times there have been calendars other than our own. The Babylonians, the Egyptians, the Jews, the Chinese, and the Romans have all had their own calendars.

The Jews, for example, date all events from the year that they once calculated the creation of the world took place. For them our year 2000 would be dated the year 5761 after the creation of the world.

The ancient Romans had two ways of dating events: 1) either before or after the date of the foundation of the city of Rome in 753 B.C., 2) according to the length of the reigns of their emperors.

In the first case, our year 2000 would be dated the year 2753 after the building of the city of Rome (A.U.C. = *aburbe conditta* = "from the building of the city"). An example of the second case can be seen in Luke's Gospel. When Luke gives the date of the beginning of John the Baptist's preaching he says:

It was the fifteenth year of the rule of Emperor Tiberius; Pontius Pilate was governor of Judea, Herod was ruler of Galilee, and his brother Philip was ruler of the territory of Ituraea and

Dionysius Exiguus

Why do we no longer follow the Roman calendar? Is it because Rome is no longer the great capital of the world that it used to be? Or because there are no longer any Roman emperors? Or because the modern world needed a better calendar? History tells us that we date our calendar the way we do because of the Roman monk and astronomer Dionysius Exiguus, which means Denis the Little.

By using the time line above we can see how some important historical events were dated, not according to our calendar, but according to the ancient Roman calendar.

Dionysius and the Christians of his time had been using the Roman calendar. But they were convinced that an historical event had taken place infinitely more important than the foundation of the city of Rome.

For them the most important event in the history of the world was the birth of Jesus. They believed that the center of all time and all history was the time of Jesus. Dionysius decided, therefore, to redate all events of history either before the birth of Christ (B.C.) or after the birth of Christ (A.D.). He did it in the year 525 A.D., and that is how our calendar came into existence.

Trachonitis; Lysanias was ruler of Abilene, and Annas and Caiaphas were high priests. At that time the word of God came to John son of Zechariah in the desert.

Luke 3:1–2

When Luke tells about the birth of Jesus in Bethlehem, he says it took place during the reign of the Emperor Augustus: **At that time Emperor Augustus ordered a census to be taken throughout the Roman Empire (Luke 2:1)**. According to our calendar, the Emperor Augustus ruled from 27 B.C. ("before Christ") to 14 A.D. (*anno domini*—"in the year of the Lord").

The World Says Yes!

In the course of the centuries, almost all the nations of the world accepted Dionysius' calendar. In time events automatically came to be dated either before Christ (B.C.) or after Christ (A.D.).

For an idea of what they went through, compare the two time lines on pages 6 and 8 and consider how people had to readjust their thinking once they realized that everything in history centered around Jesus. What they encountered might be compared to the trouble it is causing us to change to the metric system with its liters in place of quarts, meters in place of yards, and kilometers in place of miles.

■ How does the focal point of history differ on the Roman and the Dionysian time lines? Why do you think so much of the world has adopted the Dionysian calendar?

The Greatest Influence

Christians went to all the trouble of changing their calendar because they believed that Jesus was the one who put all history into its proper perspective. If we reckon the importance of great persons by their influence on our lives, then no person in the history of the world can be said to be a greater influence than Jesus. He is the one who gives us the ultimate truth about ourselves, about others, about the world, and about God. As an unknown author put it:

"Here is a young man who was born in an obscure village, the child of a peasant woman. He grew up in still another village. He worked in a carpenter shop until he was thirty, and then for three years he was an itinerant preacher. He never wrote a book. He never held an office. He never owned a home. He never put his foot inside a big city. He never traveled 200 miles from the place where he was born. He never did one of the things that

2500	**2550 B.C.** Cheops' Pyramid
2400	
2300	
2200	
2100	
2000	
1900	
1800	
1700	**1750 B.C.** Abraham
1600	c. **1680 B.C.** Isaac — c. **1620 B.C.** Jacob
1500	**1550 B.C.** Israel in Egypt
1400	
1300	
1200	**1240 B.C.** Exodus
1100	
1000	**1000 B.C.** King David
900	**975 B.C.** King Solomon — **935 B.C.** Kingdom Splits
800	**867 B.C.** Elijah
700	**753 B.C.** Founding of the City of Rome — **738 B.C.** Isaiah
600	**681 B.C.** Money Invented
500	**597 B.C.** Jeremiah **586 B.C.** Babylonian Exile — **509 B.C.** Roman Republic
400	
300	**340 B.C.** Aristotle — **332 B.C.** Alexander the Great
200	
100	
B.C.	**37 B.C.** Herod the Great — **27 B.C.** Caesar Augustus
A.D.	**14 A.D.** Tiberius **32 A.D.** St. Paul Converted — **70 A.D.** Rome Destroys Jerusalem
100	**166 A.D.** Great Plague in Rome
200	
300	**313 A.D.** Christianity Legalized — **324 A.D.** Constantine
400	**410 A.D.** Rome Falls

usually accompany greatness. He has no credentials but himself.

"While he was still a young man the tide of public opinion turned against him. His friends ran away. He was turned over to his enemies. He went through the mockery of a trial.

"He was nailed to a cross between two thieves. While he was dying, his executioners gambled for the only piece of property he had on earth, and that was his coat.

"When he was dead he was laid in a borrowed grave through the pity of a friend.

"Nineteen centuries wide have come and gone, and today he is the central figure of the human race and the leader of the column of progress.

"I am far within the mark when I say that all the armies that ever marched, and all the navies that ever sailed, and all the parliaments that ever sat, and all the kings that ever reigned, put together, have not affected the life of man upon this earth as has that ONE SOLITARY LIFE."

In Search of Truth
Truth—about human persons, about the world, about God! Everyone wants it. Everyone values it. Everyone is looking for it. Philosophers, scientists, psychologists, and theologians have busied themselves for centuries searching for it. They know that truth iluminates, warms, energizes, and sometimes also frightens a person. The truth is much more than the stuff that dreams are made of. It is reality. When we find it, it can help us guide our lives. It can give us the vision and the energy to lead a rich and full existence.

The truth about people, the world, and God is deep; the task of finding it is sometimes difficult. That is why we are constantly asking who and what we are; who and what God is; and what is the purpose of this world and our existence in it.

For Christians the New Testament, which is also called the Christian Scriptures, is crucial because it is in it that we find Jesus' response to these questions. We learn through what he said, through what he did, and through his attitudes and approaches towards people, the world, and his Father. That is why Christians have been reading and studying the Christian Scriptures for the last two thousand years.

The Christian Scriptures are presented as a collection of divinely inspired books, each with its human author or authors, history of composition, and literary form or forms. Such information helps one understand, as *Sharing the Light of Faith* (National Catechetical Directory) reminds us, "what meaning the sacred writers really intended, and what God wanted to manifest by means of their words."

Encounters of a Third Kind

Scientists believe that it is entirely possible that intelligent beings exist on other planets far beyond the borders of the solar system. Some science fiction writers take this for granted. Someday we may know for certain.

For the present, let us suppose some intelligent being from outer space comes to earth and asks us: "Who are you earth people? What kind of creatures are you? What is this world of yours? Where did it come from? Who controls it? What are you doing with it? What relationship do you earth people have to each other? Who is this God you worship in your churches?" What would we reply?

It may be centuries before we meet such inquisitive space people. In the meantime let us take a brief look at some of the answers Jesus offers to these questions about ourselves, our world, and God. Since Christians believe that God created the world and all people in it, Jesus' insights on these questions will be closely interrelated.

The Human Person

There are some people who say we humans are no different from the animals—just a little more intelligent, a lot more destructive, and a little better looking. Before inflation, scientists claimed that if we were to sell our bodies for their chemical content alone, each would be worth only about one dollar and sixty-seven cents. As Christians, however, we know that we are much more valuable than our chemical components.

12

In the Christian Scriptures Jesus says that God has given each person a mysterious but real share in his own divine life: **For God loved the world so much that he gave his only Son, so that everyone who believes in him may not die but have eternal life (John 3:16)**. As we shall see in the course of our study of the Christian Scriptures, God has given each person the ability to be perfect beyond anything anyone could ever imagine. The Christian Scriptures say a great deal about perfection.

□ Describe the qualities you would expect to find in a "perfect" person. Remember your definition, and as you study the Christian Scriptures see how their idea of the "perfect" person compares with yours.

This Spaceship Earth

When the astronauts on their way to the moon looked back at the earth from 100,000 miles out in space, they could see no signs of life, no signs of people, no signs of activity anywhere on planet Earth. Jokingly one of them asked: "Is it inhabited?" They all laughed because they knew it was teeming with life, filled with people, and bursting with activity. Describing the beauty of the earth as seen from the command module, one of the astronauts said: "It's like a shining oasis in the black void of space."

Scripture informs us that God created the world for us. It is his gift to us. But it is also his desire that we take the responsibility to perfect this world and make it into a beautiful place in which all humankind will be able to praise and thank the God who created it.

In the Hebrew Scriptures we find that it is God's will that we rule this earth as God would rule it; beautify it as God would beautify it; use and treasure it as a precious gift.

It is God's desire that we know the earth, build and perfect it, and make it a beautiful environment for all.

■ Stop for a moment and write down two or three things you could do to help make this world the place God wants it to be.

Relationships Among Persons

The more we watch television, listen to the radio, and read the newspapers, the more we hear about people murdering, beating, robbing, torturing, and crippling each other.

We might sometimes be tempted to think people are no good, not worth God's concern and perhaps not even our attention. Jesus says quite the opposite. He emphasizes God's love for all.

St. Paul in Romans 5:7-8, speaking about Jesus' death, says:

It is a difficult thing for someone to die for a righteous person. It may even be that someone might dare to die for a good person. But God has shown us how much he loves us—it was while we were still sinners that Christ died for us!

Again we read of God's love in 1 John 4:9 and 16:

And God showed his love for us by sending his only Son into the world, so that we might have life through him. . . . God is love, and whoever lives in love lives in union with God and God lives in union with him.

■ Reflect on how easy it is for us to have a distorted picture of others, one which does not reflect God's love, because of prejudices, hearsay, media reports, etc. Express yourself in collage, drawing, or words showing how we sometimes see people because of our prejudices and how God regards them.

Gods and God

You may be surprised at the different ideas people have about God. Some think of God as a strict judge just waiting to condemn people. Others think of God as someone sitting on a royal throne far away in the sky, or as someone who has to be prayed to or bribed.

In the Christian Scriptures Jesus describes God as our Father. He taught:

"This, then, is how you should pray: 'Our Father in heaven. . .''
(Matthew 6:9).

He says:

"So do not start worrying. . . . Your Father in heaven knows that you need all these things" (Matthew 6:31-32).

Jesus says that God is like the Father of an erring son. The parable of the Prodigal Son is the story of a son who abandoned his father until all his money was spent and he was starving. He wanted to return home where he would be warm, loved, and comfortable, but he thought his father would never forgive him. However, when he got near home, his father was waiting to welcome him. He learned that day after day, his father had gone down the road hoping to see his son returning.

God, like the father in this parable, loves us so much he is always waiting and wanting us to be with him.

A Perspective on Life

The great thing about the Christian Scriptures is that they help us to see ourselves, the world, other persons, and even God in perspective. They help explain the things we need to understand if our lives are to have genuine meaning.

John's Gospel sums it up beautifully in one incident from Jesus' life. Some of Jesus' disciples had decided to stay with him no longer. Jesus then asked the twelve apostles: **"And you—would you also like to leave?"** Simon Peter's response can be ours: **"Lord, to whom would we go? You have the words that give eternal life"** (John 6:67-68).

The Christian Scriptures are chiefly concerned with Jesus, whom we consider the most important person in the history of the world. Jesus teaches us about ourselves, others, and God. The Christian Scriptures consist of the following twenty-seven books and writings. Our study will give particular attention to those books marked with an asterisk. The list below follows the order of the New Testament in the Bible. As can be seen from our table of contents, we shall study them in a somewhat different order: first the writings of Paul, then those of the evangelists.

The Gospels
    According to Matthew*
    According to Mark*
    According to Luke*
    According to John*
The Acts of the Apostles*
Letters Attributed to Paul*
    To the Romans*
    First Letter to the Corinthians*
    Second Letter to the Corinthians*
    To the Galatians*
    To the Ephesians
    To the Philippians*
    To the Colossians
    First Letter to the Thessalonians*
    Second Letter to the Thessalonians
    First Letter to Timothy

    Second Letter to Timothy
    To Titus
    To Philemon*
Other Letters
    To the Hebrews
    Of James
    First Letter of Peter
    Second Letter of Peter
    First Letter of John
    Second Letter of John
    Third Letter of John
    Of Jude
Revelation

Open a Bible to the table of contents for the New Testament and notice these twenty-seven writings. Observe the difference in their lengths. Note also that some of these writings are gospels, others are letters. Two writings are neither gospels nor letters: the Acts of the Apostles, a sort of history of the earliest Christians, and the Book of Revelation, a highly imaginative description of God's action in history.

Challenges

Ray Hart, the author of Unfinished Man and His Imagination says: "We live out of the future, but we understand out of the past." Express your agreement or disagreement in terms of your own personal experience.

Suppose that you are living at the time of Dionysius Exiguus. Some people are complaining about the new calendar he is introducing. Would you join them or would you defend Dionysius? Give reasons.

This chapter's title maintains that the Christian Scriptures are not only valuable but that they make up "the most important book for Christians." How do you evaluate this claim?

Prayer
Reflection

Lord, open my mind and my heart to your presence in the Scriptures. I am told that in the first part of the Bible, the Hebrew Scriptures, you begin to reveal the truth about yourself and your loving relationship with your people.

I believe that in the Christian Scriptures you continue your revelation in Jesus of Nazareth.

The study of the Christian Scriptures which I am about to undertake is no ordinary study. Help me to read faithfully and discover the message inspired by you, the living God. May I share in the spirit of the first Christians, who experienced your inspired word in this way:

The word of God is alive and active, sharper than any double-edged sword. It cuts all the way through, to where soul and spirit meet, to where joints and marrow come together. It judges the desires and thoughts of man's heart.
Hebrews 4:12

2

Paul, the Traveling Apostle

Looking Into the Future

Most of us want to know what the future holds. For some people, knowing it is so important that they consult fortune-tellers and astrologers. Some read their horoscopes to gain insights into the next day's events.

■ Look at yesterday's newspaper and read your horoscope. Did its predictions come true? To what extent do you think stars influence and guide a person's life?

According to the Acts of the Apostles, St. Paul came to know his future not from fortune tellers or his horoscope but from God himself.

Paul the Persecutor

The story of St. Paul's conversion from persecutor of Christians to follower of Christ has been told many times, but it never ceases to amaze us.

The Acts of the Apostles gives us a glimpse of what the early Christians thought of Paul before his conversion to Christianity on the road to Damascus.

There was a Christian in Damascus named Ananias. He had a vision in which the Lord said to him, "Ananias! . . . Get ready and go to Straight Street, and at the house of Judas ask for a man from Tarsus named Saul. He is praying. . . . Ananias answered, "Lord, many people have told me about this man and about all the terrible things he has done to your people in Jerusalem. And he has come to Damascus with authority from the chief priests to arrest all who worship you." The Lord said to him, "Go, because I have chosen him to serve me, to make my name known to Gentiles and kings and to the people of Israel. . . .

Acts 9:10–19

What Ananias said was true. Until the day before Ananias went to see him, Paul had been travelling from city to city persecuting Jews who had become Christians.

You see, Paul was raised a devout Jew. As a boy he went to Jewish schools and had Jewish teachers. As a man he became a leading Pharisee and a teacher of the Jewish religion.

Paul knew the history of his own people and his own religion and, like most other Jews, believed in the first Commandment of the Jewish Law: **"I am the Lord your God. . . . Worship no god but me" (Exodus 20:2–3).** In Paul's eyes, Jews who became Christians were worshipping a man called Jesus as Lord, in addition to the one true God. This infuriated Paul so much that he set out to persecute Jews who worshipped Jesus as Lord.

What seems strange to us is that Paul thought persecuting Christians was something God wanted him to do. But we should not be too harsh in condemning

Experiences Which Transform

An individual's life can be changed enormously by the influence of a single person. You probably have seen such stories on television or in the movies many times. For example, a teacher inspires a discouraged student to continue studying, thereby enabling the student to make a success of life. A high school coach takes a so-so athlete and puts the player on the road to greatness. Friends by their ideals and respect for others inspire those close to them.

In Helen Keller's life we find a vivid example of a transforming experience. At the age of seven, her future was dramatically changed by a woman named Anne Mansfield Sullivan, a school teacher.

When Helen was two years old she became blind, deaf, and dumb. She lived in a tunnel of darkness and silence with no exit to the outside world of light and sound and language.

Anne Mansfield Sullivan came to teach her. With finger taps in her palm, she spelled into Helen's hand the words for doll, mother, father, wood, water, and a hundred other words. But there was no way for Helen to understand that the tapped-out words represented things.

It was almost hopeless, but Anne continued. One day, someone was drawing water at a well. Anne put Helen's fingers under the gushing water and spelled out the word "water." No reaction. She did it again more rapidly. Helen stood transfixed. She understood. The letters spelled out on her hand had signified "water"! Anne's fingers in her hand had opened an exit to the world outside.

Paul. He was a good man. He was just unable to see how his fellow Jews could worship Jesus as Lord. Like other Jews, he believed that by persecuting Christians he was putting an end to false worship.

■ To know what Paul thought about himself as a law-abiding Jew who persecuted Christians, read Philippians 3:5—6 and Galatians 1:13—14. On a sheet of paper tell how you think Paul would change as he grew in the Christian life.

With Anne's help, Helen completed her education through college and university, gave lectures, wrote books, and travelled widely. In a world she would never see or hear, she became an inspiration to millions.

■ Think of how your life or that of someone you know has been changed by a special person. What qualities, ideals, or values did this special person have in order to exert such an influence?

From Persecutor to Disciple

When Paul encountered Jesus his life also was dramatically changed. Paul himself tells what happened as he was on his way to Damascus to arrest Jewish Christians and bring them back to Jerusalem for punishment.

As I was traveling and coming near Damascus, about midday a bright light from the sky flashed suddenly around me. I fell to the ground and heard a voice saying to me, "Saul, Saul! Why do you persecute me?" "Who are you, Lord?" I asked. "I am Jesus of Nazareth, whom you persecute," he said to me. . . . I asked, "What shall I do, Lord?" and the Lord said to me, "Get up and go into Damascus, and there you will be told everything that God has determined for you to do."

Acts 22:6–10

From that day on, Paul had no doubt about his future. The transforming experience on the road to Damascus had opened up a new world for him. From persecutor of Christians he became a Christian himself and one of the greatest preachers of Jesus in the history of Christianity. What Paul accomplished after his conversion is a story that has inspired Christians to spread the Good News of Jesus throughout the world.

A Walkathon for Christ

Paul gave himself totally to spreading the Good News of Jesus. He was probably the first person to ever make a walkathon for an important cause. Look at the map on page 25. The arrows show Paul's miles of travel for Christ.

To appreciate Paul's missionary work, imagine yourself traveling three or four times across the length of the United States with primitive means of transportation (a donkey or a camel or by foot for land travel and a small boat to take you over the water). Imagine going from city to city without a permanent home or a regular place to sleep at night. Imagine finding yourself thrown in jail, whipped, stoned, forced to hide out like a common criminal, and ending up facing execution. That is what happened to Paul after he encountered Jesus on the road to Damascus.

As Paul traveled those many miles, his message was that Jesus Christ is the risen Lord and Son of God. Believe in him, live as he wants you to live, and your life will take on new meaning.

Paul believed so intensely in Jesus that his whole life was taken up with preaching about him. As Paul himself said: **For what is life? To me, it is Christ (Philippians 1:21).** In all, Paul spent a good twenty-five to thirty years preaching Christ, establishing Christian communities, and writing letters to help the new converts to become followers of Christ, like himself.

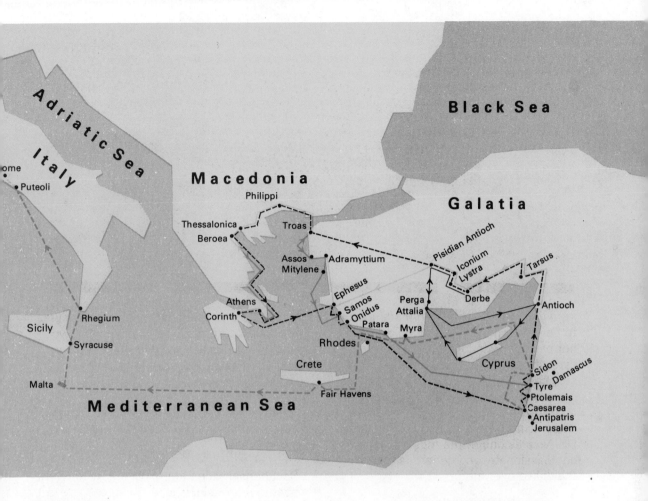

Life Is Christ!

Paul, as we mentioned, said: "For me, life is Christ." An athlete might say: "For me, life is basketball." A scientist like Albert Einstein might say: "For me, life is to discover the formula for general relativity in order to help solve the problems of the physical universe." A person like Mother Teresa of Calcutta might say: "For me, life is to care for the poorest of the poor."

Life has a special meaning and value for people who dedicate themselves to a worthy goal, and their lives touch so many others. Take for instance Dr. Alice, another example of those who dedicated their lives to service to others. Not many people are acquainted with her, but the people in the small New England town where she lives know and love her.

As a young girl, she decided to become a doctor. In medical school and throughout her career, her patients' sickness and grief caused her personal anguish. Yet she knew that helping people was her life.

As a young doctor she had made a promise to her dying mother: she would treat all her patients with love and take special care of those who could not afford medical services. She never failed in keeping this promise. The people of her hometown, many of whom were brought into the world by her, cured and comforted by her, know Dr. Alice as one of the most loving, compassionate, and generous persons they have ever met.

When Dr. Alice was 65 years old, she suffered a stroke. Because of blood clots, her leg was amputated. The surgeons said she would never again practice medicine. But medicine and healing were her life. She overcame the effects of her stroke and with an artificial leg learned to walk and drive and carry on normally. She returned to her practice and continued as before.

Dr. Alice is now in her 70's and her life's meaning is still the same as it was when she was young: to live is to practice medicine as a way of helping people.

■ List some things which make your life worth living at this time. Explain why two of these items are both worthwhile to you and can be worthwhile to others.

Paul the Community Builder

Paul wanted people to form active Christian communities and live as followers of Jesus Christ.

Paul himself does not explain how he went about establishing these Christian communities. But Luke does. In the Acts of the Apostles Luke tells us that Paul began by preaching in synagogues to Jews and to Gentile converts to Judaism. His efforts there, however, resulted in little more than his being thrown out of the synagogues, whipped, waylaid in alleys, and beaten.

Most often Paul went to places where there were no Christian communities as yet. There he instructed the Gentiles and spent much time helping them to organize Christian communities. At Ephesus, for example, he rented a hall and taught for a full two years.

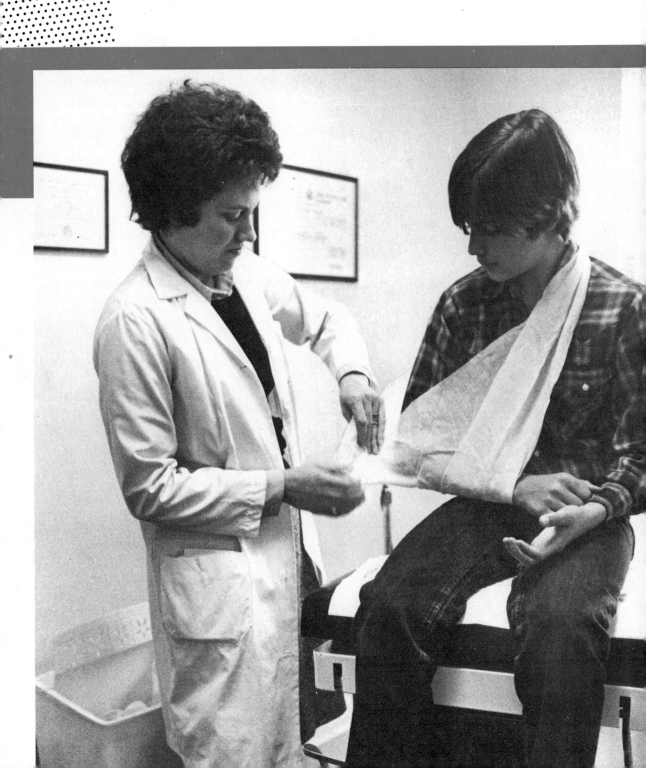

We are not sure what other meeting places Paul used when preaching the good news of Jesus. He might have preached on street corners. He probably sought out groups of people as he did in Athens on the hill called the Areopagus (Acts 17). Paul was a tentmaker, and he may have talked about Jesus and the Christian faith to the people who came to buy his tents.

In order to understand Paul's teachings, which are found in his letters, it may be important that we imagine ourselves in his place. Try to sense:

● the uncertainty he must have felt as he entered a new place and began preaching to people who did not even believe in the one true God;

● how he would not only have to teach about the one true God, his risen Son, Jesus, and the Holy Spirit, but would also have to convince the Gentiles to abandon the gods they had worshipped and believed in for centuries;

● how he would have to work closely with them, continually helping them to learn how Christians live and believe;

● how close Paul would become to the converts and how he would feel responsible for their progress in and fidelity to Christianity after he left and moved to another community.

28

■ Read Acts 9:20–25 and try to get a sense of how Paul must have felt as he started out his new life with such enthusiasm and found himself rejected by those he loved.

29

The Troublemaker

As Paul preached the good news of Jesus he often got into trouble. He had difficulties with the Jews, with the Gentiles, and even with his own companions. The nature of his message as well as his own personality could explain some of the opposition he met.

Following his conversion, Paul went first to synagogues to preach the good news of Jesus. But just as before his conversion he did not understand how Christians could worship Jesus as Lord, so his listeners could not understand how Paul could accept and preach that Jesus was indeed Lord and Son of God. As a result, they drove him out of the synagogues and tried to kill him.

Let's take a look at some of the difficulties Paul experienced in towns where he preached the good news.

Antioch (Acts 13:13–52)

In Antioch in Pisidia, the Jews were jealous because of the large crowds listening to Paul. What Paul said to the Jews did not help matters any.

He told them that since they refused the good news of Jesus, the Gentiles who accepted it would become God's chosen people. The Gentiles were elated, but naturally the Jews were resentful and this led them eventually to expel Paul from the city.

Iconium and Lystra (Acts 14:1–20)

In Iconium, the Jews planned to stone Paul and Barnabas, his companion and co-worker. Fortunately, they heard about the plan and escaped. Paul, however, was not so lucky in other places. In Lystra, when he cured a man, the people tried to worship him as a god. Wanting none of this, Paul attempted to stop them. Some Jews from Antioch turned the crowds against him and, instead of worshiping him as a god, the crowds stoned Paul and dragged him out of the town, thinking that he was dead.

Philippi (Acts 16:11–40)

In Philippi a slave girl who was a fortune-teller kept following Paul and his friend Silas, shouting at them. Paul was annoyed and he demanded that the spirit which allowed her to tell fortunes depart from her. It left, and her slave master was enraged. The crowds joined the man, stripped Paul and Silas, whipped them, and threw them into jail.

■ The outcome of this episode is found in Acts 16:25–40. Notice Paul's reaction in verse 37. How does this fit with his character?

Ephesus (Acts 19:1–40)

In Ephesus, Paul's preaching started a riot among the pagan silversmiths who earned their livings making statues of gods. When Paul preached that pagan gods did not exist, many of the people believed him. Naturally, they ceased buying the statues. The unhappy silversmiths rioted for two hours until the town clerk was able to quiet them.

Troas (Acts 20:7–12)
Paul might have been in serious trouble in
Troas but for the help of God. As usual,
Paul was preaching. He was so intent
on getting his message across that he kept
talking till after midnight. The length of
his talk caused one of his listeners to go to
sleep and fall from a window.

■ Read this unique story in Acts 20:7–12
and see how Paul got himself out of
trouble this time.

Antioch (Acts 15:36–41)
Paul had a disagreement with his close
friend and companion Barnabas. It was
over Barnabas' cousin John Mark, a
young disciple who had been traveling with
them. At Pamphylia John Mark left
them. Later on, at Antioch in Syria, when
Barnabas wanted to take John Mark along
again, Paul flatly refused. The argument
resulted in Paul and Barnabas splitting up.
Barnabas took John Mark, Paul took
Titus (another believer), and they went
their separate ways.

■ These stories show Paul's bluntness
and lack of sensitivity in dealing with
people. Do you think Paul was justified
in being so unbending: towards the Jews at
Antioch in Pisidia; towards the Gentiles
at Philippi and Ephesus; and even towards
his companions at Antioch in Syria? Share
your analysis with others in the class.

Final Arrest (Acts 21:27 ff.)

Strangely enough, the opposition that led to Paul's death was not something he himself caused. His reputation as a troublemaker must have been well-known, because when Paul arrived in Jerusalem the Jews were already presuming the worst about him.

It started when Paul was in the Temple at Jerusalem. Some Jews had seen him earlier with a Gentile friend from Ephesus, and they presumed they had both gone into the Temple, a sacred place for all Jews; Gentiles were never allowed into certain of its areas.

Paul was innocent, but the crowds could not have cared less. They rioted and attacked him. Luckily, Roman soldiers arrived and dispersed the mob. The Roman commander thought Paul was an Egyptian who sometime before had caused a riot and led bandits into the desert. Paul eventually explained himself, but as usual he could not leave well enough alone. He infuriated the Jews by telling them about his conversion to Christianity on the road to Damascus, and they began to chant: **"Away with him! Kill him! He's not fit to live!" (Acts 22:22).** The outcome was that Paul once again landed in prison.

Some of Paul's opponents vowed not to eat or drink until they had killed him. A friend who heard of the plot told the Roman commander, who ordered 200 infantrymen, 70 calvalrymen, and 200 spearmen to protect Paul on his trip to Caesarea where he was to stand trial. Needless to say, Paul arrived safely.

Paul was kept in prison in Caesarea for two years while the Jewish leaders tried to find grounds for having him executed.

Eventually, Paul appealed to Caesar and was sent to Rome to plead his case before the emperor. We do not know how the trial turned out. All we are told is that Paul was under house arrest in Rome for another two years and spent this time preaching about Jesus to anyone who would listen to him. We have no written records of Paul's last days on earth. But we do know from tradition that he died in Rome.

The Warm Side of Paul
You might think people would be frightened by a person as unbending as Paul. Yet despite his brusque personality, he had many friends who loved him deeply. We saw evidence of this in the above stories when people tried to save him from his enemies.

Acts 20:17–38 tells us how Paul said goodbye at Miletus to friends who came from Ephesus to be with him for most likely the last time. Acts also tells us how they expressed their sorrow at his leaving.

■ Envision yourself as a close friend of Paul from Ephesus who has just learned of his death in Rome. Write a profile to send to Christians throughout the lands he traveled, describing the kind of person you feel is the real Paul of Tarsus.

Challenges

People like Paul who achieve things beyond the ordinary are sometime called "driven"—driven by ambition or anger or love or some subconscious psychological force. Imagine yourself as Paul. What do you think drove him?

Paul made trouble of some kind almost everywhere he went. How would you evalute Paul as a troublemaker? Explain.

Not everyone would want to imitate Paul's personality or lifestyle. To what extent do you find who he was and what he did attractive? Name someone who you think is a modern parallel to Paul. Explain.

Prayer
Reflection

Yes, God called St. Paul in an extraordinary way. I too am called, as is every person God has created. This may at times require that I change my plans or give up some present security.

The poet Robert Frost tells how he feels about meeting such a challenge:

"The woods are lovely, dark and deep.
But I have promises to keep,
And miles to go before I sleep,
And miles to go before I sleep."

As Paul traveled he must often have felt like staying when he passed through beautiful peaceful places in Greece or Syria or Palestine. But he moved on because he had promises to keep.

God calls me. It may be for great things or little things. However and whenever he does, may I be ready to respond as Paul did. For this, Lord, I ask both light and strength. Amen.

3 Paul, the Letter Writer

Getting Mail

Pretend you have just received three letters—one from a parent, one from a past teacher, and one from a friend. You don't know which letter is from which person; there are no return addresses, no postmarks, no signatures, and all the letters are typewritten on the same kind of paper with the same kind of typewriter. How would the tone of each letter and the experiences related in it help you determine who had written each one?

For a different kind of example, read the following letter to Sam from his friend John.

Dear Sam,
Joe and I went camping for a week. "Our friend" kept telling us to bring raincoats and make sure we checked in at the ranger station before going into the woods. We said yes and of course then went ahead and did what we always do.

We went to the place you liked so much last year and did all the things you enjoyed doing so much. We got lost on a side trip to Eagle's Point, but we met the man who lives in the log cabin, and he gave us directions, so we got there and back without any trouble. "Our friend" was happy when we arrived home safely and without any horror stories. Next time you've

got to come along. We missed you, and you missed a good time.

Your friend,
John

Now reflect on the following questions:
* Did you feel left out of the conversation?
* Who is "our friend"?
* What did Joe and John "always do" and why didn't they check into the ranger station?
* Where did they go camping and what things did Sam enjoy doing so much?
* Where was Eagle's Point and who was the man in the log cabin?
* Why was "our friend" happy when they arrived home safely and without any horror stories?
* Even though you may not know the answers to all these questions, were you able to understand the heart of the letter?

Early Christian Mail

When we study Paul's letters we see that Paul, like a parent, teacher, or best friend, has a certain style of writing. Paul's friendliness, beliefs, and way of dealing with people show through. Also, when we read Paul's letters, it's like reading John's letter to Sam—we are reading someone else's mail. We should not be surprised, therefore, if we do not always understand everything that Paul says to the persons to whom he writes.

Background Information

When a close friend moves away, we may feel as badly as the people of Ephesus did when Paul left them. Imagine how Paul felt each time he left his friends to travel on to a new town and to new people. As we would not quickly forget a close friend, neither did Paul. He couldn't visit them as he would like, so he did what we would do. He kept in touch by letter.

The churches on the map above show where Paul established Christian communities. The scrolls show to which churches he wrote letters. We have evidence that Paul wrote many letters, but of those he wrote, we have only seven. The letters with

Inspiration, however, does not mean that Paul's letters are any less human than the ones which we write. Just as people 2,000 years from today would have trouble figuring out some of our writings, so we too have trouble understanding all of Paul's writings.

Slavery in the First Century
One of Paul's shortest and most interesting letters has to do with a runaway slave. In those times if land was conquered, it was very possible that the inhabitants of that land might become slaves. Nationality or race did not matter. Slaves of course tried to escape, and many succeeded. But the laws were strict and dealt heavy penalties, including death, to those who were caught.

The Letter to Philemon
In reading Paul's letter to Philemon, we get the distinct impression that Onesimus, the man for whom Paul intercedes, is a runaway slave, and Philemon is his master. Evidently Onesimus, who now wants to return to Philemon, had committed some other crime in addition to escaping. Since Paul was a friend to both Onesimus and Philemon, he writes this letter to help Onesimus and Philemon be reconciled.

asterisks on page 17 are considered by scholars the authentic letters of Paul. The other Pauline letters are thought to have been written by his disciples in his name. As is all of Scripture, Paul's letters are inspired by God. Inspiration means that God and the Christian community stand behind the truth of Paul's teaching. In short, inspiration assures us that Paul's message is God's message. For this reason, Paul's letters have been accepted by the Christian community as a norm for its belief in Jesus Christ.

Read Paul's letter to Philemon. (It is so short that unless you look it up in the table of contents you may never find it.)

Let us now analyze the letter to Philemon in order to understand the form for letter writing in those times and Paul's basic style of writing. His form includes several basic ingredients, which we will now explore.

The Greeting

In Paul's time, as you notice from verse 1, the sender gave his name at the beginning instead of at the end of the letter. It is not until verse 2 that we learn to whom the letter is sent.

The Blessing

Verse 3 shows another element of ancient letter style—the blessing. Paul's blessing, of course, is done the Christian way. He calls on God the Father and Jesus to bless those to whom he writes.

The Thanksgiving

Verses 4-7 contain the thanksgiving, which is similar to the section in our letters in which we express how much we care for the person to whom we are writing.

In addition to expressing his esteem, Paul uses this section to give hints about the central topic or topics of his letters.

The Praises

In the thanksgiving section of the letter Paul tells his friends how much they mean to God, to him, and to other Christians. But as soon as he finishes praising them, he lets them know that they have some shaping up to do.

Read verses 4-7, printed below, and pay close attention to the praises in the underlined words:

Brother Philemon, every time I pray, I mention you and give thanks to my God. For I <u>hear of your love</u> for all of God's people and the <u>faith you have</u> in the Lord Jesus. My prayer is that <u>our fellowship with you</u> as believers will bring about a deeper understanding of every blessing which we have in our life in union with Christ. <u>Your love</u>, dear brother, has brought me <u>great joy and much encouragement</u>! You have <u>cheered the hearts of all of God's people.</u>

Now read verse 8:

For this reason I could be bold enough, as your brother in Christ, to order you to do what should be done.

At first glance it may seem underhanded to praise people and then criticize them. But look at it this way. Paul is the one who brought them the Good News about Christ. He feels responsible for making sure that they act like Christians, and he certainly does not enjoy telling them he has doubts about their Christian response. In verse 8 he states that he has the right to order what ought to be done. But in verse 9 he softens what he says: **But because I love you, I make a request instead**.

Study verse 21 to determine how Paul respects his friends and, even though he has doubts, still has faith in their goodness. It is the respect, love, and faith he has in his friends that is shown in the praises of the thanksgiving section.

The Clues

Paul uses the thanksgiving section also to hint at the main topic of his letters. Note the subtle suggestion to Philemon in verse 6 about understanding **every blessing which we have in our life in union with Christ**. The blessings Paul is pointing out are the blessings which Philemon, Apphia, and Archippus have received from Christ that will enable them to forgive the runaway slave Onesimus.

In verse 7 Paul hints at what he wants them to do. He tells his readers the hearts of God's people have been cheered

through them. Onesimus, likewise, has become a Christian, one of God's people! It follows, therefore, that Onesimus' heart, and Paul's as well, would be cheered if they will forgive and take Onesimus back. Follow the development of Paul's earnest request in verses 10-20.

Signing Off

Paul ends his letter much the same way we do. He gives regards to Philemon, Apphia, and Archippus from their friends. We might say: "Dan and Joan send their best. Sincerely yours. . . ." In addition, Paul wishes them the grace of the Lord Jesus Christ.

What Happened

As we said, when we read Paul's letters we are actually reading someone else's mail and we cannot expect to understand everything that is said. For example, when reading the Letter to Philemon do we know: What did Philemon, Apphia, and Archippus do to show their love for all of God's people and the faith they have in the Lord Jesus? How were the hearts of God's people cheered through them? Why is Paul in prison? Why did Onesimus leave his master? What has Onesimus done that Paul would have to pay for? Why does Philemon owe Paul his "very self"?

Even though we do not know the answers to all these questions, we certainly can understand the heart of the letter.

■ What is your response to the following questions:

● What happened to Onesimus after he escaped from Philemon?
● What does Paul mean when he says that, in sending back Onesimus, he is sending back his "heart"?
● What does Paul expect Philemon to do for Onesimus and why does he expect him to do it?
● What does Paul mean in verse 16 when he says to Philemon about Onesimus: **how much more he will mean to you, both as a slave and as a brother in the Lord?**

Philemon and Me
Paul tells Philemon to treat Onesimus as a brother in the Lord. Slavery is not legal in the United States, as it was in the Roman Empire, but what Paul says applies to us as much as it applied to Philemon. Paul's message is: all people are brothers and sisters in the Lord; treat them as such.

For example, what difference do you think it made to Onesimus to have Philemon accept him as a person "in the Lord" instead of as a runaway slave who must be punished?

Do you look upon the people around you as "in the Lord"? If you do, it will make a significant difference in how you treat them.

Thessalonians
In Arkansas back in 1969, a group of people who thought the world was coming to an end within a year sold everything they had, gathered together in one place, and waited for the end to come. Something similar to this happened in one of the Christian communities which Paul began.

In 50 A.D. Paul founded a little community of Christians in the city of Thessalonica in northern Greece. Six months later Paul was in Athens longing to hear from this new Christian community. He sent Timothy to bring back news and in the meantime moved on to Corinth (1 Thessalonians 2:17-3:2). While Paul was in Corinth, Timothy returned with this startling news: the Thessalonians believed that the end of the world was coming soon!

Timothy reported also that some Thessalonians were refusing to work—they were sitting around doing nothing, just waiting for the end to arrive. Others were living immorally, ignoring the Commandments as if they had gone out of style, and trying to make the last days on earth one big party!

Timothy said also that certain Thessalonians were upset because some of their friends and relatives had died. They had the strange idea that in order to go to heaven they had to be alive when Jesus returned. If they died before, they were out of luck. Thus, from a distance Paul is faced with loafers, high-livers, and worriers in a community for which he feels some responsiblity. Paul was so busy with the Corinthians that he could not go to Thessalonica. Instead, he wrote a letter which turned out to be the earliest of all his extant letters and the earliest of all the writings in the Christian Scriptures.

▢ Think of what your parish or school would be like if a number of its members were loafers, high-livers, and people worried about the resurrection and the end of the world. What effect would these people have on the life of the parish or school? Would the parish or school be able to function as it should? What steps could be taken to remedy this situation?

A Basic Method

When studying the Scriptures, it is important for us to understand the inspired author's message. In our study of the Christian Scriptures, therefore, we recommend the following steps:

- *Read* the book of the Christian Scriptures which we are studying.
- *Analyze* passages which are key to understanding the book's message.
- *Reflect* on the importance of the inspired message both for those for whom it was originally written and for ourselves today.

46 We will apply this method first of all to our study of Paul's letter to the Thessalonians. In this letter he deals with loafers and high-livers in 1:1-4:12; with the problems of those who die before the second coming of Christ in 4:13-18; and with the time of the end of the world and the second coming of Christ in 5:1-11.

1 Thessalonians 1:1–10
From our study of the letter to Philemon, we know Paul's style. In reading 1 Thessalonians 1:1-10 pick out:

- the greeting and the blessing;
- the phrases Paul uses to show his esteem for the Thessalonians;
- the hints which show that he will have something to say about working; about living a good moral life; and about the end of the world and the second coming of Christ.

1 Thessalonians 2:1-20
Read 2:1-20. Notice especially verses 9 and 10. In 2:9 Paul indirectly criticizes the loafers when he says: **Surely you remember, our brothers, how we worked and toiled! We worked day and night so that we would not be any trouble to you as we preached to you the Good News from God.**

Verse 2:10 is a rebuke to the high-livers: **You are our witnesses, and so is God, that our conduct toward you who believe was pure, right, and without fault.**

In 1:6–7, Paul had praised the Thessalonians for becoming imitators of Jesus and himself and for setting a good example to others around them. The loafers, however, were doing nothing, and the high-livers were hardly giving good example.

■ Why do you think Paul wrote 2:9-10? What impact do you think he had on the loafers and high-livers by reminding them of the kind of life he had led when he was with them?

1 Thessalonians 4:1-12
Here Paul reprimands the loafers and the high-livers. Read these verses and give examples of modern-day situations to which Paul's message could apply. Note especially the underlined phrases.

Finally, our brothers, you learned from us how you should live in order to please God. This is, of course, the way you have been living. And now we beg and urge you in the name of the Lord Jesus to do even more. For you know the instructions we gave you by the authority of the Lord Jesus. God wants you to be holy and completely free from sexual immorality. Each of you men should know how to live with his wife in a holy and honorable way, not with a lustful desire, like the heathen who do not know God. In this matter, then, no man should do wrong to his fellow Christian or take advantage of him. We have told you this before, and we strongly warned you that the Lord will punish those who do that. God did not call us to live in immorality, but in

holiness. So then whoever rejects this teaching is not rejecting man, but God, who gives you his Holy Spirit.

There is no need to write you about love for your fellow believers. You yourselves have been taught by God how you should love one another. And you have, in fact, behaved like this toward all the brothers in all of Macedonia. So we beg you, our brothers, to do even more. Make it your aim to live a quiet life, to mind your own business, and to earn your own living just as we told you before. In this way you will win the respect of those who are not believers, and you will not have to depend on anyone for what you need.

1 Thessalonians 4:13-18
In 4:13-18 Paul deals with the Thessalonians' worries about their dead relatives and friends. Read what he says in 4:13-15:

Our brothers, we want you to know the truth about those who have died, so that you will not be sad, as are those who have no hope. We believe that Jesus died and rose again, and so we believe that God will take back with Jesus those who have died believing in him. What we are teaching you now is the Lord's teaching: we who are alive on the day the Lord comes will not go ahead of those who have died.

■ Explain in your own words what you think Paul was saying about those who died before the second coming of Jesus.

How do you understand the underlined words in 4:16-18?

There will be the shout of command, the archangel's voice, the sound of God's trumpet, and the Lord himself will come down from heaven. Those who have died believing in Christ will rise to life first; then we who are living at that time will be gathered up along with them in the clouds to meet the Lord in the air. And so we will always be with the Lord. So then, encourage one another with these words.

Some people understand this scene of 4:16-18 as a blow-by-blow description of the end of the world. They expect some day to see Jesus coming on the clouds of heaven with trumpets blasting and armies of angels filling the skies. Paul, however, does not know anymore than we do when the end of the world will take place or what it will be like.

His description of the end-time is a dramatization. He makes these verses sound like stage directions for the last act of the history of the world. The best way to understand his language is as the language of drama.

In 4:16, for example, Paul presents Jesus as the greatest person in history. When important dignitaries visit the United States, they are welcomed with music, singing, and military bands. When Paul uses words like "the archangel's voice," and "God's trumpet," what he is trying to say is that when Jesus comes at the end of the world he will come as the greatest person of all time!

1 Thessalonians 5:1–28

Paul deals with the timing for the end of the world in 1 Thessalonians 5:1–11, asserting that nobody knows the date but that everyone should be in a state of readiness for whenever it happens.

Paul ends his letter with some advice and his usual expression of regards.

■ Read 5:12–28 and jot down the piece of advice that means the most to you. Explain why.

Challenges

To what extent do you think that Paul's relationship with Christ had a great deal to do with his concern for the runaway slave Onesimus?

Paul reprimanded those Thessalonians who were refusing to work and were making themselves a burden on the community. Would you agree with Paul that putting in an honest day's work is part of being a good Christian? Explain how this may apply in our complex economic world today. You may wish to compare your answers with others in your class.

Paul gave attention in his teaching to people who held slaves, to those who lived immorally, and to those who were worrying about the resurrection and the end of the world. Choose one of these groups and explain why it was important that Paul address them and their situation.

Prayer
Reflection

May we reflect prayerfully on some of the concerns which Paul experienced in his ministry to Christian communities:

- A concern for a slave who needed an advocate with his master. May we speak and act on behalf of those who have little voice or power of their own.
- A concern for the everyday responsibilities of human living. May we cultivate what talents we have and put them to good use both for ourselves and for others.
- A concern for appropriate moral living. May we recognize our need to observe God's commandments as a help to full human and Christian life.
- A concern for patience and trust that God will give us a new heaven and earth in God's good time. May we look forward to an eternity with God as his sons and daughters.
- A concern that death be understood not as an end but as a beginning. May we realize that our own death will be a passage to fuller life with God.

4 Paul, the Trouble Shooter

Live Issues

In the spring of 1979, something went wrong with the nuclear reactor on Three Mile Island near Harrisburg, Pennsylvania. For almost a week, there was the prospect of a "China Syndrome"—that the atomic core would melt its way through the bottom of the reactor, and down into the earth.

The immediate danger passed and people relaxed. Yet this accident heightened a great debate throughout the world. Is the use of nuclear power so critical to the energy crisis that nations should take the risk of an atomic accident that could pollute the atmosphere, scorch the earth, create disease, and perhaps kill a great many people?

Cosmopolitan Corinth

After Paul left Corinth in the fall of 52 A.D., it was something like Harrisburg after Three Mile Island. This alive city became the center for controversial issues provoked by his preaching of the good news of Jesus Christ.

Paul had set up his headquarters in Corinth eighteen months before because the city was a perfect location for an apostle like him. Look at the map of churches on page 38 and locate Corinth. As you see, the city is located near the Isthmus of Corinth, which provided a shortcut to western Greece. It was thronged, as a result, with merchants, shippers, sailors, and tourists from all the far-flung sea lanes of the Mediterranean.

Recall for a moment the problems the loafers, the high-livers, and those worried about the resurrection and the end of the world caused in the little community at Thessalonica. They were nothing compared to the problems at Corinth.

Paul had so much trouble with the Corinthians he felt obliged to write them at least four letters. We do not have the texts of the first and third. We know about them only because Paul refers to them in the two letters which we do have (1 Corinthians 5:9 and 2 Corinthians 2:3–4). His second and fourth letters are known to us as First and Second Corinthians.

Paul not only wrote letters to the Corinthians, he also sent Timothy and later Titus to work with them (1 Corinthians 4:17 and 2 Corinthians 7:6–7). He went back to Corinth a second time, in 56 A.D., and a third time, in 57 A.D., to try to help them better understand Christianity (2 Corinthians 12:14).

Troubling News

Paul was in the town of Ephesus in Asia Minor (modern Turkey) when news reached him that the community in Corinth was experiencing turmoil. Check the map of churches on page 38 for the location of Ephesus in relation to Corinth.

- true wisdom and genuine teachers (chapters 1–4)
- conscience (chapter 8)
- the eucharist (chapter 11)
- charismatic gifts (chapters 12–14)
- the resurrection (chapter 15).

Praise and Reprimand

As usual, Paul begins his letter by praising those who will be reading it. Read chapter 1:1–9 and pick out the verses which praise. Look for the hints which Paul gives about the topics he will address in the rest of his letter. As you can see, Paul's praises, unfortunately, are brief. Early in verse 10 of chapter 1, he faces head-on one of the problems in Corinth.

According to Chloe, the community was breaking up into competing cliques, some siding with one favorite teacher, others with a second. If this trend continued, Paul realized, there would soon be no community at all!

Paul tells them clearly that they must be united, otherwise they are dividing Christ (1 Corinthians 1:10–17). Paul tries to get to the root of the problem. He warns the Corinthians that they are missing the heart of Christ's message. They are thinking of themselves and their favorite teachers when they should be concentrating on the crucifixion of Christ. Jesus' suffering and death is real wisdom because Jesus did God's will even when it meant the sacrifice of himself unto death.

Chloe, a woman who was very active in the Christian community in Corinth, was well-informed about developments there. Some members of Chloe's family from Corinth were the first to bring him the bad news (1 Corinthians 1:11). Still later, three of Paul's friends—Stephanus, Fortunatus, and Achaicus—came from Corinth to Ephesus and told Paul about the troubling situation. With the reports from Chloe, Stephanus, Fortunatus, and Achaicus still ringing in his ears, Paul wrote the letter which we now know as 1 Corinthians. The letter is sixteen chapters long and covers many subjects. We will deal only with the following selected topics:

Some Corinthians were saying that salvation through Jesus' death was foolishness. They were trying to replace God's wisdom with human logic. It was not a good situation.

Logic Versus Christian Wisdom

To understand this issue, try putting yourself in the place of a serious-minded Corinthian.

Situation: You are a logical-minded Greek. As far as religion goes, you have never so much as heard of the one true God. You believe that there are many gods: some good, some bad. You have studied the works of the great philosophers Socrates, Plato, Aristotle, and others. You think as they do. You believe only what is logical, only what makes sense and what is reasonable.

Now Paul comes along and preaches the good news of Jesus. You accept most of it because it makes good sense. But then Paul drops a bombshell! He claims that Jesus' death on the Cross is central to God's wise plan for the salvation of all humanity. You were brought up to believe only what is logical; you cannot accept the idea that dying on a cross is wise. You think it is foolishness!

■ Read 1 Corinthians 1:18—2:16 and see what Paul answers in reply to your contention that the Cross is foolishness. You may wish to write out your answers before discussing them.

● Whose wisdom does Paul say is foolishness?
● Paul states that a person does not understand the wisdom of the Cross through human wisdom or logic. According to Paul what does one need to understand truly the wisdom of the Cross?

● Some people live by the rule "Do good unto others as long as it is to your own benefit." Using Paul's argument in 1:18—2:16, explain why such a rule runs counter to the wisdom of the Cross.

Real Teachers (1 Corinthians 3—4)

In the early days of television there was a program called "This Is Your Life" which honored outstanding people. One evening the guest was a retired school teacher. One former student after another thanked her for all that she had done for them. She was overwhelmed to tears and could not understand why her students were so grateful. Her answer to all their praises was: "But all I ever did was love them."

"Loving them" is what Paul is talking about in chapters 3 and 4 of 1 Corinthians. Paul is blunt with the trouble-making teachers and preachers who are causing divisions in the community. Teachers and preachers, he says, are the *servants* of the community. Their job is to build up the community, not tear it down!

Teachers and preachers, Paul contends, are:

. . .Christ's servants, who have been put in charge of God's secret truths. The one thing required of such a servant is that he be faithful to his master.
1 Corinthians 4:1–2

Being "faithful to his master" means sacrificing oneself for others, thinking and caring about others before oneself, loving others for themselves. It is a hard lesson to learn.

■ As you read chapters 3 and 4, pick out the qualities Paul says are necessary in order to be good Christian teachers and preachers. Think of teachers and preachers whom you have liked best. List personal qualities that made them good teachers and preachers. Share your list of experiences with others.

What Is Permitted? (1 Corinthians 8)
Paul next goes on to discuss a problem the Corinthians themselves presented to him in a letter.

"Is it all right," they asked, "to eat meat which has been offered up in sacrifice to pagan gods?" Some Corinthians claimed it was permissible because pagan gods did not exist. Paul agreed with them. But these same Corinthians also thought it was perfectly all right to take part in pagan worship and all the immorality that went with it. Paul draws the line there.

■ Read carefully what Paul says about conscience in 1 Corinthians 8:1–3 and answer the following questions:

● On what basis does Paul say that the Corinthians have the *right* to eat idol meat?
● On what basis does he claim that they should give up, not their *right,* but the *use of their right* to eat idol meat?
● What is the meaning of Paul's statement: **Such knowledge, however, puffs a person up with pride; but love builds up (8:1)?**

The Eucharist (1 Corinthians 11:17–34)
Another troublesome issue which the Corinthians faced was the way in which they celebrated the Eucharist. In the earliest days of Christianity, the Eucharist took place as Jesus had celebrated it—at a meal. At Corinth, however, the meal part of the Eucharist was getting out of hand. As reported to Paul, the Corinthians were not considerate of one another at the Eucharistic meal. Some started eating before everyone arrived, some drank too much, some did not share their food with the poor who could bring little or nothing to the meal.

Paul was very unhappy with the reports he received and he told the Corinthians: **In the following instructions . . . I do not praise you . . . (11:17).** Instead he reminds them that Jesus gave us the Eucharist as a remembrance of his death—a death which was a giving up of himself for others. People who eat before the others, drink excessively, and ignore the poor, Paul tells them, are thinking only of themselves. They are far from giving up anything for others. Paul asks them squarely: **. . . would you rather despise the church of God and put to shame the people who are in need? (11:22).**

■ Read 1 Corinthians 11:17–34 to get a deeper understanding of Paul's teaching on the Eucharist. Is your own understanding of it similar?

When you go to Mass, to what extent are you aware that the Eucharist is a remembrance of Christ's death and a reminder to you to make sacrifices for others and especially the poor? Discuss your answers.

Charismatic Gifts (1 Corinthians 12—14)

When someone has an ability to get things done or to help others or to create something new, we say that he or she is gifted or talented. In the Christian Scriptures, when someone uses his or her gift or talent for the good of the community, this means that they have a special charism. "Charism" is simply the Greek word for favor or gift.

The Corinthian community had an all-star roster of talented individuals. They had gifted apostles, teachers, preachers, and organizers. They had people with the gift of healing, the gift of prophecy, and the gift of speaking in tongues.

But unfortunately many of them were too proud of their gifts. They looked down on others who did not have the same gifts they had.

Paul talks about gifts in general in 1 Corinthians 12. He stresses the importance of using gifts with love in chapter 13.

Paul tries to help the Corinthians understand these issues by making five points. Pick them out as you read 1 Corinthians, chapters 12—14:

● Gifts are not charismatic unless used for God under the guidance of the Holy Spirit.
● Gifts are not charismatic unless used for the building up of the Christian community.
● Like a body which has many different organs and members all working together for its good health, the community has many different members with diverse gifts. All these gifts should work together for the common good of the community.
● Some gifts, like some parts of the human body, are more important than others. Yet as we do not think less of the less vital bodily organs, so we should not regard any gifts as unimportant within the community.
● Without love the other gifts are useless. Without love nothing that really counts ever happens. For Paul, then, love was the underlying factor.

Earlier in the letter, Paul had said: **Such knowledge, however, puffs a person up with pride; but love builds up.** Here, he might have said: "Such *gifts* puff a person up with pride, but love builds up."

Bodily Resurrection

For Christians, Easter is the fulfillment of all their faith and hope in Christ. Every year on Easter Sunday, Alleluias ring out from every Christian church, and the promise of personal resurrection after death fills the hearts of all the Christian faithful.

Some Corinthian Christians, however, did not welcome the thought that some day they too would rise from the dead. Although they wanted to be immortal, they did not want their bodies to share in it. To understand why they were so fearful, imagine yourself as a new Corinthian convert.

Situation: Before you became Christian you belonged to a religion which said that all spiritual things come from a good god and that all material things have their source in an evil spirit. It taught that as spirit you come from the good god but your spirit has been trapped and imprisoned in what was considered an evil material body from which there is only one way to escape. Someone from the good god must bring you the "secret knowledge" that will release you from your evil body and all other evil material things.

When Paul begins to preach that Jesus has come from the good God to save you, you are excited. You accept his message and feel sure that now you possess the "secret knowledge" which you need to be free from your evil body. Now you "know" and you can do with your body as you wish. You can punish it if you want or you can use it to enjoy yourself.

But then Paul surprises you by declaring that everything created has been brought into being by the good God. He quotes you Genesis 1:31, which says: **God looked at everything he had made, and he was very pleased.** As though this were not enough, Paul tells you that after death your body will rise again and you will live forever in your body. He knows this because it happened to Jesus and, as he states in 1 Corinthians 15:1–8, he and many others witnessed Jesus alive in his body after his resurrection from the dead. Read Paul's forceful answer to those who would not accept his teaching in 1 Corinthians 15:12–20.

■   As a new Christian convert in Corinth, write a letter to a friend explaining how you felt about your body before your conversion and what you believe about the body after Paul's instruction.

Paul realized that the Corinthians would want to know: How can the dead be raised to life? What kind of body will they have (2 Corinthians 15:35)?

Paul was not personally involved with this kind of scientific explanation. He had no design for our resurrected bodies. What he was certain of, however, was that our resurrected bodies would be real bodies, filled with the spirit and the power of God (1 Corinthians 15:35–46). The one thing Paul would not budge on was this: Jesus rose in a body, and so shall we!

■   Reflect on the words of the Creed, which express our belief in the resurrection.

Try, Try Again (2 Corinthians)

If at first he does not succeed, Paul tries and tries again. Even if it takes four letters, three visits, and the sending of such colleagues as Titus and Timothy, he does not give up.

As we saw in Paul's First Letter to the Corinthians, they had a way of inventing their own versions of Christianity. First they would get the basic message of Christianity all twisted around to suit themselves. Then they would find that they could not tell a true apostle from a false one.

What appears to have happened is something like this. Around 56 A.D. Paul left Ephesus and went back to Corinth to see for himself what was going on in the Corinthian Church. He soon discovered that some missionaries from Jerusalem had come to Corinth and were claiming that they, not Paul, were the true apostles of Jesus and that their version, not Paul's, was the true version of the gospel.

These Jewish Christian missionaries have been called "Judaizers" because, in the opinion of scholars, they were teaching people that salvation comes by obeying Jewish laws and customs rather than by belief in Jesus.

Some Corinthians preferred the Judaizers' version of the gospel. When Paul heard this, he was upset. His whole personal experience had been the opposite: Jesus, not the Mosaic Law, frees us from sinfulness. There is no way of knowing exactly what happened when Paul met up with these missionaries from Jerusalem. But it must have been a bruising run-in. Paul left Corinth with a heavy heart.

Back in Ephesus, he wrote his third letter to the Corinthians. This letter, as mentioned, has been lost. But in 2 Corinthians, Paul gives us a glimpse of what he wrote in the third letter. Read especially 2 Corinthians 2:3—4.

We suspect the cause of Paul's "greatly troubled and distressed heart" and "many tears" was the fact that some of the Corinthians deserted him and joined the new missionaries from Jerusalem.

Paul wrote 2 Corinthians from somewhere in Macedonia. It was his fourth attempt to instruct his troublesome converts. His aruguments are long and involved. We will study only one part of the letter—the section which gives us the heart of his message: 2:13—7:4. Here Paul defends his gospel by explaining who is really qualified to be an apostle of Jesus Christ.

Who Is Qualified?

When we read Paul's letters, we often find he repeats himself, but with good reason. Some aspects of Christianity are more difficult to understand than others. Identifying a true apostle is one of these.

■ Read the following passages from 2 Corinthians and notice the qualities Paul mentions to help the Corinthians recognize a true apostle:

- 2 Corinthians 1:17
- 2 Corinthians 4
- 2 Corinthians 5:11—21
- 2 Corinthians 6:1—7:1

From what you read in these passages, construct a definition of what a true apostle is, according to Paul. Read 2 Corinthians, chapters 10—13, and explain to what extent you think Paul has measured up to his own description of a true apostle.

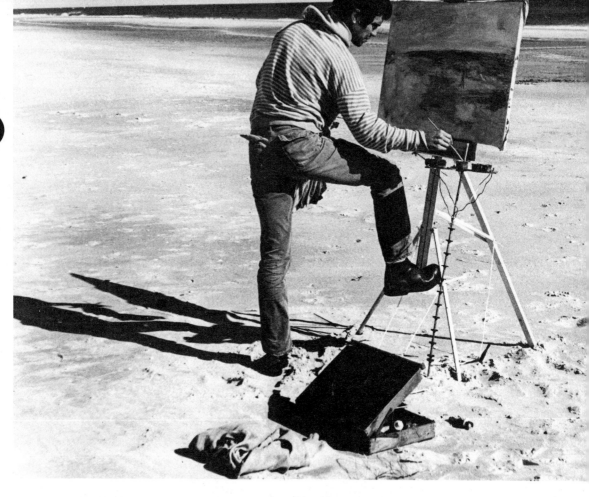

Studying Paul's letters to the Corinthians makes us aware of how easy it is to miss the central message of Christianity: "Love God with all your heart, mind, soul and strength, and love your neighbor as yourself." To do this one must constantly try to become the perfect disciple described by Paul in 2 Corinthians.

■ Can you think of one or two famous Christians from history who have come close to measuring up to Paul's description of a true apostle? Can you think of a modern-day Christian who seems to be living Paul's description of a true apostle?

Challenges

Explain what you understand by Paul's teaching about the wisdom of the Cross in 1 Corinthians 1 and 2. Do you think God could have chosen a wiser way to prove his love for us? Please explain.

In 1 Corinthians 8 – 10, Paul deals with conscience and rights. Do you agree that a Christian should be willing to give up the use of his or her rights for the good of another? Please explain.

Prayer
Reflection

There are gifts which we get. They come from outside ourselves and to some extent they stay outside us. A stereo, a ten-speed, a camera are mine but they are not me.

There are other gifts which we are. They come from within us and to some extent they grow along with us. A personality, a talent, a sensitivity are not only mine, but they are also me.

Writer Ernest Larsen helps us think about being authentic and genuine with these words:

"There is all the difference in the
            world
between one who teaches
and a teacher,
one who plays an instrument
and a musician,
one who goes to church
and a believer."

A key to Paul's understanding of what our gifts are meant to be is that God works through us for others by way of them. As he told the Corinthians:

Here we are, then, speaking for Christ, as though God himself were making his appeal through us. . . .
                    2 Corinthians 5:20

May we pray:
Lord, teach me how I can allow you to reach others through my talents and qualities. May I be in my own time and in my own way something of the apostle that Paul was. May we all in the Christian community look upon the gift which each one of us is as a sign of God's active presence for the good of the whole community. Amen.

5 Paul, the Theologian

Religious Bookkeeping

"The boss is God. He owns the company. If you're going to get anywhere, be a yes man, play ball—it's smart.

"The purpose is to buy shares in the company. To buy you go through certain motions, keep certain laws. You don't have to really *mean* them, just do them. Punch into church like a timeclock—it insures good standing.

"Play the game and you get paid. The pay is grace. Build up a big bank roll. The boss, God, keeps close tabs on your account. When the business deal is over, he checks out the books; if you have enough in the

old grace-roll you get a cool place called heaven. (At least everyone says it's cool.)

Paul recognized the danger that such a bookkeeping attitude could arise. If his Galatian Christians thought they could be saved simply by keeping the law, they were dangerously close to thinking they could *buy* God's friendship and *buy* their own salvation.

They may not have put it so crudely, but the Judaizers who arrived in Galatia were preaching that the only way to be saved was to keep the Jewish law.

The Letter to the Galatians

When Paul heard that the Galatians were accepting the Judaizers' version of the gospel, he was furious.

Read Galatians 1:1–10 and notice that he is so angry that after the blessing he goes right to the issue at hand. He does not even take time to include his usual thanksgiving section.

In the rest of the letter, Paul uses every argument he can think of to make the Galatians understand that salvation is not bought simply by obeying the law; that Christians are free from the Jewish law; that faith in Jesus is essential for salvation.

In the first two chapters of Galatians, Paul presents four good arguments for his contention that salvation is not something to be bought by observing the law but something given freely by God.

First Argument (Galatians 1:11–244)
Paul begins by establishing the fact that his gospel is the only true gospel because he received it directly from Jesus and not from any mere human.

Read Galatians 1:11—24 and explain the line of argument Paul uses to prove that he did not receive his gospel from anyone other than Jesus. From what we read here, what evidence do we have that Paul himself did not buy God's friendship and his faith in Christ but received it as a gift?

Second Argument (Galatians 2:1—5)
Paul's second argument comes from a meeting he had in Jerusalem with the other apostles. There it was decided that Paul's companion Titus, who was a Greek and a Gentile, did not have to observe the Jewish law of circumcision.

Read Galatians 2:1—5 and answer the following: If Titus, a Gentile, did not have to submit to circumcision, what is Paul telling the Gentile Galatians who are giving in to the Judaizers' insistence that they have to keep the law in order to be saved?

Third Argument (Galatians 2:6—10)
Paul's third argument supports his position against giving in to the Judaizers. Paul points out to his readers that after fourteen years of preaching his gospel of faith in Jesus, Church leaders in Jersualem found nothing wrong with his gospel.

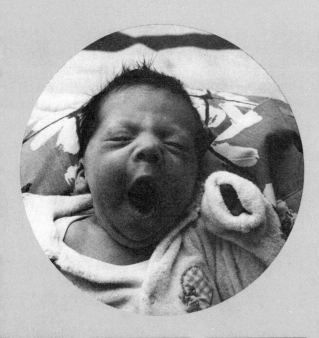

eating with the Gentiles out of fear of offending these strict law-observers.

Paul uses the incident as an argument in favor of his gospel that salvation is freely given by God though faith in Jesus. He argues that Peter, a Jew and the head of the community, was right in the first place when he ate non-kosher food with Gentiles. By doing so publicly he showed that he was not bound to the Jewish law. Why then should they, Gentile Galatians, who were not even Jews to begin with, feel bound to obey the Jewish law?

■ Read Galatians 2:11–14. Discuss how this argument strengthens Paul's claim that salvation depends on faith in Jesus and not on strict observance of the law.

More Evidence
In Galatians 3:1–5, Paul reminds the Galatians that they were Gentiles at the time when they became Christians. As Gentiles they certainly had not been obeying Jewish laws and customs. Perhaps they were even unaware of them. Therefore they were converted not because they kept the law, but because they believed the gospel which Paul preached. The important thing was their faith in Jesus.

In Galatians 3:6–14, Paul supports his teaching with statements from Genesis. Read Genesis 15:1–6 and 17:1–14 for answers to the following questions which make up Paul's line of reasoning:

● Was it because Abraham had himself circumcised or because he believed what God promised him that God was pleased with him and accepted him? (Genesis 15:6.)
● Did God give Abraham the promise of salvation before or after he demanded circumcision?
● What does Genesis 17:10-14 say is the purpose of circumcision?

Read Galatians 2:6–10 and explain how this argument supports Paul's claim that his gospel, not that of the Judaizers, is the correct gospel.

Fourth Argument (Galatians 2:11–14)
Paul's fourth argument comes from a disagreement he had with the great apostle Peter.

When Paul came to Antioch, a city in northern Syria, he discovered that Peter, Barnabas, and other Jewish Christians had been disregarding the Jewish law by eating non-kosher foods with the Gentiles. However, when the Judaizers came along, Peter and the others stopped

■ Explain how Paul's use of the story of Abraham in Galatians 3:6-14 is a valid argument that faith in Jesus is a free gift from God and is not something bought by observance of the law.

Freedom from/Freedom for

The thought of what civilization would be like if we were not subject to law makes some people shudder. They see a world of violence, injustice, and terrorism. They argue, as a consequence, that Paul does not really mean what he says in chapters 5 and 6 of Galatians. Yet Paul does mean exactly what he says: Christians are free from the law; they do not need the law. Those who understand what Paul really has in mind agree with him completely when he uses the words "Christian," "law," and "freedom." If we understand the reasoning behind the following statement we will also understand the meaning of Paul's point that Christians are not bound by the law: It is true to say that if Christians did not cheat, steal, or lie, there would be no need for Christians to obey laws that say do not cheat, steal, or lie.

As we can see in Paul's message to the Galatians, Christians are free *from* the law *for* a higher purpose. Read Galatians 5:13–15 and explain what Paul wants his "free-from-the-law" Christians to be free for. Spirit-guided Christians do not need laws because, as Paul says: **the Spirit produces love, joy, peace, patience, kindness, goodness, faithfulness, humility, and self-control. There is no law against such things as these (Galatians 5:22).**

For some Christians the law remains necessary as a reminder that they are not yet what they should be.

■ Towards the end of his letter to the Galatians Paul includes a practical reminder. He warns the Galatians that no one can deceive God. What a person really is determines what his or her reward will be. Read Galatians 6:7–10. Discuss to what extent Paul's point makes good sense to you.

Letter to the Romans

When Paul wrote to the Christians in Rome, about 58 A.D., the city was the capital of the world, the heart of civilization, and the center of political power. Rome was to the ancient world what Peking, Washington, and Moscow are to the modern world.

Paul established churches at Thessalonica, Corinth, Philippi, and the district of Galatia and wrote letters to the Christians in those cities.

However, if we look at the map of churches on page 38 we do not find a church symbol at Rome. The Christian community there had already been established when Paul wrote his letter. Why then, if Paul did not found the Roman Church, did he write his longest and most theological letter to the Christians in Rome?

Paul had intentions of visiting Rome on his way to Spain, and we presume, but are not certain, that he was afraid that others

would get to Rome ahead of him and cause him the same grief as in Corinth and Galatia (cf. Romans 1:10-15 and 15:23-28). Fearing this, Paul wrote ahead to introduce himself and his gospel to the Romans before visiting the great capital.

A Theological Mount Everest
Every year hundreds of mountain climbers risk their lives. They live dangerously because they like the challenge. Asked why he wanted to climb Mount Everest, the highest mountain in the world, an experienced mountain climber replied: "Because it's there!"

For theologians, Paul's letter to the Romans is "there". It is the theologian's Mount Everest, one of the greatest theological challenges in the world. Saint Augustine, a great theologian, got confused reading Romans. Even some of our best modern scholars still find Romans very complicated. Mount Everest has been climbed. Romans is still waiting to be conquered.

Mountains are not conquered with a single leap, and Paul's letter to the Romans will not be conquered with a single reading. The long journey to the top begins as it ends—with a few brave steps. In asking you to study Romans, we would like you to take those first brave steps.

Three Systems

A preliminary for taking our first steps in understanding Romans is to realize that Paul is talking about different systems or means of salvation.

Paul begins by stating the central truth of salvation, which reminds us of his message to the Galatians.

I have complete confidence in the gospel; it is God's power to save all who believe, first the Jews and also the Gentiles. For the gospel reveals how God puts people right with himself: it is through faith from beginning to end. As the scripture says, "The person who is put right with God through faith shall live."

Romans 1:16-17

After such a forceful statement, Paul explains that the pagan and the Jewish systems of salvation do not work because, as the old saying puts it: "You cannot pull yourself up by your own bootstraps." Faith in Jesus, which is Paul's system, consists in letting go of our bootstraps and holding out our arms to God in trust and love—and this system works.

The Pagan System (Romans 1:18-32)

In dealing with the inadequacy of the pagan system, Paul shows that the pagans, despite their confidence in philosophy, do not successfully understand and respond to God's greatness and power. Even though they philosophize about creation and the world around them, most pagans worship all kinds of idols in place of the one true God. They depend on themselves for salvation. Paul's argument is that with Christ the pagans go *away* from God rather than *toward* him.

■ Read Romans 1:18−32. Tell why the pagan way of salvation does not work by explaining what Paul says about:
● God's part in the plan of salvation for the pagans;
● the pagans' response to God's self-revelation;
● the consequences of their choice to reject God.

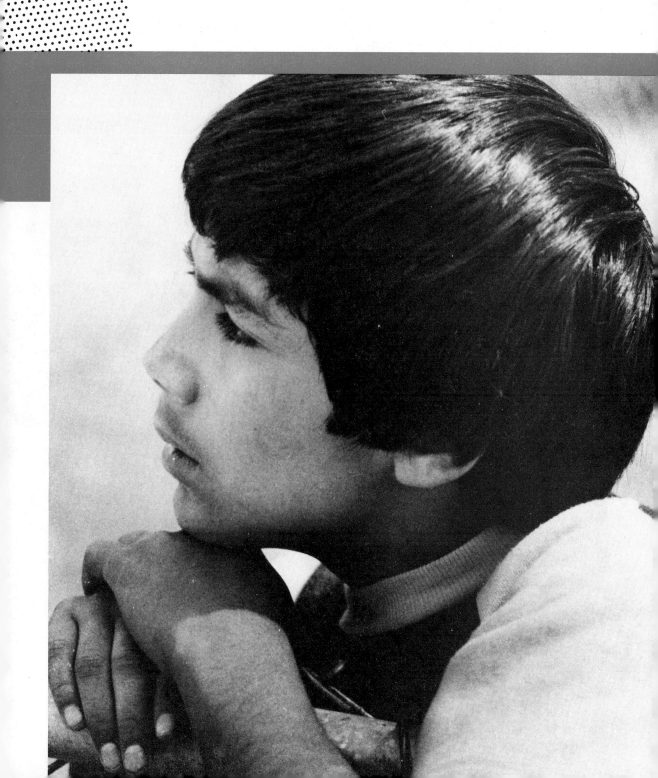

Also explain how this section affirms the Christian belief that:

● God creates everyone with a free will;

● God never violates this freedom by forcing anyone to love and accept him;

● each of us must accept the consequences of our free decisions.

The Jewish System (Romans 2:1-3:20)
Paul continues arguing for his system of salvation by showing that most of the Jews, with their system of justification through the keeping of the law, succeed no better than do the pagans. They do not fall into immorality and corruption like the pagans, but neither do they keep the law they boast so much about.

The Jewish system comes down to the
same error: dependence on self rather
than on God for salvation. This is
bootstrap theology rather than faith
theology.

Paul's System (Romans 3:21-26)
Paul summarizes his system of salvation
through faith in Jesus in Romans 3:21-26.
Read this section and note the parts of
this passage which express the following
key elements of Paul's system of
salvation:
- Jews and Gentiles alike are sinners;
- Jews and Gentiles alike can be put
right with God through faith in Jesus;
- Jesus saves through his death on
the cross.

The DNA Molecule

Faith for Paul means trusting God. Being "put right by faith" means God loves people so much that he gives to those who trust him the gift of sharing in his life. A good way to understand the importance faith has in Paul's system is to compare it with the DNA molecule.

In the early 1950s, two scientists, James Watson and Francis Crick, helped us to understand the mystery of the DNA molecule, the chemical carrying the universal genetic code. Even though they could not see, touch, or photograph it, Watson and Crick figured out correctly what it looked like, how it worked, and why it was so fantastically important.

The DNA molecule is important because it contains the genetic code which provides complete instructions for all the other cells in our bodies. It literally runs the show in our physical life. It tells our cells what shape, size, and weight we are to be. It determines the color of our eyes, the size of our nose, and the length of our legs. When we get sick, it sends out instructions to find the disease, repair the damage, and create new cells. It is the wonder molecule. For discovering it, Watson and Crick received the Nobel prize in 1953.

Faith may be compared to the DNA molecule of people's spiritual life. Paul states that without faith nothing happens. With it a person begins to live a life of trust in God and becomes alive with love for others.

When that happens, whatever good works are done are done not to *earn* salvation as a reward, but rather, to love God in return.

Consider how important faith and trust are in our own lives. How would we feel if we could trust no one to be concerned about us, care for us, and worry about us?

We might say, or at least think, "We can get along by ourselves." But with a little thought we would most likely realize that even for our physical and psychological life we need to depend on and trust others. For our spiritual life, there is no other way. If we do not trust God, we are left tugging at our bootstraps. We never get off the ground, religiously speaking.

Ask yourself: "Do I really believe God loves me? Can I really trust him to be concerned about me at all times no matter how imperfect I am or how often I may turn from him?"

Love, Sin, and the Law (Romans 5–8)

In the second part of Romans Paul does two things. First, he shows why God can be trusted (5:1–11 and 8:1–39). Second, he answers the objections to his system of faith in Christ (cf. 6:1,15; 7:7).

Paul says that the reason why we should trust and believe in God is because he loves each of us so much that he sent his only Son to die for us.

■ Read Romans 5:1–11 and 8:1–39. Note especially what Paul says about:
● God's love in sending his Son to save us while we were sinners (5:1–11);
● living according to human nature (8:1–17);
● hope for the future through an indestructible relationship with God (8:18–39).

In terms of Pauls' explanation choose which system makes most sense to you:
● remaining pagan;
● remaining law-observing Jewish Christians;
● following Paul's system of salvation through belief in Jesus.

Explain your choice.

The Jews and Jesus (Romans 9–11)
''How odd of God to choose the Jews!'' Hilary Belloc, an Englishman, coined this mischievous little couplet almost fifty years ago. If Paul had read it, he would have said: ''Not at all so odd of God.''

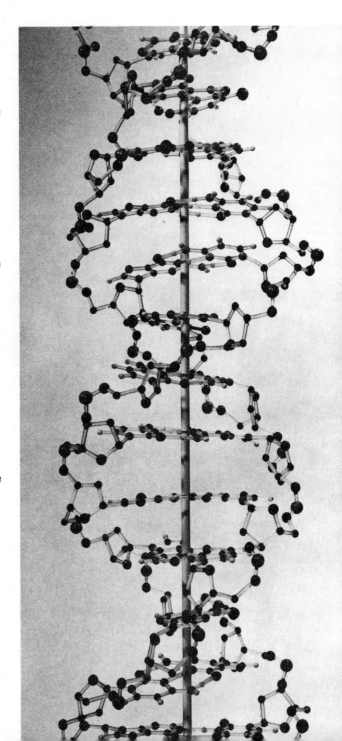

God is free to choose whomever he wants. What Paul found odd was something else. Why, he asked himself, did the Jews not choose Jesus and the good news?

Even today, 1900 years later, Christians may wonder, though not nearly as much as the early Christians, why it happened that the Jewish nation as a whole did not recognize and accept Jesus as the Messiah foretold to them by their prophets.

Indeed Jesus was accepted by many of his fellow Jews—the twelve apostles, hundreds of early disciples and, according to Luke in the Acts of the Apostles, thousands upon thousands of Jews in Jerusalem and Judea. But the fact remains that in the first century many Jews did not accept and believe in Jesus.

For Paul, who deeply loved his Jewish brethren, their rejection of Jesus was heart-breaking. In Romans 9–11, he takes up the problem and explains how God's plan for the salvation of the world includes even so strange an event as Jesus' own people not accepting him.

Their rejection of Jesus, Paul explains, is only temporary. He is of the opinion that when the Gentiles have accepted Jesus the majority of the Jews will come to accept and believe in him as well.

When this will happen, Paul neither says nor knows. But he is sure of God's love for the chosen people. As he says in Romans 11:29: **God does not change his mind about whom he chooses and blesses.**

Life in God's Service (Romans 12–16)

The last part of the letter to the Romans is filled with Paul's advice on how to live a truly Christian life. It is not heavily theological like chapters 1–4, 5–8, and 9–11, and it makes great reading for anyone who would like to be a "Pauline" Christian.

The letter ends in chapter 16 with Paul's greetings to friends and with the beautiful doxology which sums up his Christian belief: **To the only God, who alone is all-wise, be glory through Jesus Christ forever! Amen**.

■ Think back on what Paul has said in his letter to the Romans about God's love for people. What personal experiences led Paul to make and believe in these statements? To what extent do you feel that God's love has touched your life so that you also would want to say: **To the only God, who alone is all-wise, be glory through Jesus Christ forever! Amen.**

Challenges

What is your own evaluation of "bootstrap theology"?

G.K. Chesterton said: "Christianity has not failed, it has not yet been tried." Explain how Paul's vision of a Christianity that goes far beyond anything the law can demand is the kind G.K. Chesterton was talking about.

If you had been a Christian in Rome and never met Paul, to what point of his letter would you have reacted most positively? What point would you most have questioned? Explain.

Prayer
Reflection

For our prayer may we reflect on the personal experience of St. Augustine. Reading Paul's letter to the Romans played an important part in his life.

Somewhat like Paul's conversion on the road to Damascus, Augustine's experience of God in Jesus Christ happened dramatically. In his book entitled *Confessions* he describes it this way:

"For I felt that I was still enslaved by my sins, and in my misery I kept crying, 'How long shall I go on saying "Tomorrow, tomorrow"? Why not now? Why not make an end of my ugly sins at this moment?'

"I was asking myself these questions, weeping all the while . . . when all at once I heard a voice say, 'Take it and read, take it and read' . . . I stemmed my flood of tears and stood up, telling myself that this could only be God's command to open my book of Scripture and read the first passage on which my eyes should fall . . . I seized the book containing Paul's Letters. I opened it, and in silence I read the first passage on which my eyes fell: **'Take up the weapons of the Lord Jesus Christ, and stop paying attention to your sinful nature and satisfying its desires.' (Romans 13:14)**. I had no wish to read more and no need to do so. For in an instant, as I came to the end of the sentence, it was as though the light of faith flooded into my heart and all the darkness of doubt was dispelled."

May we pray:
Lord, open my life to your presence in your Son, Jesus Christ. May I understand the writings of your apostle Paul in the only way really possible—by experiencing your love and by responding to it in faith.
Amen.

6

Paul, the Prisoner

A Letter from Prison

It is difficult to imagine what it is like to be alone and facing death, but we can try.

Think of yourself in a distant country. You have been arrested falsely. You are in prison, and all efforts by your family, friends, and country have failed to get you out. You are told that in a few days you will be executed.

One thought dominates your thinking. You will never be able to see or speak to your family and friends again. You are allowed, however, the opportunity to write one last letter. The situation is that you are clearly threatened with death.

Write this letter. When you have finished answer the following questions. (You may keep the letter and answers confidential if you wish.)

● Did you write to the person(s) you love the most?
● Did you talk about things most important to you?

● Did your letter have some happy sections?
● Did you try to cheer up the person(s) you wrote to?
● Did you say any positive things about your death?
● While writing your letter, were you thinking more of the person(s) you were writing to than of yourself?
● Did writing this letter put your values into clearer focus?

If you answer *yes* to all these questions, your letter was written in much the same style as Paul's letter to the Philippians. Let us study his letter closely.

A Joyful Letter

Paul is in prison when he writes to the Christians in the city of Philippi. We do not know why or where, but we do know that he thinks he may be about to die (1:20−24; 2:23). From his prison cell, Paul writes his most joyful letter.

He writes neither to preach nor to teach. Naturally he is feeling depressed when thinking about his friends and how much he misses them (4:1). He writes to thank the Philippians for all that they have done for him and to share his last thoughts.

Read the entire letter to the Philippians and notice that Paul shows deep affection.

Paul does not complain about the Philippians. Instead he talks about the great help that they have been to him in spreading the gospel and encourages them to continue their good work. He regards them as partners, especially in 1:3−5, 1:30, 2:2, 2:17−18, and 4:3.

Paul does not send Timothy and Epaphroditus to the Philippians as troubleshooters. Rather, he sends them as friends who share his own ideals and experiences (2:19−30, 4:10−20).

■ This letter of Paul differs a good deal from his others which we have seen. Explain something which you find different in it.

Oftentimes when people are about to die they want to talk to someone who will understand the things that matter the most to them. When Paul writes from prison, he writes to the Philippians because they are his favorite Christian community. They understand what he has done with his life. They share his ideals and his sufferings. They will not be shocked when Paul tells them he *wants* to die! (1:21–24).

We do not often meet people who look forward to dying. Death is usually not a welcome event. People about to be executed are not usually bursting with joy. But there are exceptions. St. Ignatius, the bishop of Antioch in Syria in the second century, faced the lions in the arena with the confident thought that he was like wheat about to be ground into flour for the Eucharistic bread.

Death was joyful for Ignatius because it meant for him a passage from something good to something better. As Paul writes to the Philippians, he thinks that death is at his doorstep and he too is joyful!

Read the following verses taken from his letter to the Philippians (1:21–24) and direct your attention to the underlined sections.

For what is life? To me, it is Christ. Death then, will bring more. But if by continuing to live I can do more worthwhile work, then I am not sure which I should choose. I am pulled in two directions. I want very much to leave this life and be with Christ, which is a far better thing; but for your sake it is much more important that I remain alive.

■ What is the "more" Paul wishes to die for? Discuss Paul's reason for wanting to die.

Death with Joy

Paul's letter has a "newsy" tone. He tells what happened to him, how he feels, and what good has come from his being in prison. (See especially 1:12–14.)

We might ask ourselves: Why should a newsy thank-you letter be included among the books of sacred Scripture? If we study Philippians closely, we will see that even though it is a friendly thank-you letter, it is also deeply theological. As a matter of fact, the message of this letter is in some ways the hardest of all for Christians to grasp and accept because it deals with a positive attitude toward death and dying.

Experiencing Death

"Death and dying" has become a new and exciting field of study. In the past many people hesitated to talk about death. Recently, however, people have been speaking about it more openly. One reason has been the testimony of some men, women, and children who apparently had died and yet were revived. One such person is Joanne Costello.

Joanne Costello is a wife and a mother of four children. One day she was in a serious automobile accident. After the rescue squad got her out of her car, in which she had been pinned for several hours, she was rushed to the hospital.

For two weeks, the doctors did not know whether she would live or die. Then she took a turn for the worse. Her husband was called in and told that she had only a few minutes to live. Apparently she then died. The doctors, however, made one last attempt to bring her back to life.

While the doctors were working to revive her, Joanne claims that she had the experience of leaving her body, watching the doctors work over her, then going down a long dark hall with a bright light shining at its end. As she drew near the light, a voice said to her: "Joanne, you must go back to your husband and children."

She remembers begging the voice to let her stay because she felt so peaceful and joyful in this place. But the voice once again said: "You must go back because I have plans for you on earth. I want you to do my work." Then she recalls returning to her body and responding to the doctors' efforts to revive her. Joanne Costello is sure that her experience was a glimpse of God and heaven. From that day on she has never feared death and looks forward to the day she will return to "the other world."

■ How do you react when persons like St. Paul and Joanne Costello say that they not only do not fear death but actually welcome it? To what extent does their Christian faith influence their attitude?

The Important Things

It is said that people who come close to their death see their past life flash before their eyes like a movie. Apparently what flashes before Paul's eyes, however, is not the past but the future.

Paul is thinking about what will happen to the Philippians when he is gone. He tells them how much he loves them and he talks to them about his deepest concerns.

Paul's first concern is the spreading of the Good News of Jesus. The miles he traveled and the sufferings he underwent have not discouraged him from wanting everyone to know the Good News. Since he thinks he is about to die, he asks his closest friends, the Philippians, to carry on his work.

■ Read Philippians 1:1—8 and 1:12—14 and discuss how much it means to Paul that the Philippians continue to share the gospel with others.

Paul's second concern is that the Philippians make progress, day by day, in becoming more and more like Christ. He says: **Now, the important thing is that your way of life should be as the gospel of Christ requires . . . (1:27).**

Paul sums up his idea of being worthy of being called a Christian in the following words:

Don't do anything from selfish ambition or from a cheap desire to boast, but be humble toward one another, always considering others better than yourselves. And look out for one another's interests, not just for your own.
Philippians 2:3—4

To make sure that the Philippians understand what he means by **looking out for one another's interests,** Paul tells them: **the attitude you should have is the one that Christ Jesus had (2:5).**

A Hymn to Christ Jesus
Paul then quotes, in Philippians 2:6—11, a hymn about Jesus sung by the early Christians. Because of its beauty and its importance as a piece of early Christian literature, we will examine it in parts, offering comments and questions in between.

He always had the nature of God,
     but he did not think that by force he should try to become equal with God.

Suppose that the Incarnation had happened this way: Jesus becomes man as a great conqueror. He goes throughout the world exercising his power as God and forces everyone to accept him as their savior and ruler.

He lays down rules and commandments and demands that they be strictly obeyed so that all people will act in a right and just way toward each other.

Jesus could have acted this way and he could have ruled this way. He could have forced his "Godness" on people and made them subject to him. It would have been the easy way.

**Instead of this, of his own free
will he gave up all he had,
and took the nature of a
servant.
He became like man
and appeared in human
likeness.**

Jesus came into the world in humble surroundings. When he preached the Good News he did not say: "I am God. I created you. Listen to me. I know all the answers." He was divine and equal to God the Father. Yet instead of seeking to be treated and served as Lord and Master of the world, he served others.

**He was humble and walked the
path of obedience all the
way to death—
his death on the cross.**

Jesus is God, the Lord of heaven and earth, the ruler of all. Yet he allowed himself to be arrested, mocked, crowned with thorns, spit on, stripped of his clothes, and nailed to a cross.

Jesus had the power to put a stop to all this. But he did not use his divine power precisely because he came to earth to show his love for all people, even if it meant giving up his life in this terrible fashion. As we shall see when we get to John's Gospel, Jesus meant what he said when he declared: **"The greatest love a person can have for his friends is to give his life for them"** (John 15:13).

**For this reason God raised him
to the highest place above
and gave him the name that
is greater than any other
name.**

The Father's plan for Jesus did not end with his death on Good Friday. Recall what Paul had said to the Christians in Corinth about Jesus' resurrection and our own. How important do you think it is for Christian faith that in our thinking we always join together death and resurrection—and not just end with death?

And so, in honor of the name of Jesus
    all beings in heaven, on earth,
      and in the world below
will fall on their knees,
and all will openly proclaim
    that Jesus Christ is Lord,
  to the glory of God the Father.

This hymn reaches its climax in these final verses (Philippians 2:10–11). They say something about Jesus and they say something about us. With regard to Jesus, they attribute to him the name "Lord," which in the Hebrew Scriptures was reserved for Yahweh alone. Jesus is Lord, the center of the universe, the focal point of human history.

With regard to ourselves, the hymn tells us indirectly that the pattern of Jesus' life should be the pattern of our own. We too are called to go through our own deaths and resurrections. The "deaths" occur when we put ourselves out for others at a cost to ourselves. The "resurrections" are the times of growth which we experience in our relationship with God and with others. They all prepare us for our own final death *and* resurrection. In this way we **proclaim that Jesus Christ is Lord, to the glory of God the Father.**

What the World Could Be

To help us understand what Paul meant by being humble like Jesus, reflect upon the following questions:

● What kind of family life would we have if all members of families thought first of others?

● What would the world of labor be like if all employers were concerned more for the welfare of their employees and less with making money for themselves?

● What would society be like if all doctors, lawyers, teachers, politicians, and others thought first of the people they serve and second of their own interests?

▪ We may be tempted to say: all this sounds nice, but that's not the way things are—I have to watch out for number one, myself.

In what way does the teaching of Paul to the Philippians face this temptation directly? How did Paul by his own example respond to such a temptation?

Running with Christ (Philippians 3—4)

In Philippians 3:2—21, Paul talks about another way to grow in Christ. He shares with his readers what faith in Christ means to him:

I reckon everything as complete loss for the sake of what is so much more valuable, the knowledge of Christ Jesus my Lord. For his sake I have thrown everything away; I consider it all as mere garbage, so that I may gain Christ and be completely united with him.

Philippians 3:8—9

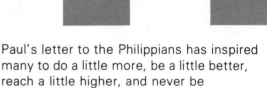

He then encourages his friends to have Jesus as their goal and to keep running with him. He cautions them about being sidetracked by false teachers (cf. 3:12–21).

Finally, in Philippians 4:8, Paul suggests a wonderful way to keep running with Christ. He says:

In conclusion, my brothers, fill your minds with those things that are good and that deserve praise: things that are true, noble, right, pure, lovely, and honorable.

Paul's letter to the Philippians has inspired many to do a little more, be a little better, reach a little higher, and never be satisfied with being just a "run-of-the-mill" kind of Christian.

■ We have now studied sections of Paul's seven letters. Using what we know about Paul and his inspired message, work on the following projects:

● Take a map of the United States or the world. From newspapers, magazines, and your memory write on the map with a brightly colored pen human situations found in various areas of the world today which need to be remedied.

● Now plan a missionary trip for Paul. With a pen of another color circle one location for Paul's headquarters and draw arrows indicating the order of his journeys.

● Briefly outline who he will be speaking to at each place and what his message will be.

It is easy to recognize a situation which has to be remedied. But for us to take part in the cure is more difficult.

Recall the situations you mentioned above and the messages you felt might help remedy them. Discuss ways in which you might take part in helping the message reach one of the groups.

Other Christian Scriptures

When people think about the Christian Scriptures, most often they think of:

● the four gospels and the Acts of the Apostles, which we will study in the second half of this book;

● the seven authentic letters of St. Paul, which we have just studied;

● the letters written by Paul's followers in his name, e.g., 2 Thessalonians, 1 and 2 Timothy, Titus, Ephesians, and Colossians, and the letter to the Hebrews, which we will not have time to study in this book.

But there is even more to the Christian Scriptures. There are: two letters written by disciples of St. Peter, three letters by disciples of St. John, two very short letters attributed to St. James and St. Jude respectively, and the strange apocalyptic book, called Revelation, attributed to St. John. Scholars date these writings to between 75 and 100 A.D.

These other writings of the Christian Scriptures are all inspired, just as are the authentic letters of St. Paul and the four gospels. We recommend, therefore, since we do not have space to treat them in this book, that these other Christian Scriptures be read at your leisure.

Challenges

When Paul writes to the Philippians, he believes he is about to die. In such a situation, people are especially honest about what they want to say. Of what Paul said, did anything surprise you? Did he omit anything that you may have expected him to say? Give specific examples.

List ways Paul suggests to grow in Christ. Which do you find has the most meaning for you? Explain.

Think of the seven Pauline letters we have studied. List the central message from each. Which do you think most needs repeating in our world? Explain.

Prayer
Reflection

A time for change is a time for taking
inventory. When we move into a new
room or a new house we ask ourselves:
"What will I take with me? What will I
discard?"

For Paul, his approaching death gave him the
opportunity to take stock of his whole life.
He expressed his inventory of personal
values in these strong words:

**I reckon everything as complete loss for
the sake of what is so much more
valuable, the knowledge of Christ
Jesus my Lord. For his sake I have thrown
everything away; I consider it all as
mere garbage so that I may gain Christ
and be completely united with him.**
Philippians 3:8–9

May we pray:
Lord, help me to take this occasion to make
a small inventory of my own personal
values. May I have the wisdom to see
things for what they are really worth. May I
have the courage to cultivate what has
true value and to discard or at least put in its
place what I have over-esteemed. Finally,
may I experience the joy and freedom
which come with living out such an
inventory. Amen.

7 Introduction to the Gospels

Pyramids and Gospels

2850 B.C.—a thousand years before Abraham—the dawn of civilization! The Egyptians have just completed the great pyramid of Cheops to enshrine their dead Pharoah. Year after year, thousands of human slaves have quarried granite, shaped it into blocks, transported the blocks 500 miles down the Nile river, and put them into place to construct the great marvel we call a pyramid.

Almost 3000 years later—the first century A.D.—the dawn of Christianity! Matthew, Mark, Luke, and John have constructed monuments we call gospels—literary monuments whose words enshrine but the living Christ!

"What," you may ask, "have pyramids and gospels in common?" More than you might think. Look at it this way. First of all, both pyramids and gospels need quarries for construction material. Without quarries, there would be no stone to shape into building blocks. Without shaped building blocks, Egyptian architects would be unable to construct pyramids.

It is the same for the four gospels. Without Jesus, the quarry, there would be no miracles, parables, sermons, and famous sayings to be shaped into stories for the evangelists to use in writing the gospels.

It may help us to see these developments in parallel form. From what has just been said, we can draw similarities between the steps in the construction of a pyramid and a gospel:

Pyramids	Gospel
Quarry	Jesus
Stone	What Jesus said and did
Shaped blocks	Stories about what Jesus said and did

As we read in *Sharing the Light of Faith:* "The books of the New Testament, especially the Gospels, enjoy preeminence as principal witness of the life and teachings of Jesus, the Incarnate Word. Everyone, according to ability, should become acquainted with the infancy narratives, the miracles and parables of Jesus' public life, and the accounts of His passion, death, and resurrection" (#60).

Eyewitnesses and Authors

Envision this situation. At an airport you see a jetliner crash on take-off. You are an eyewitness because you actually saw the event. Reporters interview you and write up the story of the accident for their newspapers, using the information you give them. You are their source.

Almost all writings about historical events follow the same process. However the authors of the gospels lived 1900 years ago, and wrote between 70 and 100 A.D.—some 40 to 70 years after the resurrection—when very few Christians were still alive who had actually seen or heard Jesus personally. Consequently, when Matthew, Mark, Luke, and John wrote their gospels, it was not easy to find or to interview eyewitnesses.

What the evangelists did was to gather together stories about Jesus that people had heard from their parents, from traveling missionaries, and from their church leaders who were either eyewitnesses themselves or had heard about Jesus from eyewitnesses.

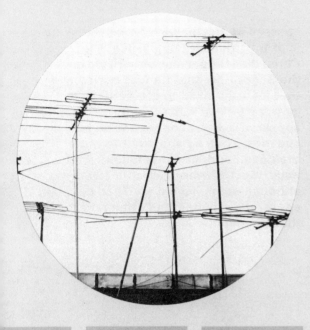

In studying Paul's letters we saw how Paul adapted his one message of faith in Jesus Christ to meet the particular needs and concerns of the Christians in Thessalonica or Corinth or the region of Galatia. The evangelists did something similar. It is because of the special concerns of the Christians in his particular community that:

- Matthew wrote "The Idealist's Gospel";
- Mark wrote "The Realist's Gospel";
- Luke wrote "The Joyful Gospel";
- John wrote "The New-Life Gospel."

This explains to some extent why we find stories in one gospel which are not found in the others, or why we find different versions of the same stories in different gospels.

Some examples are: only Matthew has the story of the Roman soldiers guarding Jesus' tomb (28:11–15); only Luke has the parables of the Lost Son and the Good Samaritan (15:11–32 and 10:25–37); and only John has the story of the raising of Lazarus (11:1–44).

Now look at some different versions of the same stories.

- Compare the Beatitudes of Matthew and Luke (read Matthew 5:3–10 and Luke 6:20–22).
- Compare Matthew's version of the Our Father with Luke's (read Matthew 6:9–15 and Luke 11:2–4).
- Compare the location of Jesus' Beatitude sermon in Matthew with the same sermon in Luke (read Matthew 5:1 and Luke 6:17).

There are numerous other differences which we will explain as we study each evangelist's personal viewpoint of Jesus.

Each evangelist then chose for his gospel the stories and versions of stories he thought would best help his readers understand Jesus.

Different Viewpoints

In studying the four gospels it is important to keep in mind that one gospel differs from another because each evangelist wrote his gospel for a particular Christian community with particular needs. Also, each author brought his own experience and personality to his writing.

The Positive Differences

For many who lived at the time of Pope John XXIII his death came as a great disappointment. They felt that he was a pope of the people, a person who understood their needs and hardships. Pope John had given to thousands of people a fresh and exciting look at Christianity. He showed Christian men, women, and children that they were indispensable to God, to each other, and to our world.

When Pope John died, these people who had come to appreciate their self-worth did not want to lose the encouragement and friendship of this great man of God. They wanted to know more about him and keep his memory with them.

Reporters interviewed Pope John's family and friends. They spoke with the people he ministered to in parishes as a priest, bishop, and cardinal. They even consulted world dignitaries who had met him and had been influenced by him.

As you can imagine, people closest to Pope John, such as his family and close friends, saw him from a different viewpoint than those who knew him as a parish priest or those who knew him as a result of a brief meeting or interview. From the reports of all those interviewed, however, the world came closer to knowing the real Pope John. The differences in viewpoints, when put together, added up to a plus—a clearer picture of this unique pope.

A Living Tradition

In the years between 30 and 58 A.D. when Paul was preaching, traveling, and writing his letters, many people were still alive who had witnessed Jesus' sermons, parables, miracles, and even his passion, death, and appearances after the resurrection.

For example, Paul in the year 55 A.D. describes to the Corinthians how he knows about Jesus' resurrection from others as well as from his own experience. Note how he uses the verbs "receive" and "pass on," which is what we mean by tradition:

I passed on to you what I received, which is of the greatest importance; that Christ died for our sins, as written in the Scriptures; that he was buried and that he was raised to life three days later, as written in the Scriptures; that he appeared to Peter and then to all twelve apostles. Then he appeared to more than five hundred of his followers at once, most of whom are still alive, although some have died. Then he appeared to James, and afterward to all the apostles.

1 Corinthians 15:3–7

Anyone who examines the four gospels carefully will find many stories people were telling about Jesus, many of Jesus' parables retold by his followers, and all kinds of things which the early Christians talked about when they spoke to others about Jesus. One thing is sure, people said a great deal more about Jesus than has been written down in the Christian Scriptures. John says at the end of his Gospel:

Now, there are many other things that Jesus did. If they were all written down one by one, I suppose that the whole world could not hold the books that would be written.

John 21:25

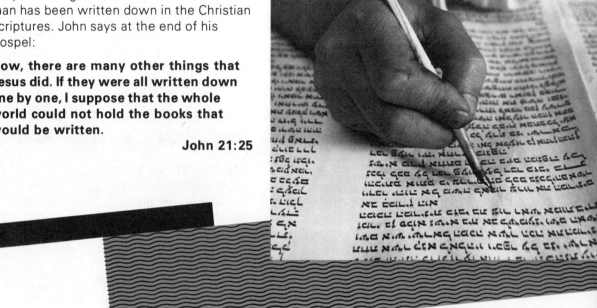

All things considered, the different viewpoints we have about Jesus from the Christian Scriptures are a definite plus; together they give us a wonderful many-sided picture of Jesus and his message of good news.

Basics Which Are Constant

The core of what people were saying about Jesus is found in the gospels of Matthew, Mark, Luke, and John. As a matter a fact, it is from the gospels that we learn the following basics about Jesus in his historical ministry with which we are all familiar:

- Jesus came into the public eye for the first time in Galilee about the year 27 A.D.
- Jesus was a traveling preacher who taught about God, humankind, and the coming of the Kingdom of God.
- Jesus was conscious of a unique personal relationship with God, his Father.
- Jesus was conscious also of a unique authority residing in himself, an authority which gave him the right to call all people to believe in him and follow him, and to demand of people that they place in him their personal destiny and the destiny of all humanity.
- As a teacher Jesus taught through stories called parables.
- Jesus had an extraordinary concern

for the poor, the sick, and the disadvantaged, and he sometimes even worked miracles to help them.

● Jesus insisted that the law of laws for every individual is to love God and to love one's neighbor as oneself. Jesus opposed the abuses of those in authority and as a result was considered by them to be a radical and a revolutionary.

● Because of his teachings, Jesus was brought to his death by the leaders of the organized religion of his nation.

● According to the testimony of his followers, Jesus was seen living again, resurrected from the dead, shortly after his death.

■ Without opening the gospels, make a list of some things which you recall from Jesus' life. Next to each of your recollections, select the item from the above list of basics to which it most closely relates. Which basic of Jesus' life did your memory recall first? Were there any basics for which you had no recollection? Please explain.

Specifics Which Vary

As we study the four gospels, we may notice that the basics are constant but that the specifics vary. To understand why the specifics change we have to understand what a gospel is and how it should be read.

Sharing the truth about Jesus is what a gospel is all about. Between the years 70–100 A.D. many "gospels" were written. But not all were accepted as inspired by God. As a result, most just went out of circulation. With the inspired gospels of Mark, Matthew, Luke, and John it was different. They were faithfully copied and recopied year after year from the time of the authors right down to the present day. Consequently, the four gospels as we have them today are almost the same as the original manuscripts written by the inspired authors themselves.

How to Read a Gospel

The difficulty in understanding the inspired gospels is knowing from what viewpoint each author interprets the truth. To solve this, we have to learn how to read a gospel intelligently.

A wise approach to reading a gospel follows these three steps:

1. read it as dramatized history;
2. follow the underlying movements;
3. know its structure.

Dramatized History

The gospels are neither straight biography nor straight history in the sense that we use these terms. The evangelists make Jesus live for their readers by dramatizing his life. Each gospel is like the script of a play. It is filled with scenes showing what Jesus says and does. From Jesus' words and actions the attentive reader gains an understanding of Jesus, just as the attentive playgoer gains an understanding of the central character around whom a play revolves.

Follow the Movement

Each gospel follows the drama of Jesus' real life story. Historically, Jesus presented himself to his fellow Jews as prophet, messiah, and God's own Son. Some accepted him, others did not. Those who accepted his teachings became the earliest Christians, the beginning of the Church. Some of those who did not had him crucified. The finale of the gospel drama is Jesus' glorious resurrection. The resurrection is the climax of Jesus' life, and it is in the light of the resurrection that all the gospels are written.

It can be said that each gospel follows this movement:
- credentials
- response
- discipleship and the beginning of the Church
- passion, death, and resurrection.

These four categories will help us to follow the movement and development of each gospel as we study it. It will also enable us to see how each author adapted the stories of what Jesus said and did in such a way that each author was able to present his own particular viewpoint and at the same time provide for the special needs of his audience.

Credentials

All four evangelists present the same basic credentials for believing in Jesus as Messiah and Son of God:

- the witness of John the Baptist (for example, Mark 1:1–8);
- the witness of the Holy Spirit (for example, Luke 3:21–22);
- the witness of Jesus' authoritative preaching and miraculous deeds (for example, Matthew 5–7 and 8–9).

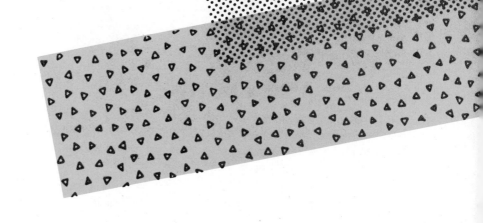

Response

All four gospels show that on the basis of his credentials Jesus had every right to expect to be accepted and believed. All four show that the apostles and many others gave a positive response to Jesus' credentials. Others did not. For example, a positive response would be Matthew 16:13—19, and a negative response would be Mark 2:1—3:6.

Discipleship

All four gospels show Jesus turning away from those who refuse to accept him, and concentrating on his disciples who believe in him. They show Jesus teaching his disciples how to model their lives after his.

Passion, Death, Resurrection

All four gospels tell the dramatic story of Jesus' arrest, trial, crucifixion, death, and resurrection. This was how Jesus' life ended and began again. All four gospels tell the same basic story but with different slants according to each evangelist's inspired theological interpretation of these most momentous events in the history of the world.

Look over each evangelist's retelling of the last days of Jesus on earth. Notice the length of each account. Notice especially, by reading the titles throughout these accounts, how each author emphasizes and elaborates different aspects of the events.

Know the Structure

By having a sense of each gospel's structure we can better appreciate the gospels as individual literary works. And we will find it much easier to understand each evangelist's specific message about Jesus.

Ready to Begin

We now have some understanding of the fundamental principles for reading a gospel, namely:

- reading the gospel as a dramatized history;
- knowing the movement of the gospel according to its four steps: credentials; response; discipleship; crucifixion, death, and resurrection.
- knowing the structure of the gospel.

Let us now apply these principles to our study of the gospels according to Matthew, Mark, Luke, and John.

Challenges

When the priest or deacon reads the gospel during the Eucharistic liturgy he begins with the words: ''The Holy Gospel according to Matthew (Mark, Luke, or John).'' Why does he say: ''according to . . .''? Why are there different gospels? Why is it to our advantage that there are different gospels?

Explain why the gospels are categorized more properly as dramatized histories of Jesus rather than as biographies of Jesus.

When we compare the gospels we see that they give us accurately the message of Jesus rather than his exact words.
From an historical point of view give reasons why this is so. From a practical point of view explain why the message itself is more important than the exact words.

Prayer
Reflection

Some things come along in our lives which we don't really plan but which can make a big difference for us: a chance to be in a play, the arrival of a new class member who becomes a close friend, a setback in our family which makes us rethink our lifestyles. That I am using this book on the Christian Scriptures now is a choice that someone else has made for me, yet it provides an opportunity for me to think, to grow, to become different. This is true especially now as we begin to encounter the person of Jesus in the gospels.

What can happen when we encounter Jesus? Sister Jane Marie Richardson describes it in this way:

"In discovering Jesus, freedom prevails; he coerces no one. Jesus simply allows more and more of his person and mission to be understood according as those who approach him are hospitable or hostile. The words of revelation are not dictated by him, but discovered by those who interact with him. He draws forth from them their own thinking and then confirms or corrects it as it echoes or not what he knows about himself."

May we pray, borrowing some words of an apostle to the poor, Archbishop Helder Camara of Brazil:

> Come Lord!
> Do not smile and say
> you are already with us.
> Millions do not know you
> and to us who do,
> what is the difference?
> What is the point of your presence
> if our lives do not alter?
> Change our lives,
> shatter our complacency.
> Make your word flesh of our flesh,
> blood of our blood
> and our life's purpose.
> Take away the quietness
> of a clear conscience.
> Press us uncomfortably.
> For only thus that other peace is made,
> your peace.
> Amen.

8

Mark: Realist's Gospel

The Challenge of Reality

As humans we have to face reality, evaluate situations for ourselves, and take responsibility for the choices we make. Less and less do others—parents, teachers, authorities—make decisions for us. Today we are launched younger and earlier on the way to becoming fully responsible for our own lives and actions.

Facing reality and making constructive decisions frequently brings us suffering. When we choose to be different from the crowd we experience the hurt of being laughed at, misjudged, excluded from the group, and even suspected by friends. Running away may be easy. Facing reality takes courage.

■ From your own experiences examine the effort involved and the encouragement needed to face the realities of becoming a mature person. List several experiences in which you or someone you know faced difficult situations. Explain why they were difficult to face. Discuss the consequences which had to be accepted for deciding to face reality.

The Realist's Gospel

Facing reality is a lifelong challenge. The readers of the gospel according to Mark were not exempt from this challenge.

In Mark's time, it was par for the course for Christians to be ostracized from their civic community, for non-Christian husbands and wives to abandon their Christian spouses, for political and religious leaders to have Christians beheaded, stoned to death, and even at times thrown to the lions in the arena. In those days it was probably just as hard to be different as it is today.

If the early Christians lived in our time, they would probably picket for their religious rights, bring injustices to the courts, and hold rallies and religious marches for freedom.

But in Mark's time, the only support Christians had came from their belief in Christ and from the mutual help Christians could give one another. Mark could see that his fellow Christians needed his support to remain faithful to Christ and to withstand persecution.

Facing reality is what Mark's gospel is all about. He wants his readers to understand, accept, and face the hardships and suffering of Christian life. He pulls no punches. He encourages his readers, but clearly says that they have to suffer for the privilege and joy of being Christian.

As far as we know, Mark was the first of the four evangelists to write a gospel. He wrote around the year 75 A.D., some 10 to 15 years after Paul's last letter. We will begin our study of the gospels with his work.

- Jesus teaches and acts with authority.
- Apostles follow Jesus.
- Synagogue leaders reject him and plot his death.

B: 3:7-6:6
- Jesus teaches and acts with authority.
- Some accept and others reject Jesus.

C: 6:7-8:30
- Jesus multiplies the loaves and disputes with the Pharisees.
- The apostles recognize him as the Messiah.

Part Two: Discipleship — 8:31-10:52

A: 8:31-9:29
- Disciples must follow Jesus.
- Disciples must trust Jesus.

B: 9:30-10:31
- Disciples must sacrifice themselves for others.
- Disciples will be rewarded.

C: 10:32-52
- Disciples must serve others rather than themselves.
- Disciples must not be like those who lord it over others.

Part Three: The Last Week — 11:1-16:8

A: 11:1-13:37
- The crowds praise Jesus.
- Synagogue leaders reject him.

B: 14:1-15:47
- Jesus' passion and death.

C: 16:1-8
- Jesus' resurrection.

■ Analyze the outline of Mark's Gospel below. Pick out the sections which form the movement of the gospel:
- credentials
- response
- discipleship and the beginning of the Church
- the passion, death, and resurrection.

Mark: The Realist's Gospel — A Structural Outline

Prologue — 1:1—13
  A. Mark's Testimony to Who Jesus Is
  B. Foreshadowing of What Is to Come
Part One: Credentials and Response — 1:14—8:30
  A: 1:14-3:6

Motivation

Few people make choices which cause hardship without believing that the decisions are worth the suffering they bring.

■ Recall the first exercise of this chapter. Analyze the motivation that prompted you or your peers to face the realities and the consequences of your decisions.

For example, was the motivation:
● fearing punishment?
● knowing that it was right?
● seeing that your self-worth and self-respect was at stake?
● other reasons?

Try to describe the motivation behind each decision.

Mark's Motivation

Jesus is Mark's motivation for accepting the hardships of Christianity. Mark, like Paul, thinks no suffering is too great for Jesus' sake.

Mark does not want his own word to be the sole basis of his readers' acceptance of Jesus. He reminds them of Jesus' credentials.

■ Read Mark 1:1-13 (the prologue) and record on a separate sheet of paper what each witness says about Jesus.
● Mark himself (1:1)
● John the Baptist (1:2−8)
● the Holy Spirit (1:9−10)
● God the Father (1:11)

A more impressive list of witnesses and testimonies would be difficult to come by! In 1:14−8:30 Mark piles evidence upon evidence to reinforce Jesus' credentials. But it is rare that anyone is accepted by everyone. Jesus is no exception. Some believe in him, others reject him.

■ Read Mark 1:14-8:30 and look for the episodes that show:
● Jesus as the Messiah and Son of God;
● those who accept Jesus' credentials;
● those who reject Jesus' credentials.

It Takes Time

It takes time to come to trust and believe in someone. It was no different for the apostles and disciples of Jesus. Their belief didn't come like magic:
● first they followed. . . (1:16−20; 2:13−14; 3:13−19).
● then they listened though they did not understand. . . (4:13; 4:34; 4:40−41; 6:45−52; 7:17−23; 8:14−21).

The above passages show how realistic Mark is in pointing out to his audience that it takes time to put one's faith in someone, even to have faith in God.

Beginning to Believe

At Caesarea Philippi, Jesus asks his apostles who people think he is. They tell him that some think he is John the Baptist; some, Jeremiah; some, Elijah or one of the Prophets.

Then Jesus asks them point-blank: **"Who do you say I am?"** Peter speaks for all the apostles and says: **"You are the Messiah" (cf. 8:27–30)**.

■ Look once again at the outline of part I of Mark's gospel on page 115 dealing with credentials and response. Explain why Peter's four words **"You are the Messiah"** are the climax of this whole section.

The Good Soil (Mark 4:1–20)

As we have seen in our study of the Pauline letters, Paul presented Jesus' credentials and many of the Jews rejected them. Mark recalls Jesus' parable of the sower (who represents Jesus himself) and the seed (which represents Jesus' message) as a way of explaining why some people continue to reject Jesus and his message.

■ Read 4:1–20 and in your own words explain Mark's teaching on what a person must do in order to accept Jesus and why some people do not accept him.

Facing Challenges

An aspirin for a headache, an airconditioner for the heat, or a vacation trip to "get away from it all."

People have always tried to avoid suffering. Mark's audience was no exception. Many of them found being rejected and persecuted for their faith difficult to accept. Others wanted to escape by saying that since Jesus had already suffered and died to save them, they could just sit back and do nothing.

Mark gives them no aspirin, no airconditioner, no vacation. He tells them the harsh reality of discipleship—in some ways they will suffer and may be persecuted as Jesus was.

Mark presents his message in basically three steps:
- disciples must serve and suffer;
- disciples must have faith in God in order to live as Jesus lived;
- disciples will be rewarded.

God's Way (Mark 8:31—9:29)
Mark begins his teaching about true discipleship with a sobering episode. It takes place as Jesus and the apostles set out for Jerusalem, where Jesus knows he is going to die. As they travel along the road, Jesus tries to instruct the apostles in the necessity of following his way of life. But each time he brings up the subject of suffering and death his disciples ignore what he says and insist on talking foolishly about the high places they expect in his glorious messianic kingdom (cf. 8:31ff, 9:30ff, 10:32ff).

The first time Jesus mentions suffering, Peter tries to get him off the topic. Jesus corrects Peter and in the presence of his disciples rebukes him severely, saying: **"Get away from me, Satan. . . . Your thoughts don't come from God but from man"(8:33)**. Jesus is saying: the human way is to think suffering is foolishness; God's way is different.

■ Read 8:31—38 and construct a sentence about how definite Mark is about each of the following:
- Jesus suffering and dying (8:31);
- Jesus wanting no part in running away from suffering (8:32—33);
- about disciples having to follow Jesus in the way of suffering (8:34—38).

Joy in the End (Mark 9:2-13)
Suffering and death is certainly not all there is to true discipleship; there are also joys and rewards. After the hard-to-accept account in 8:31-38, Mark encourages his audience by means of the transfiguration episode.

In this scene Jesus takes three of his apostles to a high mountain. A voice from

heaven says: **"This is my own dear Son—listen to him!"** **(9:7)**. The apostles understand nothing of what is happening. For Mark's readers, however, the story has two meanings:

● The voice from heaven and verses 12 and 13 are a message for them to listen to Jesus' teachings about taking up the cross and following him through suffering and even death if necessary.

● The glorified Jesus, Elijah, and Moses encourage Mark's audience by being signs of the promise of their own resurrection and eternal happiness if they obey the Father and follow Jesus.

■ Mark follows the story of the transfiguration with an incident showing how the apostles are unable to drive out evil. Read 9:14-29 and explain what two things Mark claims are required of disciples who want to imitate Jesus in the way he faces evil and suffering.

The Serving Disciple (Mark 9:30–47)

Sometime later, still on the road to Jerusalem, Jesus tells the disciples once more that he must first suffer and die and then be glorified through the resurrection. Again the disciples do not understand what Jesus so clearly tells them. They avoid the issue and talk about something else. Far from discussing Jesus' suffering, death, and resurrection, they argue about which of them will be the greatest in his kingdom! For the second time, Jesus instructs them on the necessity of suffering.

■ Read 9:30–41 and explain how Jesus' statement that **"Whoever wants to be first must place himself last of all and be the servant of all"** **(9:35)** is a

description of what a true Christian ought to be. Explain also how serving others may involve suffering. Finally, what does Jesus say in verse 41 about those who serve others in his name? As we have seen, Mark has three steps to his argument on facing the realities of discipleship:

- Mark 9:30–40 describes the "suffering servant" disciple.
- Mark 9:41 shows that disciples will be rewarded.
- Finally, in Mark 9:42-47 he presents faith as a crucial element for the loyal servant of Christ. Read 9:42-47 to see the importance Mark places on faith for discipleship.

Mark illustrates the kind of faith which Jesus has in mind by recounting an incident involving Jesus and children. Read 10:13-16 and explain how it helps us to understand the kind of faith true disciples of Jesus should have.

Three Points (Mark 10:17–31)

Now read the story of "The Rich Man" in 10:17–31 and reflect on the following questions:

● How does Jesus' request of the rich young man (verse 21) show that those who follow Jesus will have to make sacrifices?

● How is it evident that the rich young man did not have complete faith and trust in Jesus? How does Mark substantiate his claim in verse 27 that faith is essential for discipleship?

● Which verses describe the joys people experience when they make Jesus central to their lives?

A Hard Pill to Swallow (Mark 10:32–52)

As Jesus and his disciples approach Jerusalem, Jesus repeats for the third time his prediction that he will have to suffer and die. For the third time the disciples fail to get the point. On this occasion, two of them, James and John, acting as if Jesus had said nothing about suffering, ask him for high places in his kingdom. For the third and last time, Jesus patiently instructs them on God's way—the way of suffering.

■ Read 10:32–45 and explain how Mark once again puts across his threefold message:

● Disciples must serve and suffer.

● Disciples must have faith in God in order to live as Jesus lived.

● Disciples will be rewarded.

Damien the Leper

In the imposing courtyard of the new statehouse in Honolulu, there is an unusual statue. It looks like a man, but the face is barely human. The nose is gone. The eyes are sunken. The forehead bulges. The lips are bloated. The hands and feet are blobs.

To the casual tourist, the statue means nothing. To those who know, the statue tells the story of Damien the leper—a man who like blind Bartimaeus "saw" and followed Jesus along the road of suffering (Mark 10:46–52). Damien was a missionary priest on the Island of Oahu in the last half of the nineteenth century. In his spare time, he worked for the lepers on the island of Molokai, visited them, fed them, consoled and encouraged them in their horrible sufferings.

One hundred years ago, there was no cure for leprosy. To live with lepers meant contracting the disease and becoming a leper oneself. It meant being confined to the island of Molokai until death. It meant never going home to family and friends and never again living a normal human life.

Nevertheless, Damien begged his religious superiors to let him work with the lepers on Molokai. In 1873, when springtime came to the islands, he received a letter which stated: "You may stay as long as your devotion dictates."

At first, Damien was careful to avoid contracting the dreaded disease. But he knew he had to face reality. If he was really to help these people, he would have to touch them. He did touch them. He bandaged their sores, bathed their stinking bodies, placed the Eucharist on their decaying tongues, and anointed their swollen foreheads when they were about to die. He even ate the food prepared by their diseased hands.

One day in December, 1884, Damien soaked his feet in extremely hot water. He felt no pain, not even a sensation of heat. He then realized what had happened. He had become a leper!

Five years later, on April 15, 1889, Father Damien DeVeuster died of the disease he dreaded so much. His superiors had said: "You may stay as long as your devotion dictates. . ." Jesus said: **"The greatest love a person can have for his friends is to give his life for them" (John 15:13)**. Damien loved and served unto death for the sake of Christ.

■ If Mark were writing his gospel today how do you think he would use the story of Fr. Damien to put across his threefold message?

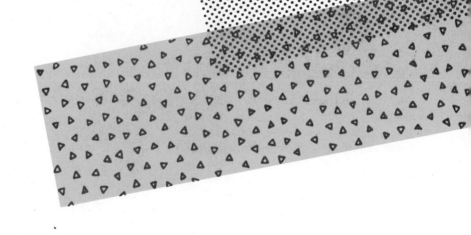

The Last Week (Mark 11–16)

Christians hear part three of Mark's gospel, Jesus' last week, every year during the liturgy of Holy Week.

It begins with Jesus arriving in triumph in Jerusalem. The crowds cheer, claiming to accept him as their king. But Jesus knows better. He tells his apostles, by cursing a fruitless fig tree, that the Jewish leaders are like trees which bear no fruit (11:1–14).

Many of them are using the Temple for their own benefit, allowing moneychangers in the Temple to make themselves rich at the expense of others. Jesus clears out the moneychangers (11:15–26).

The story continues with the Pharisees, Sadducees, and Elders looking for a way to trap Jesus and put him to death (11:27–12:40).

Chapters 14 and 15 tell the story of Jesus instituting the Eucharist at the last supper, praying in the garden of Gethsemane, being arrested, tried by the Sanhedrin, and condemned to death by Pilate, the Roman procurator.

Mark then details the scourging, the crowning with thorns, the way of the cross, the crucifixion, and finally Jesus' death and burial.

The story ends with a glorious reversal. The women go to the tomb early Sunday morning, the first Easter, and find that Jesus has risen from the dead! He is going to Galilee! There, he will rejoin his disciples (16:1-8).

A Meditation

We will not study each section and espisode of part three (Mark 11 – 16) as we did parts one and two. We invite you to read part three prayerfully and to reflect on what Jesus was experiencing during his passion:

- when he was rejected by his own people;
- when the leaders maliciously opposed him;
- when his motives were misunderstood;
- when his apostles abandoned him;
- when Judas betrayed him;
- when he pleaded with his Father to spare him from his passion and death;
- when Peter denied he even knew him;
- when he was mocked and tortured;
- when he was insulted as he hung dying on the cross.

Most of all, think of how Jesus willingly accepted the suffering and death brought on him by his enemies in order to remain faithful to his mission. Consider also how much trust Jesus had in his Father to face all the hardships of his last week on earth. Finally, try to imagine the joy and glory of the resurrection for both Jesus and his disciples.

Challenges

The example of Jesus supplies us with motivation for accepting hardships willingly. State three different ways in which Mark accomplishes this in the structure and content of his "realist gospel."

In his gospel, Mark seems to say: "Don't worry about your reward. God will take care of it. Just be concerned about following Jesus, no matter what." Explain to what extent you agree or disagree with this proposal.

Prayer Reflection

Mark's gospel can help us understand some deep truths or "realities" of human life. May we prayerfully reflect on the following:

- Doing good for others does not always bring an immediate reward. On the contrary, it can bring about, as it did in the case of Jesus, misunderstanding, persecution, physical harm, and even death.
- The evil in others is not driven out by physical force. The only thing that really overcomes evil and changes evil people into good people is love.
- Overcoming evil does not happen easily or automatically. People like Jesus who try to overcome evil by love are frequently persecuted. Only good can overcome evil. Only unselfishness can overcome selfishness.
- Suffering and unselfishness do not go unrewarded by God. This is one of the many meanings of Jesus' resurrection. It is the promise of wonderful things now and in the future for those who follow Jesus.

9 Matthew: Idealist's Gospel

Idealists

Jill Kinmont was a seventeen-year-old champion downhill skier. She was just completing the final competition which would send her to the Olympics as an official member of the U.S. ski team when she had a disastrous fall. She had fallen dozens of times during training, but this fall was different. It broke her back. On the eve of her great dream, she became paralyzed from the neck down . . . for life!

Jill, however, is an extraordinary person. Against all odds, she determined to have a useful life, go to college, get a degree, and teach children.

Filled with frustration but urged on by her ideals and assisted by her family and friends, Jill managed, ever so slowly and agonizingly, first to move a few fingers and then bit by bit to produce tiny movements in her arm. She learned to eat, to write, and to maneuver an electric wheelchair with the assistance of special prosthetic devices.

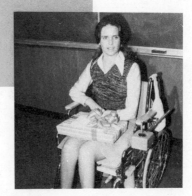

Arming herself with these few resources, she applied for college. Refusal after refusal came back claiming she was not capable of handling college life. Finally, one college admitted her ''on trial.'' With the help of those who cared, she received her degree and is today a successful teacher.

Like Jill Kinmont, Matthew the evangelist is an idealist. He writes his gospel to inspire his readers to aim high, to aim for perfection. He talks about doing God's will and doing it perfectly! There is nothing ordinary about Matthew.

A Grand Staircase

Even the structure of Matthew's gospel has a sense of nobility. It has the symmetry of a grand staircase with stairs running up each side to meet at a central landing.

Matthew's literary structure alternates between *narrative* sections and *instruction* sections, each producing a forceful step upward toward understanding what makes a ''perfect'' disciple—one who will help bring about the Kingdom of God on earth.

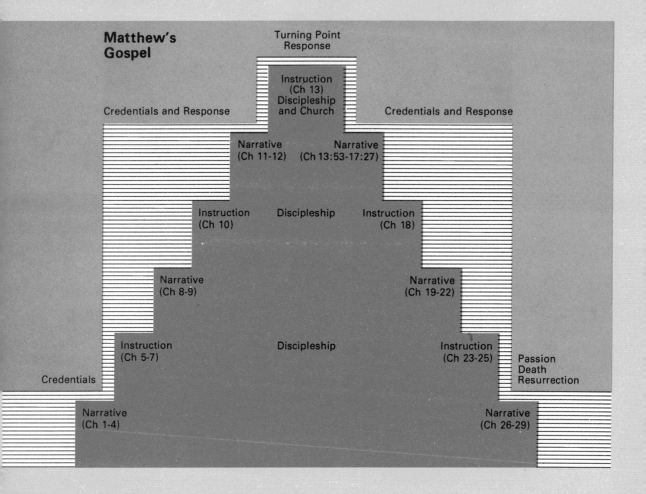

Matthew's Gospel

Turning Point
Response

Instruction
(Ch 13)
Discipleship
and Church

Credentials and Response

Credentials and Response

Narrative
(Ch 11-12)

Narrative
(Ch 13:53-17:27)

Instruction
(Ch 10)

Discipleship

Instruction
(Ch 18)

Narrative
(Ch 8-9)

Narrative
(Ch 19-22)

Instruction
(Ch 5-7)

Discipleship

Instruction
(Ch 23-25)

Passion
Death
Resurrection

Credentials

Narrative
(Ch 1-4)

Narrative
(Ch 26-29)

Look at the structure of Matthew's gospel above. Note that once again we find the four elements which form the movement of the gospel. Note also that each instruction of this gospel centers specifically on discipleship.

In our study of Matthew we will concentrate upon the following sections, which are the heart of his gospel: chapters 1–4; 5:21–48; chapters 8–13; chapter 18; chapters 23–25; 28:18–20.

The First Narrative. (Matthew 1–4)

For Jews, Moses was the ideal leader. He brought them out of slavery and led them through the desert to the Promised Land, where Israel developed into a great nation.

In chapters 1–4, the first narrative section of the gospel, Matthew shows that Jesus is like Moses. This narrative lays the foundation for his next step, the *discourse* in chapters 5–7, where he shows that, although Jesus is like Moses, he is actually infinitely greater than Moses—Jesus speaks with the authority of God.

forty days and nights, eating and drinking nothing (Exodus 34:28).
● After spending forty days and nights without food, Jesus was hungry (Matthew 4:2).

These parallels prepare Matthew's readers to listen to Jesus the way the ancient Israelites listened to Moses. But as Matthew will point out in chapter 5, Jesus is not just another teacher *like* Moses. He is the ultimate authoritative teacher for all humankind, the teacher who speaks with the authority of God and the one who can lead disciples to perfection. Matthew points this out by means of two more parallels:

● **And Moses went up the mountain to meet with God (Exodus 19:3).**
● **Jesus saw the crowds and went up a hill (mountain) (Matthew 5:1).**
● God tells Moses his will in the Ten Commandments (Exodus 20:1–17).
● Jesus tells the people his will in the Sermon on the Mount (Matthew 5:21–48).

The First Instruction (Matthew 5–7)
The Sermon on the Mount is the greatest sermon ever given on discipleship.

Matthew's subject in 5:21–48 is an idealist's delight. He tells what God expects of people at their very best! What God expects is not just surprising, it is overwhelming. In 5:48 Jesus says: **"You must be perfect—just as your Father in heaven is perfect."** Jesus not only wants his followers to be perfect, but in this great sermon he also tells them how to be perfect.

Read chapters 1–4 and the sections of Exodus indicated below. Notice the parallels between Moses and Jesus.

● Moses goes into exile in Midian (Exodus 2:15–17).
● Jesus goes into exile in Egypt (Matthew 2:14–15).
● God tells Moses: **"Go back to Egypt, for all those who wanted to kill you are dead" (Exodus 4:19).**
● God tells Joseph in a dream: **"Get up, take the child and his mother, and go back to the land of Israel, because those who tried to kill the child are dead" (Matthew 2:19–20).**
● **Moses stayed there with the LORD**

God's Will (Matthew 5:21–48)

In 5:21–48 Jesus speaks with the authority of God himself. Jesus says: **"You have heard that people were told in the past. . . . But now I tell you. . . ."** Here Jesus is contrasting his way of life with the Ten Commandments as revealed to Moses.

When God manifested his will to Moses in the Ten Commandments, he asked for the minimum. For example, the fifth commandment said: **Do not commit murder (Exodus 20:13).** Jesus, however, now asks for the maximum: **"Whoever is angry with his brother will be brought to trial" (5:22).** The sixth commandment of the law given to Moses stated: **Do not commit adultery (Exodus 20:14).** Jesus, in the Sermon on the Mount, says: **"Anyone who looks at a woman and wants to possess her is guilty of committing adultery with her in his heart" (5:28).** In the Hebrew Scriptures, God had commanded: **"Love your neighbor as you love yourself" (Leviticus 19:18).** In Matthew, Jesus commands: **"Love your enemies and pray for those who persecute you" (5:44).**

These are examples given by Jesus to explain his message. If we read 5:21–48, we notice that the meaning is clear; Jesus calls upon his followers to go to the roots of moral behavior and do away with anything at all that would lead to not loving God, neighbor, and self perfectly.

In place of roots poisoned by hatred, lust, and dishonesty, Jesus wants us to have roots nourished by love. This love to which Jesus refers is not a romantic love; it is rather an active self-giving love—a love that reaches out to do good to others, friend and enemy alike.

■ Give your opinion of the reality of Matthew's statement: **"You must be perfect—just as your Father in heaven is perfect" (5:48).**

The Second Narrative (Matthew 8–9)

In the Sermon on the Mount, chapters 5–7, Matthew affirmed Jesus' credentials by showing him *speaking* with the authority of God. Read chapters 8–9 and select the sections where Matthew adds to Jesus' credentials by showing him *acting* with divine authority.

The Second Instruction (Matthew 10)

The second instruction has four parts:

● the empowering and the sending of the apostles with authority to do what Jesus did (10:1–15);
● a warning that preaching the gospel will bring hardships (10:16–27);

● encouraging words to hearten the apostles (10:28–33);

● a warning to those who hear the apostles to listen and make a decision for Christ (10:34–42).

■ Read Matthew 10 and describe how the people who try to live by high ideals:

● would be disposed to help others the way the apostles did;

● would probably have to suffer hardships;

● would be truly consoled by Jesus' words in 10:28–33.

The Third Narrative (Matthew 11–12)

The third narrative has three sections which prepare Matthew's readers for the turning point of his gospel:

● 11:2–27: the unbelievers;

● 11:28–12:21: Jesus and the law;

● 12:22–50: once more the believers.

It would take long and detailed study to understand this narrative section completely. We will concentrate only on the theme of the narrative which prepares the way for Matthew's message about discipleship and the Kingdom of God in 13:1–52.

The Unbelievers (11:2–27)

What Matthew does in this section is show Jesus' last efforts to bring the crowds to believe in him.

He begins by bringing John the Baptist back on the scene (11:2–6) and by assuring the crowds that the Baptist is truly a prophet sent by God (11:7–15).

Once he has established that John is a true prophet, he points out how the crowds refuse to listen either to Jesus or to John the Baptist (11:16–24).

Jesus and the Law (11:28–12:21)
In the second part of the narrative Matthew shows that a major difficulty the Jewish leaders have in believing in Jesus is their objection to his compassionate interpretation of the law.

Jesus states that the law is made for people and not the other way around. As we saw when we studied Saint Paul, the Jewish leaders believe that the most important thing for salvation is to obey the law strictly, even if people are sometimes needlessly hurt.

A very beautiful and consoling section of this narrative is 11:28–30. Read these verses and see how Jesus pleads with his listeners to come to him. Two passages which reinforce the theme of Jesus' compassion are found in 12:1–8 and 12:9–14. Read these passages and explain how Jesus shows that his interpretation of the law is based on the compassionate principle that the law is made for people and not the other way around.

Once More the Unbelievers (12:22–50)
In part three (12:22–50), Matthew presents in a different way the same issues he addressed in part one (11:2–27), namely, those who do not believe in Jesus.

■ Recalling all the miracles Jesus had worked so far, how would you explain 12:38 as a perfect example for Matthew's theme that the "unbelievers" do not believe because they choose not to believe and not because of a lack of credentials on Jesus' part?

The Turning Point (Matthew 13)

Listen, if you have ears!
See, if you have eyes!
Much of the crowd and many Jewish
leaders in Matthew's gospel did neither. It is
in chapter 13 that Matthew shows that
he is a realist as well as an idealist. If people
will not believe in Jesus and are
determined to close their ears to his
words and their eyes to his deeds, Jesus
tells them he will as a consequence
turn to those who are open to accept and
understand him. It is on believers and
believers only that he will depend to
spread the message of the Kingdom of God.
Jesus himself said: **"Anyone who is not for
me is really against me; anyone who**

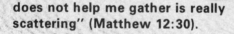

does not help me gather is really scattering" (Matthew 12:30).

The unbelief of the crowds and the synagogue leaders in chapters 11 and 12 sets the stage for chapter 13 and explains why Jesus turned to his disciples. Those who reject him certainly would not be disposed to share the kingdom of God and the message of Jesus' commandment of love. The thirteenth chapter of Matthew consists of seven different parables. *Webster's Seventh New Collegiate Dictionary* defines parable as a: "short fictitious story that illustrates a moral attitude or a religious principle."

▪ Read chapter 13 and find the parables of Jesus which describe the following statements concerning moral beliefs and religious principles. In some cases more than one parable will apply to one statement. Explain your choices.

● God's word is given to everyone, but only some accept it.
● The acceptance of God's word will make the Kingdom of God grow and flourish.
● Heaven is for those who accept and live God's word; hell is for those who refuse.
● The Kingdom of heaven is a priceless possession.

The Fourth Instruction (Matthew 18)

The fourth instruction is addressed to the apostles, but the lesson it teaches is meant for all Christians.

The apostles want to know: **"who is the greatest in the Kingdom of heaven?" (18:1).** Jesus answers by pointing to a little child. Matthew uses this story, as Mark did in 9:33–37, to show that the person who trusts God totally the way a little child trusts his or her parents is the greatest in the Kingdom of heaven. This kind of trust is real faith. The answer seems simple, yet it takes a truly humble person to admit that everything he or she has comes from God. Read 18:6–10 and see how, like Mark (9:42–50), Matthew shows the importance of this kind of faith.

In the rest of the chapter, Jesus talks about two things. First, the duty of the apostles as leaders of the people of God to seek out sinners and bring them back to God (18:10–14). Secondly, Jesus knows that his disciples will not always succeed in living up to his teachings. Read what he says about the situation in the Parable of the Unforgiving Servant (18:21–35).

■   In your own words explain the meaning of this parable and also what lesson we as Christians can derive from Jesus' words to Peter: forgive "seventy times seven" times.

The Fifth Instruction (Matthew 23–25)

People frequently find it easier to explain what they are against than what they are for. In the Sermon on the Mount, chapters 5–7, Jesus instructed Christians on what they should be for. Here, in chapter 23, he tells them what they should be against if they want to be true disciples.

■   Read 23:1–36 and list what Jesus says a follower should avoid. Then, opposite each negative item, indicate the positive quality followers should strive for in order to make progress toward becoming "perfect."

As we have seen in our studies before, Jesus' love is boundless and it invites all, even sinners, to come to him. Read 23:37–39 and explain how these verses emphasize Jesus' love even for those who do not accept his message.

In the End (Matthew 24:1–31)

Matthew is realistic about the hardships Christians will have to face. At the same time, he is confident that in the long run Christians who live their faith will triumph.

Matthew 24:1–31 is written in the apocalyptic style, a style filled with symbolic language which meant a great deal to people in the first century but which for us in the twentieth century can be somewhat difficult to understand.

Read 24:1–31. It is not necessary to understand the symbolism, but try to grasp Matthew's message according to the outline:

- Jesus leaves the crowds and speaks to his disciples on Mount Olivet (24:1–3).
- He tells them that impersonators of the Messiah will try to deceive them (24:4–5).
- He describes symbolically the sufferings his disciples will experience in their encounters with the forces of evil in the world. He tells them that, nevertheless, God will triumph in the end (24:6–14).
- Jesus again depicts symbolically the sufferings his disciples will experience and the impersonators of the Messiah who will try to deceive them (24:15–26).
- Jesus concludes by describing the coming of the Son of Man. Matthew pictures Jesus coming in triumph at the end of the world to punish the wicked and to reward the good (24:27–31).

More About Active Faith (Matthew 24:32–25:46)

Matthew knows that discipleship is difficult. To encourage his readers, Matthew records some parables of Jesus which teach perseverance in times of trial.

Read Matthew 24:32—25:30 and notice how he cites sayings of Jesus which insist that disciples must be alert and active, watching for and taking advantage of every opportunity to do good. In 25:31–46 note how powerfully Matthew expresses the need for active love of neighbor as expressed in Jesus' unforgettable Parable of the Final Judgment.

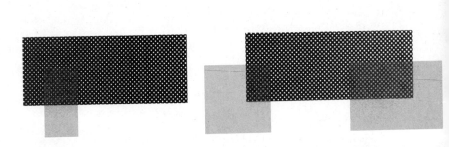

The Conclusion of the Gospel (Matthew 28:18–20)

Matthew concludes his gospel by telling how Jesus after his resurrection meets with his disciples on a mountain in Galilee and gives them his final instruction. He tells them:

"I have been given all authority in heaven and on earth. Go, then, to all peoples everywhere and make them my disciples: baptize them in the name of the Father, the Son, and the Holy Spirit, and teach them to obey everything I have commanded you. And I will be with you always, to the end of the age."

28:18–20

Jesus' last instruction contains a summary of the major themes of Matthew's gospel. Matthew began his gospel by giving the credentials of Jesus as being someone greater than Moses. Here Jesus himself declares: **"I have been given all authority in heaven and on earth" (28:18).**

Because the Jews rejected him, Jesus had appointed his apostles the new leaders of the people of God (10 and 16:17 – 19). Here Jesus, who has all authority in heaven and on earth, authorizes the apostles to go into the whole world and make disciples of all peoples.

In the short discourse of John the Baptist (3:8 – 12) and in the five long instructions (5 – 7, 10, 13, 18, and 23 – 25), Jesus had taught the apostles what is required to be a true disciple. Here, he commands his apostles to teach the whole world **"to obey everything I have commanded you" (28:19).** Obviously, Jesus is

referring to the teaching contained in the five great instructions.

In this last brief instruction Matthew has expressed in a nutshell his idealistic dream that all people everywhere do all that Jesus has commanded. He knows his dream is possible because Jesus himself has promised: **"I will be with you always, to the end of the age" (28:20).**

Challenges

Ernst Bloch, a philosopher, remarked that we all have dreams—day dreams and night dreams. We can do nothing about the night dreams, he said, but we can make our day dreams come true by putting foundations under them, by planning, working, and building for the future we dream about. In what ways is Matthew's gospel written in the spirit of Bloch's observation on dreams?

*At the end of Matthew's gospel, Jesus sends the apostles out to make disciples of all people, teaching them **"to obey everything I have commanded you"** (28:18–20) From what Jesus has taught in the five great discourses of Matthew's gospel, what would you say were the main things the apostles were to teach all people to do?*

Matthew's gospel tries to show both the similarities and differences between Jesus and Moses. Explain to what extent Jesus resembles Moses and to what extent he goes beyond Moses. Illustrate your answer with concrete examples.

Prayer
Reflection

The musical "Man of La Mancha" draws its inspiration from Miguel Cervantes' *Don Quixote.* One of the songs from the play expresses something deep in our human hearts which echoes the spirit of Jesus as portrayed by Matthew.

May we reflect upon its words and see if we can imagine ourselves taking part in this glorious quest.

"To dream the impossible dream,
To fight the unbeatable foe,
To bear with unbearable sorrow,
To run where the brave dare not go,
To right the unrightable wrong,
To love, pure and chaste, from afar,
To try, when your arms are too weary,
To reach the unreachable star.
This is my quest, to follow that star,
No, matter how hopeless, no matter how far,
To fight for the right without question
    or pause,
To be willing to march into hell for a
    heavenly cause!

And I know, if I'll only be true to this glorious
    quest,
That my heart will lie peaceful and calm
    when I'm laid to my rest.
And the world will be better for this
That one man scorned and covered
    with scars,
Still strove, with his last ounce of
    courage,
To reach the unreachable stars!"

10 Luke: Joyful Gospel

Journey of a Pope

A light rain fell as the jetliner carrying Pope John Paul II landed at Boston's Logan International Airport. At 3:02 P.M., on October 1, 1979, the "traveling" Pope stepped out of his plane and began his historic visit to the United States of America.

He was greeted by Mrs. Rosalyn Carter, the wife of the President: "This may be your first visit to our shores as pope," said Mrs. Carter, "but you do not arrive as a stranger. You have stirred the world as few have ever done before. . . At a time when materialism and selfishness threaten to overwhelm the values of the spirit, your spirit, your visit reminds us that life's true meaning springs from the heart and the soul—from purposes and beliefs larger than our individual lives."

Then John Paul began his first public speech in the United States of America:

"Praised be Jesus Christ!

"It is a great joy for me to be . . . in this land and . . . to greet all the American people of every race, color and creed. . . .

. . . I come as one who already knows you and loves you, as one who wishes you to fulfill completely your noble destiny of service to the world. . . . may the peace of the Lord be with you always—America."

For all those who know Luke's Gospel it was clear that John Paul was greeting America with joy, concern for the poor, and enthusiasm for a great commitment to Jesus, as Luke does throughout his gospel. It is Luke who says: **Glory to God in the highest heaven and peace on earth to those with whom he is pleased! (2:14)**

A Travelogue

Luke's two-part book (the Gospel of Luke and the Acts of the Apostles) is filled with journeys of joy much like that of Pope John Paul II. His characters move from town to town, city to city, and country to country. He takes his readers through Palestine, Syria, Turkey, Macedonia, Greece, and Rome. The movement is continuous, and the journeys give the reader the feeling of joy and hope that goes with putting the past behind and moving on toward a new and glorious goal.

Unlike the gospels of Matthew and Mark, which end with Jesus' resurrection, Luke's gospel continues after the resurrection with the Acts of the Apostles. The story of Jesus' ascension into heaven, which is told at the end of the gospel, and also at the beginning of the Acts of the Apostles, serves as the center of Luke's two-part book.

Look at the outline of Luke-Acts on page 147 and become acquainted with its structure. Luke's gospel is too long to discuss in detail; therefore we will concentrate on its central message of joy and on the sections which are special to Luke.

The Acts of the Apostles

Part One: The Beginning of the Church
(1:1—8:3)
  A. The Ascension, and the Birth of
the Church at Pentecost (1:1—2:47)
  B. Growth and Persecution of the
Church in Jerusalem (3:1—8:3)
Part Two: Spread of the Church to Judea,
Galatia, Samaria, and Syria
(8:4—12:25)
Part Three: Journeys and Witness of
Paul (13:1—28:31)
  A. The First Journey (13:1—14:28)
  B. The Meeting of the Apostles in
Jerusalem (15:1—35)
  C. Second Journey (15:36—18:22)
  D. Third Journey, Ending with Paul's
Trial In Jerusalem (18:23—23:11)
  E. Journey to Rome as Prisoner
(23:12—28:31)

Joy to the World

For Christians, Christmas is one of the most joyful times of the year—the time when they share unselfishly with others, when they gather food, clothing, and toys for the poor, and when, at least this once in the whole year, the world seems to be what it is truly meant to be.

Luke: The Joyful Gospel—A Structural Outline

Part One: Credentials and
Response—1:1—9:50
  A. Infancy Narrative (1—2)
  B. John the Baptist and the Holy Spirit
(3:1—38)
  C. Jesus' Miracles and Authoritative
Preaching (4:1—9:50)
Part Two: Discipleship (9:51—19:27)
Part Three: The Last Week in Jerusalem
(19:28—24:53)
  A. Preaching of Jesus (19:28—21:38)
  B. Passion and Death (22:1—23:56)
  C. Resurrection and Ascension
(24:1—53)

It is from Luke that we get our image of what the world can be: the earth bursting with joy, worshipers praising Christ, the poor filled with hope, the lonely less lonely, and all the world a kinder, warmer place.

■ Chapters 1:1—2:20 show how this hope and joy were brought to earth by God himself. Read these chapters and compare them with the account of John Paul's arrival in the United States on pages 149—150. Note how the words of Rosalyn Carter and Pope John Paul II resemble what Luke says about Jesus in these two chapters.

Joy to the Poor! (Luke 1:46—4:21)

One reason Luke's Gospel is so joyful is that it brings a special message to the poor, who have a special place in God's Kingdom. Read 1:46—2:24. In these chapters there are several passages typical of St. Luke with regard to the poor.

Only he recounts:
- how God chose Mary to be the mother of Jesus (1:46—49, 52-53);
- how Jesus was born in a manger like the poorest of the poor (2:7);
- how the message of peace was proclaimed to poor shepherds (2:8—14);
- how poor shepherds, not the rich and powerful, were the first to visit the newborn Jesus (2:15—20);
- how, when Mary and Joseph presented Jesus in the temple, they offered pigeons, the gift of the poor, and not a lamb, the gift of the rich (2:22—24).

Read 4:16—21 and explain how these verses contain more good news for the poor.

Part One: Credentials and Responses (Luke 1:1—9:50)

We have already studied the ways in which Mark and Matthew establish Jesus' credentials and describe the response of the people to him. This can help us to discover the "credentials and response" in Luke's gospel.

- Read 1:1—9:50 and express in your own words:
- the witnesses and miracles Luke uses to establish Jesus' credentials;
- the positive and negative responses given to Jesus as Messiah and Son of God;
- the journeys Luke's characters take in these chapters and show how "credentials and response" is part of the action of a particular journey.

The parable of the sower tells about different responses to Jesus' credentials—some accept him immediately, some accept him for a time and then fall away, some do not accept him at all (8:4—15). This parable readies us for part two of Luke's gospel. There Jesus turns to his apostles and disciples who, like the seed which fell upon good soil, accept him. At the same time, he turns away from those who, like the seed which fell on rocky ground, reject him.

Part Two: Discipleship (Luke 9:51—19:27)

We read about Jesus going to Jerusalem to suffer and die in Luke's gospel just as he does in Mark's. In Luke, however, the journey is different. It is terribly slow. Jesus and the apostles are always stopping along the road for one thing or another. Also, Luke brings into his journey-story so many of the things Jesus said about discipleship that, in effect, the whole trip is taken up with an explanation of discipleship.

Because Luke's account of this journey is so long we will not discuss it in detail. We will study what Jesus says a follower should be, when he talks to his disciples, and what he says a disciple should not be, when he speaks to the crowds or to the Pharisees.

Call to Commitment

John Paul II's visit to America can be compared to Luke's gospel not only in the Pope's message of joy but also in his call to commitment for discipleship.

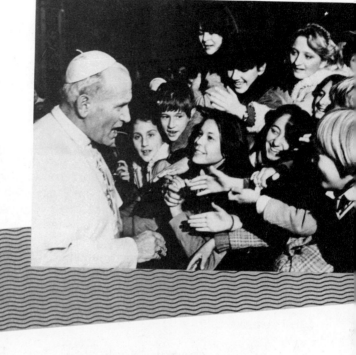

Wherever John Paul went on his whirlwind tour of the United States, thousands came to see and hear him. They were caught up in his warmth, his frankness, his sincerity, and his love for everyone.

He came with a message much like that of Luke: "To all I have come with a message of hope and peace—the hope and peace of Jesus Christ."

In his first address to America, on the Boston Common, he appealed in a special way to the youth of America:

". . .Everywhere young people are asking important questions—questions on the meaning of life, on the right way to live, on the true scale of values: 'What must I do. . .? What must I do to share in everlasting life?'. . .

"To each one of you I say, therefore: Heed the call of Christ when you hear him saying to you: 'Follow me! Walk in my path! Stand by my side! Remain in my love!' There is a choice to be made: a choice for Christ and his way of life, and his commandment of love. . .

"Do I then make a mistake, Catholic Youth, that it is part of your task in the world and the church to reveal the true meaning of life where hatred, neglect or selfishness threaten to take over the world? Faced with problems and disappointments, many people will try to escape from their responsibility. . . But today I propose to you an option of love, which is the opposite of escape.

If you really accept that love from Christ, it will lead you to God. . . to the service of love: the love of God and of your neighbor. . . ."

Luke's Call

Luke, too, starts his section on discipleship with the difficulties and joys of following Jesus.

Jesus offers his disciples the challenge to witness to the Kingdom of God. He tells his disciples that there will be difficulties as well as joys in the great work of sharing the gospel.

Read 9:51—10:37. Point out where Jesus speaks about the difficulties disciples will have to face. Note what Jesus says about loving our neighbor and compare it with what John Paul II says about love.

■   In 10:21—24, Luke talks about the joys of discipleship. Suggest ways young people today can serve God and neighbor. Explain how these ways can bring joy.

How Terrible for You Pharisees! (Luke 11:37—54)

This section gives a good description of what a disciple should not be according to Luke. For each condemnation of the Pharisees make up a "blessing of praise" for people of today which counters the failings of the Pharisees. For example, for verse 42, a blessing of praise could be: "Happy are you disciples of Jesus! You give your time and energy for others and when possible share your possessions with them. You are just and love God and your neighbor."

More About Discipleship

We have seen the strong language Luke cites Jesus as using to describe what a disciple should not be. Expressed positively, who are the true disciples? For Luke they are:

● people who, like Mary, choose to sit at the feet of Jesus and listen to him teach (10:38–42);

● people who learn to pray: **"Father. . . may your kingdom come. . ." (11:1–4);**

● people who firmly believe true happiness comes from hearing and obeying God's word (11:28);

● people who accept the hardships discipleship puts upon them (14:25–33);

● people who know that God values them highly, answers their prayers, and lovingly awaits their return when they turn away from him (11:5–13; 12:4–7; 15:11–32).

● Think of someone you know whom you think fits these descriptions of a true disciple. What motivates him or her to live in this way? To what extent would you like to incorporate these values in your life?

Wealth and Worry

In chapter 12 Jesus again speaks to his disciples. Especially important here is the Parable of the Rich Fool (12:13–21) and what Jesus says to his disciples about worrying (12:22–53).

Read 12:1–53 and reflect on the following:

● Why is the rich man in the parable called a fool?

● Why does Jesus tell his disciples not to be worriers but to be watchful servants of the Lord?

● How would you explain to someone that the rich fool is the opposite of:

—Mary, Martha's sister, who chose to sit at the feet of Jesus (10:38—42);

—those who learn to pray (11:1—4);

—those who believe happiness comes from God and not from oneself (11:28).

Luke had a thing about money. Read the parables about The Shrewd Manager and The Rich Man and Lazarus in 16:1—31. Also examine the stories of The Rich Man in 18:18—29 and Zacchaeus in 19:1—9. Of all the things Luke says about discipleship, nothing is more provocative than what he says about wealth and poverty.

What do you think Luke is really for and what do you think he is really against with regard to being rich, being poor, or being somewhere in-between? To what extent do you agree with Luke's position as you understand it?

When John Paul II spoke at Yankee Stadium in October of 1979, he specifically compared the rich man to America and Lazarus to the poor nations of the third world. How do you react to this comparison?

Part Three: The Last Week In Jerusalem (Luke 19:28—24:53)

Luke's account of the last days of Jesus' life, beginning with his triumphal entrance into Jerusalem in 19:28–40 and ending with his ascension into heaven in 24:48–52, is for the most part the same as the accounts in Mark and Matthew. Such differences as there are, however, are typically Lucan.

As we might expect, Luke's account has his characteristic human touch. He continues his message of joy for disciples by showing how much Jesus cares about people as individuals, how he weeps for them, understands them, forgives them, and even surprises them.

● It is only Luke who has the story of Jesus weeping over Jerusalem (19:41–44).

● It is only Luke who has the human story about the apostles at the last supper still disputing which of them would be the greatest in Jesus' kingdom (22:24–30).

● It is Luke alone who mentions what Jesus says to the women who follow him along the way of the cross: **"Women of Jerusalem! Don't cry for me, but for yourselves and your children" (23:28).**

● Luke alone mentions Jesus' words on the cross: **"Forgive them, Father! They don't know what they are doing" (23:34)** and his unforgettable words to the repentant thief: **"I promise you that today you will be in Paradise with me" (23:43).**

● It is only Luke who has the story about the disciples who walk to Emmaus on Easter morning. They meet up with a "stranger" who explains to them why the Messiah had to die and whom they later discover at the breaking of the bread is the risen Jesus (24:13–35). What seemed like the end was, as the two disciples now realize, only the beginning!

● Finally, it is Luke who emphasizes the account of Jesus' last journey—his ascension into heaven (24:50–53).

For Luke's readers these human touches make Jesus incredibly alive, close, and comforting. No matter how rough their own journey through life, Luke's readers know there is one who has made a rougher journey, one who understands their troubles, their temptations, their tears, and their joys, one who himself was able to weep.

The Ultimate Journey (Luke 24:36–53)

Jesus appears to his apostles, eats with them, explains the scriptures to them, and tells them to wait in Jerusalem until they are given power from above. Jesus then ascends into heaven and the apostles wait in Jerusalem for the coming of the Holy Spirit.

The ultimate journey of Jesus to heaven is not really the end at all. It begins a new and exciting section of Luke's story by linking the ascension of Jesus with the beginning of the Church. This new section is known as the Acts of the Apostles.

The Acts of the Apostles

The second part of Luke's book, which we call the Acts of the Apostles, begins with the birth of the Church in Jerusalem as the Holy Spirit comes to Jesus' followers at Pentecost (chapters 1—2). It then goes on to tell about the preaching of the apostles and the spread of the Church in Jerusalem, in the rest of Palestine, and in Syria (chapters 3—12). It continues with the journeys of St. Paul which lead him to the Mediterranean islands, to Turkey, to Greece, and finally to Rome (chapters 13—28).

Luke's story makes interesting reading. It is of course a bit one-sided. Luke tells mostly the good things about the early Church. Anyone who reads Paul's letters knows that the earliest Christians were not all saints. But Luke is not interested in the inevitable scandals that accompany all great enterprises. He sees and feels the joy and enthusiasm of true Christianity and he paints it in glowing colors.

The Birth of the Church (Acts 1—2)

Chapters 1 and 2 of the Acts of the Apostles explain how the Church, founded by Christ to bring the good news so joyfully told by Luke, began its history in Jerusalem some fifty days after Jesus' resurrection.

■ Read these first two chapters and discover the answers to these questions concerning the beginnings of the Church:

● What does Jesus say to the apostles about their mission?
● Who is elected to take the place of Judas?
● What effect does the presence of the Holy Spirit have on the apostles?

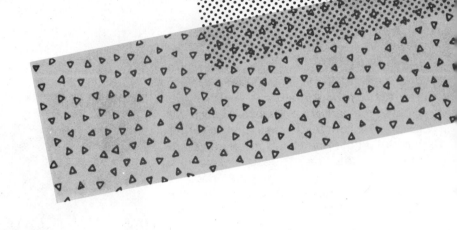

The Church in Jerusalem (Acts 3:1—8:3)
Beginning with the five thousand who experienced the Holy Spirit at Pentecost, the Church grew rapidly in Jerusalem. However, the same Jewish leaders who had plotted the death of Jesus troubled the early Church.

Read 3:1—8:3 and note these main topics:

- the arrest of Peter and John;
- the reference to the high priests, Annas and Caiaphas, plotting against the Church;
- the description of how the early Christians shared with one another;
- the arrest and imprisonment of the apostles;
- the appointment of the seven deacons (helpers);
- the arrest and death of Stephen.

The Growth of the Church (Acts 8:4—12:25)
How quickly the Church extended from Jerusalem to other parts of Palestine and to other countries we do not know. Luke gives no dates. But when Paul was converted between 32 and 35 A.D., there was already a Christian community in that capital city of Syria.

■ Read Acts 8:4—12:25, which tells how the Church spread to other parts of Palestine, and answer these questions:
- Who besides Philip preached the gospel

to the Samaritans?

● What does Luke say about the Christians in Damascus?

● Who is Cornelius and why is he important?

● Who was the apostle put to death by King Herod?

● How did Peter escape death?

The Journeys and Witness of Paul (Acts 12:1—28:31)

What is significant about Paul's journeys is that they show how rapidly the Church spread from Palestine to Syria, Lebanon, Turkey, Greece, and Rome. Luke says little about the work of the other apostles, but that is because he wanted to

impress upon his readers the example of Paul, the greatest missionary of all time.

As you read about Paul in Acts 13–28, keep in mind what we have said about him in our study of his letters. Notice also how Luke continues his journey theme—the theme that dominates the gospel, the first half of his two-part book. In the second half, the Acts of the Apostles, it dominates even more.

Luke began his book by announcing the gospel as "joy to the world." He ends it with the journeys that bring the joy of the gospel to the Gentile nations of the then civilized world.

Challenges

Pope John Paul II says the youth of today are seeking the meaning of life, the right way to live, and the true scale of values. To what extent do you find the message of Luke's gospel a help in this search? Please explain your opinion.

Luke presents the human side of Jesus. He wants his readers to realize that Jesus understands them with all their joys, their sufferings, and their weaknesses. To what degree do you sense that Jesus understands you in your humanness?

Luke wrote his two-part book especially for Gentiles who had no acquaintance with the God of Israel and the Father of Jesus Christ. He tried to make Christianity both attractive and challenging for them. In what way do you find his presentation of Jesus' message attractive? In what way is it challenging?

Prayer
Reflection

John Paul II's closing remarks on the Boston
Common sum up beautifully Luke's
presentation of what it means to be a
follower of Christ. Let us prayerfully reflect
upon his words so that we may be open
to follow where Jesus' call leads us.

". . .We could be tempted to think that
many possessions, many of the goods of
this world, can bring happiness. We
see instead in the case of the young man in
the Gospel that his many possessions
had become an obstacle to accepting the call
of Jesus to follow him. He was not ready to
say yes to Jesus and no to self, to say yes
to love and no to escape.

"Real love is demanding. I would fail in my
mission if I did not clearly tell you so. . .
Love demands effort and a personal
commitment to the will of God. It means
discipline and sacrifice, but it also means
joy and human fulfillment.

"Dear young people: do not be afraid of
honest effort and hard work; do not be
afraid of truth. . . .Open your hearts
to the Christ of the Gospels—to his love and
his truth and his joy. Do not go away
sad!"

11

John: New Life Gospel

New Life

Paula Hainesworth came from Australia to study in the northeastern part of the United States. She had never spent a winter where the trees lost their leaves, where the grass turned brown, where the world of nature looked dead.

All winter she kept remarking how depressing it was. She could not understand how people could live in such a desolate climate until. . . spring arrived! The new birth of spring was something she had never experienced.

In his gospel, John talks about a new life which transforms people much the way spring transforms nature. He talks about a life that gives to those who accept it the new life of God himself—a life that gives humans a share of the divine.

John's Audience and Style

John probably lived in Alexandria, Egypt, where there were many Gentiles and Jews. He writes his gospel in order to:

● strengthen the faith of Christians by emphasizing the value of the new life Jesus brings to the world;

● spur on those Jews who would like to become Christians but cannot make up their minds to leave the synagogue and

enter the Christian Church;
● refute the synagogue leaders who argue that Jesus is not the Messiah, not the one whom the prophets predicted, and certainly not the only begotten Son of God.

One of the pleasant ways to learn is by listening to action-filled stories. This is John's way of instructing his readers. He is a superb dramatist. His gospel is like a play in five acts, filled with dialogue between Jesus and others.

The Structure
John's gospel has the same grand staircase structure as Matthew's, where the down staircase mirrors back the scenes of the up staircase. Turn to page 162 and study the structural outline.

Like Matthew, Mark, and Luke, John begins with Jesus' credentials, goes on to show the positive and negative responses to Jesus, reveals a turning point, then emphasizes discipleship, and ends with the story of Jesus' passion, death, and resurrection. But there the similarities end. John has his own unique way of telling Jesus' story.

John: New Life Gospel —
A Structural Outline

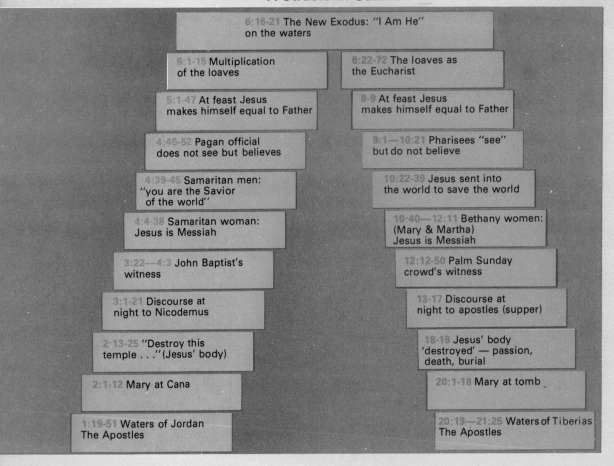

6:16-21 The New Exodus: "I Am He" on the waters

6:1-15 Multiplication of the loaves

6:22-72 The loaves as the Eucharist

5:1-47 At feast Jesus makes himself equal to Father

8-9 At feast Jesus makes himself equal to Father

4:46-52 Pagan official does not see but believes

9:1—10:21 Pharisees "see" but do not believe

4:39-45 Samaritan men: "you are the Savior of the world"

10:22-39 Jesus sent into the world to save the world

4:4-38 Samaritan woman: Jesus is Messiah

10:40—12:11 Bethany women: (Mary & Martha) Jesus is Messiah

3:22—4:3 John Baptist's witness

12:12-50 Palm Sunday crowd's witness

3:1-21 Discourse at night to Nicodemus

13-17 Discourse at night to apostles (supper)

2:13-25 "Destroy this temple . . ." (Jesus' body)

18-19 Jesus' body 'destroyed' — passion, death, burial

2:1-12 Mary at Cana

20:1-18 Mary at tomb

1:19-51 Waters of Jordan The Apostles

20:19—21:25 Waters of Tiberias The Apostles

To begin with, John describes few miracles and gives none of Jesus' parables. Instead he has long dialogues and monologues. His gospel is filled with talk. Also, John has characters never heard about in the other gospels: Nicodemus—the man "on the fence"; the Samaritan woman—married five times but with no husband; and Lazarus—the dead man who walks out of his tomb.

John's gospel differs from the others most of all in the way he presents Jesus. Matthew, Mark, and Luke present the human side of Jesus. John presents more of the divine side—the Jesus who gives new life to those who believe in him.

Act One: Credentials (John 1:1—4:3)

Because those who are rejecting Jesus do not believe in his divinity and messiahship, John is concerned from the outset of his gospel with quickly establishing Jesus' credentials. Therefore he begins by presenting a grand parade of witnesses who testify to Jesus.

■ Read John 1:1—4:3. Try to identify by chapter and verse the scenes which give witness to Jesus' credentials as Messiah and Son of God. Explain how each is a valid witness to Jesus' divinity:

Being Reborn

Johnny Cash, a famous country-western singer, was "reborn" and changed from a life of drug addiction to one of service to others.

People on retreats or at other times of prayer often experience a change and an awakening in their lives which we can call "being reborn."

When we ask someone reborn what it is like, the person is usually at a loss for words to express the excitement and the joy of the transformation. Often they answer: "You have to experience it to understand it!" Read John 3:1—21 and notice how vague Jesus is in telling Nicodemus what it is like to be reborn. The only thing Jesus says is that one must be reborn to enter heaven (3:3,5,7) and in order to be reborn one must believe in him (3:12—21).

Jesus' message to Nicodemus is the heart of John's gospel. Over and over again in the five acts of his gospel John presents Jesus struggling to persuade his audience to accept the "new life" which he has come to give all people.

- the witness of John (the author) to the preexistence of Jesus as God;
- the first witness of John the Baptist;
- the witness of the Holy Spirit;
- the witness of the apostles;
- the witness of Jesus' first miracle;
- the witness of Jesus' authority to cleanse the Temple;
- the witness of Jesus to his power over death;
- the witness of Jesus' authority in speaking to Nicodemus about the waters of Baptism;
- the final witness of John the Baptist.

Act Two: Response (John 4:4—6:15)

No one experiences rebirth automatically. Each person has to make the critical decision that will change his or her life—to believe in and accept Jesus or to reject him. The Jews and Gentiles of John's time had to make the same critical decision.

Samaritan Response (4:4–45)
John sets his scene in Samaria and shows the Samaritan woman and townspeople, unlike the Pharisees, to be honest, openhearted, and willing to listen. Because of this they recognize Jesus' credentials and believe in him.

Gentile Response (4:46–54)
In Galilee Jesus meets a government official. The official represents those Gentiles who believe in Jesus.

Read 4:4–54 and explain how Jews who were undecided as well as those who were rejecting Jesus would be made aware of the openness and trust of the Samaritan and Gentile responses to Jesus.

Jewish Response (5:1–6:15)
In Jerusalem, even when Jesus heals a paralytic, the Jews refuse to believe (5:2–18). In Galilee, even when Jesus multiplies loaves and fish to feed 5,000 people, the Jewish people misunderstand the kind of savior Jesus is and try to make him a political king (6:1–15).

Read 5:1–6:15 and explain how the responses of the Samaritans and the Gentiles contrast with those of the Jews.

Monologues for Unbelievers (John 3:10–21; 5:19–47)
As we said in explaining the differences between John's gospel and the gospels of Matthew, Mark, and Luke, John has Jesus give some rather long monologues.

John's placement of Jesus' first two monologues after incidents of unbelief form an important part of his gospel dramatization.

The first comes after Jesus' dialogue with Nicodemus, who cannot bring himself to believe in Jesus even though he would like to (3:10–21).

The second follows Jesus' healing of the paralytic by the pool (5:19–47). Instead of believing, the Jewish authorities accuse Jesus of breaking the Sabbath and of making himself equal to God (5:16–18).

From John's placement of these monologues of Jesus and from their message, it is evident that he is directing his words to certain Jews in his audience. Either they did not believe in Jesus at all, or they believed in him but could not make up their minds to make a decision for Christ. John's basic message for his undecided and unbelieving readers is this:

- God so loves the world that he sent his Son to save all people;
- the Son so loves the Father and the world that he came to save the world and, when it became necessary, even gave up his life for the salvation of the world;
- people must believe in Jesus and follow him in order to gain eternal life.

Act Three: The Turning Point (John 6:16–21)

One can assume that when God makes a promise, he will keep his word. God promised Abraham, Isaac, Jacob, and Moses that the savior would come through Israel.

John's turning point in 6:16–21 is designed to show his audience that God has kept his word. Salvation does come through Israel—Jesus is an Israelite and so are his apostles. Jesus has turned away not from Israel, but only from those Israelites who refuse to accept him.

The third act of John's drama is only six verses long (6:16–21), but it is packed with meaning. In it Jesus walks on the waters of the Lake of Galilee and brings his apostles safely through the storm to the opposite shore.

The incident may seem to be one miracle among many, but to John's Jewish readers it has so many reminders of the Exodus that they would immediately think of the crossing of the Reed Sea and their ancestors' escape from Egypt. To understand the turning point the way Jewish readers would understand it, we shall have to recall the symbolic meaning of water and the story of the Exodus.

Waters of Life

When U.S. space satellites sent back pictures of the moon, Mars, and Jupiter, all eyes searched for the smallest traces of water on their surfaces. Scientists were eager to discover if life could exist in outer space. Their criterion was that where there is water there can be life.

John's criterion is much the same: where there is the water of baptism, there is eternal life.

Read Exodus 3:1–15 and chapter 14. Study the following parallels and note how John's readers would see the walking on the water scene as the New Exodus of the new people of God, led by Jesus to a new life.

Exodus
- Moses is *afraid* (3:6).
- God identifies himself as *"I AM"* (3:14–15).
- The Exodus miracle takes place *at night on the sea* (Exodus 14:20).
- God's presence is made known to the Israelites through a *strong* wind (Exodus 14:21).
- God brings the Israelites safely to the *other side of the sea* (14:29).
- Because of God's power, the Israelites *believe* in the Lord and in Moses (14:31).

John
- The disciples are *afraid* (6:19).
- Jesus identifies himself as God when he says, *"It is I,"* which has the same meaning as *"I AM"* (6:20).
- Jesus comes to the apostles *at night on the sea* (John 6:16–17).
- When Jesus comes to the disciples there is a *strong wind* (6:18).
- Jesus brings the apostles safely to the *other side of the sea* (6:21).
- After Jesus demonstrates his power by walking on the water, the apostles willingly take him into the boat. This symbolizes their *belief* in him (6:21).

When John's readers reach the turning point in 6:15–21, they know John is saying that the apostles and their followers are the new people of God who, led by Jesus, have been brought through the storm at sea to a new life, just as the Jews of old in the Exodus were led by God to a new life as the people of God.

Act Four: Defense (John 6:22–12:11)
In Act Four of John's gospel, Jesus refutes nine counts of an indictment brought against him by the leaders of the Jews. When John wrote his gospel, at the end of the first century, a sizzling tension existed between Judaism and Christianity. Many Jews wanted to become Christians. The synagogue leaders responded by threatening excommunication upon all who believed in Jesus.

John dramatizes the tension by means of an informal trial setting. As Jesus preaches in Jerusalem and in Galilee, the Jewish leaders make accusations, the crowds listen and sometimes make comments, and Jesus refutes the accusations. The confrontation follows the pattern below.

168

The Indictment

- He claims he is the true bread come down from heaven and that whoever eats this bread will live forever. We cannot accept this claim, on the grounds that it is insane to think of eating human flesh and blood.
- He claims to teach with authority the things of God, but we know he has not received this authority from any of our rabbinical schools.
- He claims to be the Messiah but according to some of our teachers no one will know from where the Messiah comes. Others say he will come from Bethlehem. He cannot be the Messiah because we know he is from Nazareth in Galilee and not from Bethlehem.

- He testifies on his own behalf. This is not valid in our court of law.
- He is possessed by the devil. You just have to see and hear him to know this is true.
- He claims to be greater than Abraham, because he lived before Abraham. We know he was born just thirty or forty years ago.
- He claims to come from God, but this is impossible because he does not keep the Sabbath.
- He is guilty of blasphemy. He is only a man, but he claims to be God.
- He claims that whoever believes in him will live even though he dies. He is only a man, and no man can make a claim to such power.

The Refutation

- If the Father can send manna from heaven through Moses, then he has the power to send me from heaven as bread for eternal life (6:22–71).
- My teaching authority does not come from any rabbinical school but directly from the Father himself (7:14–24).
- You do not know where I am from. You think I am from Nazareth but I actually come from God (7:25–52).
- My testimony is valid. Besides, the Father also testifies for me. Two testimonies are certainly valid (8:12–20).
- I am not possessed, because I do the work of the Father (8:48–51).
- Before Abraham was born, "I Am" (8:52–59).
- I cured the blind man on the Sabbath because I am the good shepherd who loves and cares for my sheep. And I am willing even to die for my sheep (9:1–10:21).
- I am doing the Father's work. If you believe in my work, you will believe in me because the Father is in me and I am in the Father (10:22–39).
- I raised Lazarus from the dead. I do what I have said I could do (11:1–12:11).

Act Five: Discipleship, Passion, Death, and Resurrection (John 12:12–21:25)

For a week or more in the month of October the forests of the northern hemisphere glow with the last spent fires of summer. For nature lovers it provides an almost mystical experience to watch nature put on a final glorious display of life before surrendering to the winds of autumn and the long wintry sleep that precedes the resurrection of spring.

Act Five of John's gospel provides readers with a similar but much more profound mystical experience. It deals with the themes of life, death, and new life in the context of the last momentous week of Jesus' life.

It begins with Jesus' royal entry into Jerusalem (12:12–19). There follows his long discourse at the last supper in which he speaks of "love unto the end," his "new commandment," his "going away and returning again," his "glorifying the Father and the Father glorifying him" (13–17).

After the supper, soldiers arrest him (18:1–12). Caiaphas and Pilate put him on trial and condemn him (18:13–19:16). He is put to death on a cross, and buried in a new tomb in a garden (19:17–42). It seems like the end, but on Easter Sunday he rises from the dead! (20:1–21:25).

You have already read the story of Jesus' last week on earth in the gospels of Matthew, Mark, and Luke. John's account is similar in many ways, different in others. We will concentrate on the most remarkable differences:

- John's long farewell discourse in chapters 13–17;
- John's account of Jesus' resurrection in chapters 20–21.

The Farewell Discourse (John 13—17)

John's account of Jesus' words at the last supper is long for a practical reason. In John's gospel little has been said about discipleship up to this point. Here in the farewell discourse, Jesus instructs his apostles on the meaning of discipleship at the same time that he prepares them for his death.

Why John saves what Jesus says about discipleship until his farewell discourse is not difficult to explain. Last words of great persons are treasured. Last words are remembered. What better time, then, for an instruction on discipleship than the night before Jesus' death!

The Washing of the Feet (John 13:1–17)

Jesus' washing his apostles' feet puts John's account of the farewell discourse on discipleship into focus. It may seem like a simple lesson in humility, but humility is only half of it. The washing symbolizes far more than a simple cleansing—it symbolizes Jesus' love unto death. Read chapter 13:1–17, and notice especially Jesus' reference to his death in Verses 1, 3, and 7, and Peter's understanding of "later" in verse 7.

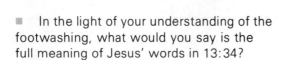

■ In the light of your understanding of the footwashing, what would you say is the full meaning of Jesus' words in 13:34?

Encouragement and Support (John 14—16)

Jesus knows the apostles will be confused and disheartened when he dies on the cross and again when he leaves them after his resurrection.

Read 14:1–31 and explain how the words "a place for you," "I will come back," "a Helper," and "Peace is what I leave with you" must have encouraged the disciples in the dismal days following Jesus' departure from the world.

The allegory of the vine and the branches contains several truths critical for an understanding of discipleship. Read 15:1–8 and pick out the verses in which these truths are expressed. **"If the world hates you, just remember that it has hated me first. . . . If they persecuted me, they will persecute you too. . ." (15:18,20).**

Read 15:18—16:33 for Jesus' warnings of what his disciples may anticipate. Notice how Jesus encourages his disciples by promising to send the Holy Spirit. How would you say that John's emphasis on the role of the Holy Spirit brings out the theme of his gospel that Jesus brings "new life"?

The Resurrection (John 20—21)

John's account of Jesus' resurrection differs in a number of ways from those of Matthew, Mark, and Luke. We will look at only one of these differences; the way he describes a meeting of Jesus with his apostles at the Lake of Galilee.

John's gospel began with Jesus and the apostles at the waters of the Jordan (1:19—51). It ends at the waters of the Lake of Galilee. Several of the same apostles are again with Jesus, and Peter, who is to be the head of the Church, again has a prominent part. In 1:42, Jesus looked at Peter and said: **"Your name is Simon son of John, but you will be called Cephas." (This is the same as Peter and means "a rock.")**

In 21:15—17, Jesus three times asks Peter if he loves him and three times says to him: **"Take care of my sheep."**

The words are significant because, in John's gospel, Jesus spoke of himself as the good shepherd (10:1–21). When Jesus tells Peter: **"Take care of my sheep,"** what he is telling him is that from now on he is to be the shepherd of the flock in place of Jesus. He is to be the leader of all those who have received the new life brought by Jesus. It is because of words like these and the words of Jesus in Matthew 16:17–19 about Peter being the rock upon which Jesus intended to build his Church that we believe that Peter and all his successors are special leaders in the Church.

Challenges

In the First Letter of John the author says: **God is love, and whoever lives in love lives in union with God and God lives in union with him (4:16).** *In what way does this one verse summarize the main themes of John's gospel?*

Which part or parts of John's gospel do you think would best help convince the Jews to believe in Jesus and follow him?

How apt do you find the title of this chapter ("John: The New-Life Gospel")? Explain what you understand by "new life" in terms of the symbols and images found in John's gospel.

Prayer Reflection

Chapter 17 of John's gospel is one of the most beautiful prayers ever written. Jesus is praying for his apostles on the night before he died. A commentary on this prayer would only take away from its profound meaning and impact.

To appreciate this passage, put yourselves in the place of the apostles. Try to experience the feelings, such as love, wonder, gratitude, sadness, apprehension, and fear, which you probably would have had on hearing Jesus speaking to the Father in this manner. Then reflect on the meaning this prayer has for you.

Reading: Jesus Prays For His Disciples (17:1–26).

May we pray:
Father, may what Jesus asked of you the night before he died still have effect in our lives and world today. May we be one in belief in Jesus Christ; one in love for you and for one another; and one in sharing the eternal life which you have given to us through your Son Jesus. Amen.

12

Conclusion: A Discussion

Perspectives

In our study of the Christian Scriptures we have described Mark's Gospel as realistic, Matthew's Gospel as idealistic, Luke's Gospel as joyful, and John's Gospel as announcing new life. Each of the gospel writers had his own perspective of Jesus; each brought to his gospel something of himself, his background, his own distinctive personality. In Paul's writings too, we see his fiery personality reflected as he described his dealings with his fellow Jews and the new Christian communities.

Imagine, for a moment, Paul and the gospel writers gathered together for a round table discussion. As we know, such a meeting never took place. However, this final chapter may sum up some of the insights we have gained if we imagine ourselves present at such a discussion. We can use what we have learned of their different perspectives, styles, and personalities to imagine what they might have said to one another about their own works and those of the others. Do you think they would always fully appreciate one another's viewpoint? Would their personalities always blend—or would they clash at times?

Let us free our imaginations to picture an honest exchange among these men that would bring out their separate, often contrasting viewpoints as we have discovered them. We could imagine that they might joke with one another, disagree, feel misinterpreted or misunderstood at times—all in a spirit of love of Christ and a desire to explain and share their faith in him.

Peter, as the head of the community, is the moderator and directs the discussion. The other panelists are Paul, who will discuss his letters, and the four gospel writers, each of whom will talk about his particular gospel account.

Peter: Gentlemen, we. are here to discuss your writings about Jesus. Our first speaker will be Paul. As you know, he is reputed to be the world's greatest theologian and, speaking from my own experience with Paul at Antioch, I'm sure he would not disagree with that judgment. You gentlemen may not agree, but I ask you in all fairness to hear him out.

Paul: Colleagues, the most important single duty of an apostle is to preach to the world the good news of Jesus Christ. That, in short, is the reason I traveled so much, preached so often, and wrote so many letters.

Some of you, I know, are not too happy with my letters. Our moderator himself, in one of his letters, has remarked about my writings that there are some difficult things in them which ignorant and unstable people explain falsely. But, gentlemen, as you well know, it is not enough to convert people to Christianity. You have to help them grow in Christ. You have to help them become mature Christians.

criticisms, because maybe, like so many others, you have not really understood what I was writing about.

Peter: Thank you, Paul. We appreciate your feelings and we hope we have not misunderstood you. Now, gentlemen, Mark, the author of the realist's gospel, will say a few words.

Mark: Thank you, Peter. Paul, we know you're a great theologian. In fact, you may even be the greatest who ever lived. But I would like to point out, Paul, that you talk too much about yourself. That in itself does not bother me unduly. What bothers me is you say so little about Jesus. I read all your letters and I do not find a single parable of Jesus. I do not find a single account of any of his miracles, except for the resurrection. Couldn't you have quoted Jesus more often? Couldn't you have quoted from the Sermon on the Mount or from John's last supper discourse? Really, Paul, if you had your writing to do over again, I think you might do it differently. (At this point, Paul is waving his hand furiously.)

Peter: Paul, I know you want to respond to Mark, but he has the floor. You will have an opportunity for rebuttal later. All right, Mark, tell us about your own gospel.

Christians must become adults in every way. That means maturity in the things of God as well as in the things of God's good world. Christianity is not just baptism and a few pious words about how a person should follow Jesus. Christianity is being Christ in the here and now with its troublesome people, agonizing problems, and intricate human relationships.

I have nothing against children, except "children" who refuse to grow up in their faith. I write for Christians who want to become adults in Christ. I am proud of my writings. You may not agree with me and you may point to all the problems my letters have caused. But I can live with your

Mark: As for my own gospel, it is short. People have called it "the grim gospel" and "the realist's gospel." A lot of people ignore it and insist on studying Matthew and Luke's gospels because they say Matthew and Luke borrowed half their material from my gospel. I wrote my gospel to concentrate on what was crucial—the fact that Jesus out of love for us died on the Cross. None of you here would have written any of your letters or gospels if Jesus had not gone to the Cross. There would be no sense talking about discipleship if Jesus had not been the perfect disciple of the Father.

If anyone really wants to follow Christ, there's only one way to do it. That's why I use the words *"Take up your cross and follow me."* That is symbolic language, I admit. I could have said: "Take up the difficulties you have every day. Take seriously what Jesus said about serving others, about doing things for others instead of expecting others to do things for you."

It sounds grim. I admit it. But it's realistic and, what's more, it is good news. Some people think that I over-emphasize suffering and service, but that depends on how you look at suffering. There is involuntary suffering—the aches, the pains, the illnesses we all have to put up with. I'm talking about *voluntary* suffering, voluntary giving of ourselves as Jesus did. That is glorious suffering! That is Jesus' way. Even Paul would agree, it's the only way.

That's all I have to say. I believe in dealing with the essentials, with reality, and that's what I did in my gospel.

Peter: Thank you, Mark. We do appreciate your gospel. We think, however, you're a little hard on Paul. (Paul smiles.)

Now, gentlemen, I would like to introduce Matthew, the author of the idealist's gospel.

Matthew: My dear colleagues, I could not agree more with Mark's criticism that Paul wrote too little about Jesus. In addition to what Mark has pointed out, let me say I'm particularly unhappy about Paul's de-emphasis of the law. (Paul tries to get the floor, but again to no avail.) In my gospel, I make it abundantly clear that you can't please God just by talking. If you want to please God, you must *do* what God commands. You will notice that I ended up the last long discourse of Jesus in my gospel with the Parable of the Final Judgment. In that judgment only one thing will count: active love of neighbor. When Jesus at the last judgment says, *"Away from me, you that are under God's curse!"* he will be speaking to people who did not *do* God's will, who did not visit him when he was sick, did not feed him when he was hungry, and so on.

I like your gospel, Mark. I certainly would not have borrowed so much material from it if I did not! I should like to point out also that I do not contest your claim that the most important *event* in history is Jesus' death on the Cross. Yet I must insist that the most important *reality* in history is the Kingdom of God or, if you prefer, the reign of God's will in our hearts and minds. That is what is crucial. My gospel is called "the gospel of the kingdom." After all, Mark, Jesus came to do his Father's will, not his own. It's more important therefore to emphasize the Father, to emphasize *his* reign through Jesus over all humankind for all time.

I am not happy with people who speak of my gospel as so idealistic as not also to be realistic. Is it too much to ask people to respond perfectly to God? God deserves the best!

It's for that reason, gentlemen, that I ended my gospel with the words of Jesus to his apostles: *"Go, then, to all peoples everywhere and make them my disciples. . . and teach them to obey everything I have commanded you."* In my humble opinion, it is important to emphasize the "everything."

It is also important to tell people *what* Jesus taught. I hesitate to say this, but I think

it's clear to most of you that neither Paul nor Mark has done one-tenth as much as I to tell the world *what* Jesus taught.

Peter: Thank you, Matthew. Now gentlemen, I present our beloved Luke. I call him that because people always speak of him as "our beloved Luke."

I think you all know why, so I will not belabor the point. I would rather give the time to Luke and let him speak for himself.

Luke: Thank you, Peter. Before I say anything about my gospel, I would like to agree in the main with the criticisms of my colleagues, Mark and Matthew, concerning Paul. I would like you to know, however, that while I agree with their criticisms, I have the greatest admiration for Paul. In the second half of my gospel, which is now known as the Acts of the Apostles, you will notice I give more space to Paul than to anyone else, including Peter.

But I must admit he is a bit too vehement. Why must he continually argue with people? A little sweetness, Paul, would have gone a long way in your letters, particularly in your Letter to the Galatians and in your Second Letter to the Corinthians. You really were not too kind to your enemies in those letters. You might, I think, have done better if you had followed your own advice in Romans when you said: *"Conquer evil by good."* (Once again, Paul tries to get the floor, but to no avail.)

Concerning my own gospel, I would like you to understand that if I am called "beloved Luke," it is not because of anything wonderful about me, but because of the kind of gospel I wrote.

As you will certainly agree, Jesus is good news in person. And good news is joyful, so I wrote a joyful gospel. Good news means having somebody who loves you. When I wrote about Jesus, I emphasized his kindness. All of you gentlemen brought this out to a certain extent in your writing. But for me, it is simply the most important thing about Jesus. It's not enough just to *talk* good news; we have to *be* good news, as Jesus was.

When I wrote my gospel, I wanted to make sure that this trait, which is for me the brightest side of Jesus, came out loud and clear.

Peter: Thank you, Luke. We appreciate your remarks. You said nothing, however, about the second part of your gospel. Could I ask you to say a few words about the Acts of the Apostles?

Luke: Certainly, Peter. I'd be happy to do that. In the first part of my gospel, from the first chapter on, I expressed my conviction that Jesus came to bring good news of the Father's love to all the people of the world.

In the second part of my gospel, now called the Acts of the Apostles, I wanted to make it equally clear that the Church Jesus founded was for all nations. I wrote the Acts of the Apostles to show that, just as the Spirit guided Jesus, so the Spirit guided the apostles at Pentecost. And I reminded my readers of Jesus' words to the apostles: *"You will be witnesses for me in Jerusalem, in all of Judea and Samaria, and to the ends of the earth."* I think these words show people that the Church of Jesus is for all nations.

Peter: Thank you, Luke. It is always a pleasure to listen to you.

Gentlemen, John has written what has been called "the New-Life Gospel." It is, however, a strange gospel when compared with those of our colleagues Matthew, Mark, and Luke. John will now explain why he wrote such a different gospel.

John: Thank you, Peter.

My friends, I am delighted with the gospels you have written. What more can I say? The few criticisms I might find are so inconsequential that I will not take up your time discussing them.

I address myself rather to our illustrious moderator's expression "a strange gospel." Critics consider my gospel strange, I believe, because for reasons of their own they think I overemphasize Jesus' divinity and equality with the Father.

But, gentlemen, is not Jesus' divinity the heart of the matter? Am I to be considered strange because I go below the surface of Jesus' life and dramatize what is surely the core of all Christian theology—the incarnation of the Son of God and the very life of the Trinity?

My gospel is in substance quite simple. If I may use the word "work" to summarize my theology, you could say that I describe the "work" of the Father as giving his Son Jesus out of love for the salvation of the world. I describe the "work" of Jesus as doing the will of the Father out of love by accepting the death plotted for him by those who could not accept him as divine. And I describe the "work" of human beings as a work of believing in Jesus as the Son sent by the Father for the salvation of the world.

When Jesus on the Cross said *"It is finished!"* he was speaking about his "work." Our work is to bring others to believe in him. That is the sole reason for the existence of the Church.

For me, it was crucial to do two things. First, to refute the false allegations of our friends from the synagogue concerning Jesus.

Second, to try to persuade Jesus' followers that there is only one sure way to convince the world that Jesus was truly sent by the Father—that is the way of Jesus, by giving ourselves for others. I explain this at the end of chapter 17, but I summarize it earlier in chapter 13 in Jesus' words: *"I give you a new commandment: love one another. As I have loved you, so you must love one another."* The key words, as everybody knows, are: *"as I have loved you."* It is asking a great deal. But, if I may paraphrase my colleague Mark, "God's way is not man's way."

Peter: Thank you, John. The summary of your thinking was masterful.

The remaining time, gentlemen, is limited. I would like to give you all time for rebuttals, but in all fairness to Paul, who has suffered your criticism with good grace if not with great patience, I think the time remaining should be given over to him. (Paul is already on his feet.)

Paul: My esteemed colleagues, let me draw your attention to several points you all seem to have overlooked. First, unlike you, I preached and wrote my letters in the *earliest* years of the Church. I was preaching Jesus in the synagogues within five years after the resurrection, forty years before Mark wrote his gospel and five or six years before the rest of you were born. All of you were still going to school when I wrote my letters in the middle fifties.

Second, you gentlemen wrote your gospels for settled Christian communities. I preached to people who had never heard the name of Jesus, and I wrote my letters to newly formed and very confused Christian communities. You, on the contrary, had the luxury of writing your gospels 40 to 70 years after the resurrection for second- and third-generation Christians. By that time the dust had settled and many of the great controversies about Jesus were resolved and over. You never had to write for the kind of people I wrote for. I rather suspect you might not be so critical if you had to write for people like the Corinthians and the Galatians.

Third, you complain that I talk too much and you insinuate that I knocked heads about a bit too often. That may be so. But I am a preacher, and what else does a preacher do but talk a lot and knock heads when necessary?

Let us be fair, my dear colleagues. Your situation and mine were worlds apart. I had little time to write my letters. Yet I get the impression from the masterful literary style and organization of your gospels that you had abundant time to research your material and to edit, arrange, and structure it. I would guess each of you spent at least a year writing your gospel.

Fourth, and most surprising of all, you all implicitly fault me for one thing—I did not, like you, write a gospel. Gentlemen, I was a missionary! You were the dramatists, the storytellers, the literary artists. I was a preacher of the Word. For every letter I wrote, I preached dozens of sermons. I had no time like you to sit down and spend a leisurely year or two writing a gospel. I not only did not have the time, I did not feel the need to write a gospel. In my sermons, I told my audiences time and time again about Jesus' miracles, parables, and controversies with the synagogue leaders.

When I wrote my letters, I was addressing myself to the immediate and critical concerns of my converts. Would you have written a gospel to settle the problems the Thessalonians had about the second coming of Christ? Would you have written a gospel while egotistical teachers at Corinth with their strange ideas about morality, the eucharist, and the resurrection were causing serious trouble for the Corinthian community?

You would not, I am sure, have satisfied the Galatians' and Romans' misgivings about faith, justification, and the Jewish question by writing a gospel!

Let us admit that my situation and yours differed drastically. You wrote for settled Christian communities two generations after the resurrection. I wrote for fledgling Christians just beginning to stretch their wings and fly. I fretted and worried about them. Think of what Jesus said: *"Jerusalem, Jerusalem!. . . How many times I wanted to put my arms around all your people, just as a hen gathers her chicks under her wings, but you would not let me."*

That is how I felt in those early years when my beloved Thessalonians, Corinthians, Galatians, Philippians, and Romans were wrestling with the meaning of the good news and often misunderstanding the message of life I was bringing them from Jesus.

It is people who count, my dear colleagues, and we must deal with them as they are, where they are, and with all their immediate difficulties and problems. That is what I tried to do as an apostle of Jesus. That is what every apostle must try to do.

I have used the word *apostle.* If the world remembers me as an apostle rather than as a writer, so be it. I am more than satisfied. The good Lord chose me to be his apostle to the Gentiles.

He did not ask me to write a gospel. I suppose he felt that was a job for better writers than me. And, gentlemen, in all sincerity, as I look around at this small but illustrious gathering, I am sure he was right. I thank you all for your attention. (All nod their heads in approval of Paul's words.)

Peter: Thank you all for your explanations, gentlemen. Thank you also for your patience and charity. It is clear that each of you has given us a unique picture of Jesus, reflecting your individual personalities and opinions. It is equally clear that we are united in a way that goes beyond words and opinions. We are united in Jesus, who makes us one as he and the Father are one. May his peace and joy remain with us always.

Challenges

In this study of the Christian Scriptures we have characterized:

- *Mark's Gospel as realistic;*
- *Matthew's Gospel as idealistic;*
- *Luke's Gospel as joyful;*
- *John's Gospel as bringing new life.*

How would you characterize Paul and his message?

The authors of the Christian Scriptures can be compared to artists, each of whom paints a somewhat different portrait of Jesus. How would you rank them according to the way in which their portraits have helped you to know Jesus and to grow in Christian faith? Please explain.